Undoing Property?

Sternberg Press

Agency
David Berry
Nils Bohlin
Sean Dockray
Rasmus Fleischer
Antonia Hirsch
David Horvitz
Marysia Lewandowska
Mattin
Open Music Archive
Matteo Pasquinelli
Claire Pentecost
Laurel Ptak

Florian Schneider
Matthew Stadler
Marilyn Strathern
Kuba Szreder
Marina Vishmidt

CONTENTS

PREFACE

Today, across the world people are engaged in exploring the bounds of locality, community, and commons. From Ramallah and Holon to Caracas and New York, these partly forgotten notions are being both revisited and retrieved. This revival is a sign of the urgent need to find contemporary ways of dealing with existence under capitalism in crisis. *Undoing Property?* forms part of this widespread urge. Specifically, it gives the urge more fuel through its specific focus on property, usually thought of as either untouchable or unshakable, and how it can possibly be undone. Here, undoing takes the form of an attitude. This attitude is not of critique, or hammering problems, but of a criticality that seeks out and weaves together minor but yet multiple possibilities, emerging between the fissures.

A unique and very timely collection of essays, art projects, and conversations, *Undoing Property?* was conceptualized and carried out over a four-year period by artist Marysia Lewandowska and curator Laurel Ptak. The project has slowly evolved in a purposeful way, allowing a space for conversations, resilience, and careful negotiations. These have been constituent parts of an artistic practice, evidenced through Lewandowska's work and guided by Ptak's curatorial attentiveness to cultural practices at the edges of contemporary art. The publication has involved several of the key agents in recent debates on the contested relationships between culture, political economy, immaterial production, and the public realm. Its perspective is multifaceted, yet grounded in the fields of art, cultural production, and activism. Together, the contributions set forth propositions—ranging from the imaginative and visionary to the abstract and concrete—on modes of thinking about how things can be different, and how to act accordingly. Brought together in this book, they exceed the so-called reputational economies of authorship (as forms of property) by creating positions that share affinities with collectively authored works.

Undoing Property? is part of the multiyear project COHAB (2012–2014), which investigates meaningful ways in which artists and organizations can be deeply invested within their local contexts and at the same time form close dialogues in an international arena. Drawing on areas of commonality, such as the "situated" ways of working of the three institutions involved—namely Casco – Office for Art, Design and Theory, Utrecht; Tensta konsthall, Stockholm; and the Showroom, London—COHAB is a framework for inquiry about cohabitation. This book sheds light on and enacts forms of cohabitation itself. This has been apparent in the process of its production, which included four seminars in the series "Publishing in Process: Ownership in Question," which the editors conceived and realized with an unusual degree of precision and care at Tensta konsthall during the spring of 2012, and which acted as the springboard for the publication. In turn, the publication will offer itself as another point of departure for various forms of activities to be organized at Casco, the Showroom, and perhaps elsewhere.

As directors of these organizations we would like to extend our warmest thanks and admiration to the editors for their engagement with the issues at hand and for their hard work in making them public. Our gratitude extends to the publisher Caroline Schneider for her unwavering support and to Konst & Teknik, the designers who gave the publication its shape. Marysia Lewandowska's and Laurel Ptak's insistence on the conditions of property being at the core of any discussion about a future other than one that extends the present remains an inspiration within our multiple contexts. The book leads us toward exploring, problematizing, and expanding the commons, and challenges us to embed these in our work.

Binna Choi, Maria Lind, Emily Pethick

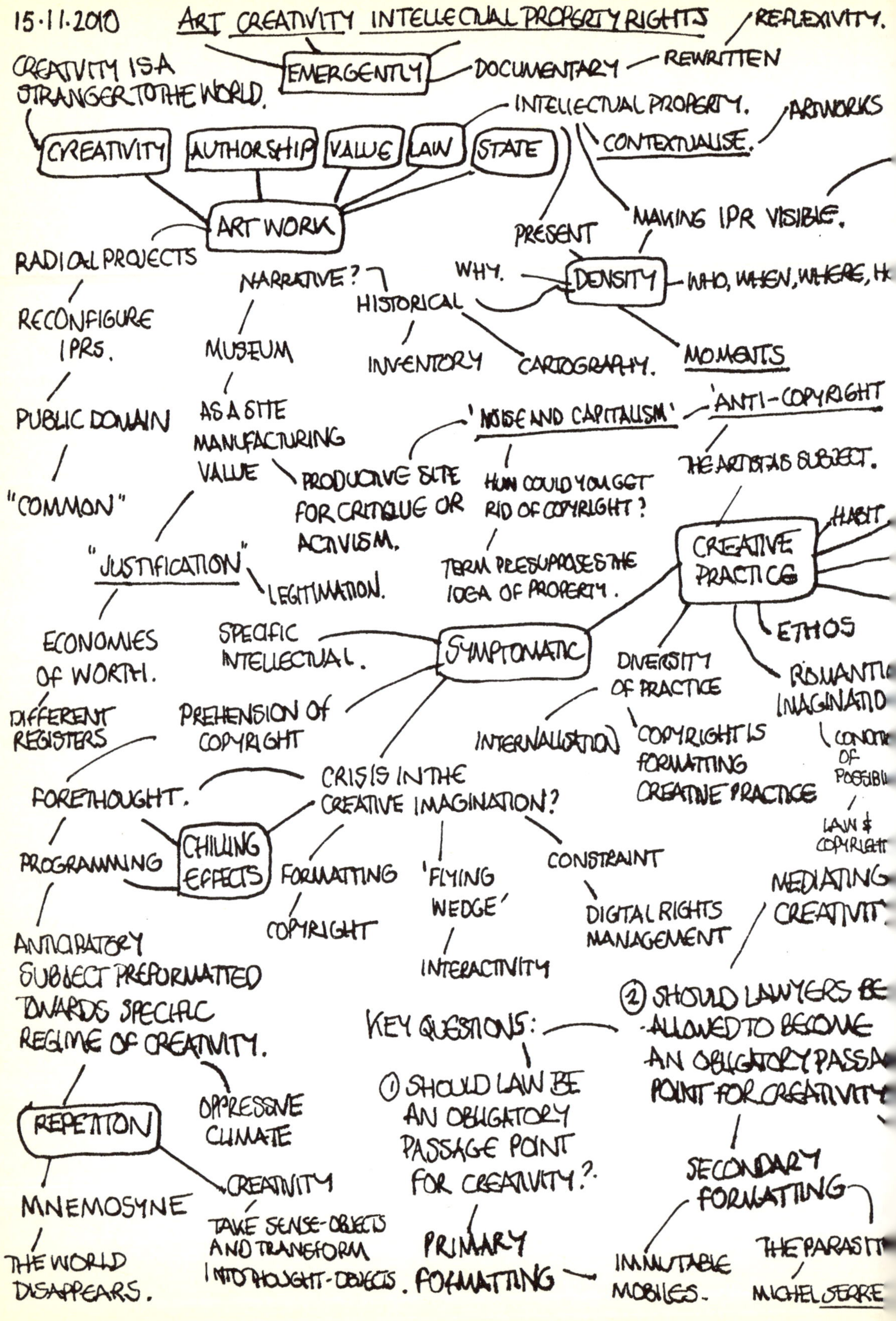

15·11·2010
ART CREATIVITY INTELLECTUAL PROPERTY RIGHTS
REFLEXIVITY.
EMERGENTLY
DOCUMENTARY
REWRITTEN
CREATIVITY IS A STRANGER TO THE WORLD.
INTELLECTUAL PROPERTY.
CONTEXTUALISE.
ARTWORKS
CREATIVITY
AUTHORSHIP
VALUE
LAW
STATE
ART WORK
MAKING IPR VISIBLE.
PRESENT
RADICAL PROJECTS
NARRATIVE?
WHY.
DENSITY
WHO, WHEN, WHERE, H
HISTORICAL
RECONFIGURE IPRS.
MUSEUM
INVENTORY
CARTOGRAPHY.
MOMENTS
PUBLIC DOMAIN
AS A SITE MANUFACTURING VALUE
'NOISE AND CAPITALISM'
'ANTI-COPYRIGHT
THE ARTIST AS SUBJECT.
"COMMON"
PRODUCTIVE SITE FOR CRITIQUE OR ACTIVISM.
HOW COULD YOU GET RID OF COPYRIGHT?
HABIT.
CREATIVE PRACTICE
"JUSTIFICATION"
LEGITIMATION.
TERM PRESUPPOSES THE IDEA OF PROPERTY.
ETHOS
ECONOMIES OF WORTH.
SPECIFIC INTELLECTUAL.
SYMPTOMATIC
DIVERSITY OF PRACTICE
ROMANTI IMAGINATIO
DIFFERENT REGISTERS
PREHENSION OF COPYRIGHT
INTERNALISATION
COPYRIGHT IS FORMATTING CREATIVE PRACTICE
CONDITI OF POSSIBI
FORETHOUGHT.
CRISIS IN THE CREATIVE IMAGINATION?
LAW & COPYRIGHT
PROGRAMMING
CHILLING EFFECTS
FORMATTING
'FLYING WEDGE'
CONSTRAINT
MEDIATING CREATIVIT
COPYRIGHT
DIGITAL RIGHTS MANAGEMENT
ANTICIPATORY SUBJECT PREFORMATTED TOWARDS SPECIFIC REGIME OF CREATIVITY.
INTERACTIVITY
KEY QUESTIONS:
② SHOULD LAWYERS BE ALLOWED TO BECOME AN OBLIGATORY PASSA POINT FOR CREATIVITY
① SHOULD LAW BE AN OBLIGATORY PASSAGE POINT FOR CREATIVITY?
OPPRESSIVE CLIMATE
REPETITION
SECONDARY FORMATTING
CREATIVITY
MNEMOSYNE
TAKE SENSE-OBJECTS AND TRANSFORM INTO THOUGHT-OBJECTS.
PRIMARY FORMATTING
IMMUTABLE MOBILES.
THE PARASIT
MICHEL SERRE
THE WORLD DISAPPEARS.

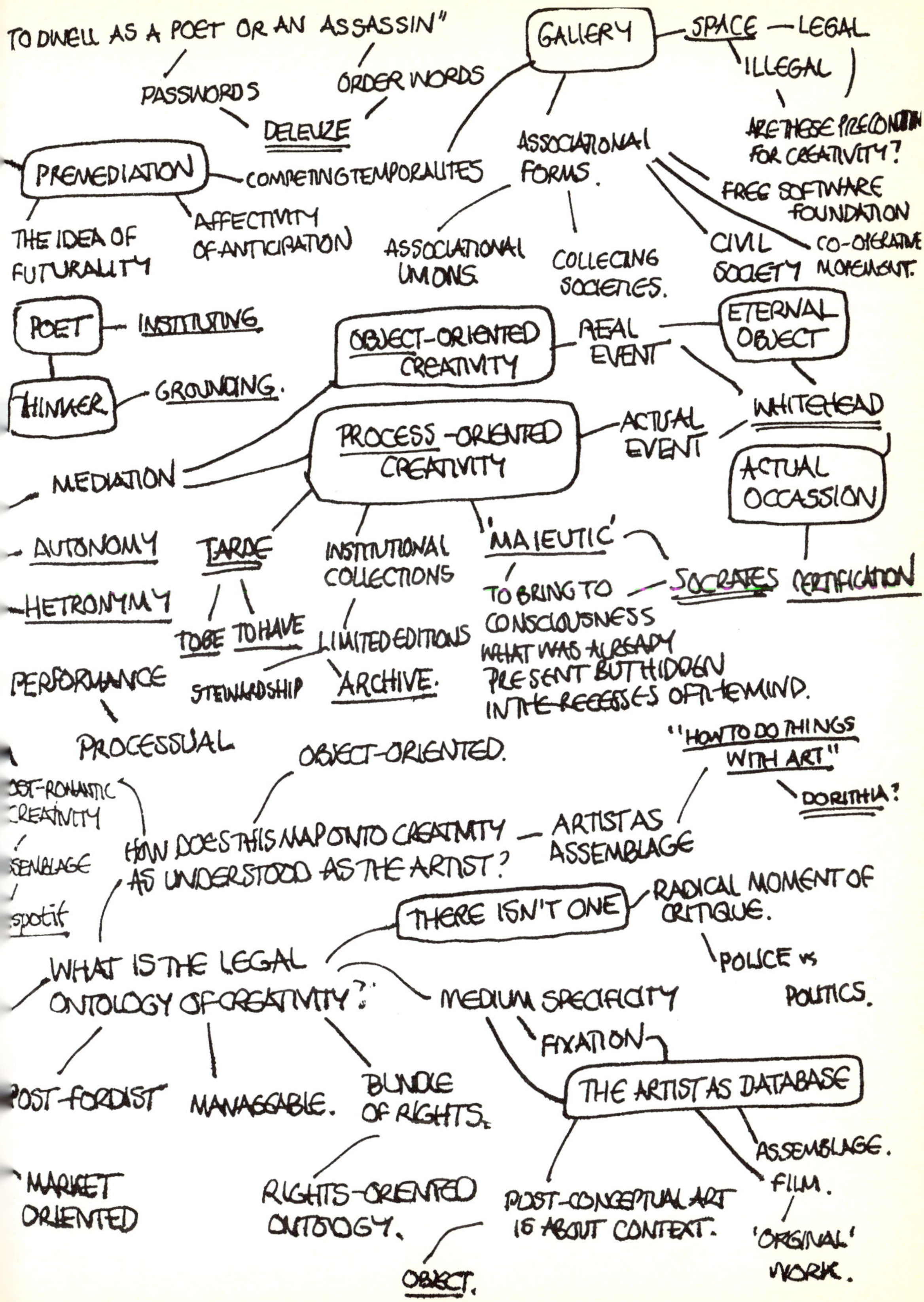

"TO DWELL AS A POET OR AN ASSASSIN"
PASSWORDS
ORDER WORDS
DELEUZE
GALLERY
SPACE — LEGAL
ILLEGAL
ARE THESE PRECONDITIONS FOR CREATIVITY?
PREMEDIATION
COMPETING TEMPORALITIES
ASSOCIATIONAL FORMS.
FREE SOFTWARE FOUNDATION
THE IDEA OF FUTURALITY
AFFECTIVITY OF ANTICIPATION
ASSOCIATIONAL UNIONS
COLLECTING SOCIETIES.
CIVIL SOCIETY
CO-OPERATIVE MOVEMENT.
POET
INSTITUTING
THINKER
GROUNDING.
OBJECT-ORIENTED CREATIVITY
REAL EVENT
ETERNAL OBJECT
WHITEHEAD
PROCESS-ORIENTED CREATIVITY
ACTUAL EVENT
ACTUAL OCCASSION
MEDIATION
AUTONOMY
HETRONYMY
TARDE
TO BE
TO HAVE
INSTITUTIONAL COLLECTIONS
LIMITED EDITIONS
STEWARDSHIP
ARCHIVE.
'MAIEUTIC'
TO BRING TO CONSCIOUSNESS WHAT WAS ALREADY PRESENT BUT HIDDEN IN THE RECESSES OF THE MIND.
SOCRATES
CERTIFICATION
PERFORMANCE
PROCESSUAL
OBJECT-ORIENTED.
"HOW TO DO THINGS WITH ART"
DORITHIA?
POST-ROMANTIC CREATIVITY
ASSEMBLAGE
spotif
HOW DOES THIS MAP ONTO CREATIVITY AS UNDERSTOOD AS THE ARTIST?
ARTIST AS ASSEMBLAGE
THERE ISN'T ONE
RADICAL MOMENT OF CRITIQUE.
POLICE vs POLITICS.
WHAT IS THE LEGAL ONTOLOGY OF CREATIVITY?
MEDIUM SPECIFICITY
FIXATION
THE ARTIST AS DATABASE
POST-FORDIST
MANAGEABLE.
BUNDLE OF RIGHTS.
ASSEMBLAGE.
FILM.
'ORIGINAL' WORK.
MARKET ORIENTED
RIGHTS-ORIENTED ONTOLOGY.
POST-CONCEPTUAL ART IS ABOUT CONTEXT.
OBJECT.

Introduction

Marysia Lewandowska
Laurel Ptak

PUBLISHING IN PROCESS

In 1793, in the middle of the French Revolution, the Musée du Louvre opened its doors—transforming a private palace into a public museum. Art was mobilized to embody the government's movement from a monarchy to a democracy. An art collection, previously privately owned, was now shared publicly. Inside, civic, financial (via taxation), and social relationships between the state and museum-goer arguably stirred a sense of mutual agency, responsibility, and collectivity. In stark contrast, today we see a drive on the part of many governments toward private interests in nearly all aspects of our lives—from art, to housing, to health care, to education. What we are experiencing right now feels like a near reversal of the Louvre's gesture—a turn away from a collectively owned culture.

More than 200 years later, in 2009, we began thinking about making a book. Informed by our histories and practices as artist and curator, we started to ask ourselves: who owns culture, information, and knowledge, and what are the conditions, politics, and economies of its production and circulation today? We wanted to bring attention to a growing number of artworks, texts, and initiatives problematizing existing notions of property inside contemporary capitalism. We were also interested in how the possibilities of digital technologies and networked distribution affected these issues. Additionally, we set out to explore art's current models of ownership, collectivity, publicness, and value already at play. These were not just theoretical concerns: we wanted to test if the context of art itself could be a productive site for critique or action.

We worked collaboratively and sought to acknowledge the many collective social processes that underlie the making of a book. This four-year inquiry connected numerous contributors and took on several forms. For instance, we negotiated with our publisher a generous set of non-exclusive rights and the release of a digital version of the publication to circulate for free alongside its traditional printed form. Over a communal pot of soup, we hosted a series of public seminars at Tensta konsthall in Stockholm to discuss the making of the book. Presentations, led by Antonia Hirsch, Florian Schneider, Matthew Stadler, and Marina Vishmidt, known as "Publishing in Process: Ownership in Question," nurtured this book's development as together we scrutinized what production, property, exchange, and ownership mean to us today.

Somewhere along the way, however, the stakes changed. By 2011, the very question of what is privately owned and what is publicly shared in society began to animate intense political struggles and social movements unfolding in numerous parts of the world. This much seemed vivid: capitalism had been steadfast in naming, separating, and enforcing property for decades in such a way that it confused and destabilized our notions of what might be collective, shared, and afforded to everyone equally, versus what was private, owned, or monopolized.

Inside the context of art, how we thought about property had its own particularities. Artists have experimented endlessly with the terms of ownership and authorship. Many refused the notion that an object's value should be equal only to the alienated labor that produces it. There are long-standing structures in place for the shared support, care, and experience of artworks. In short, art had often attempted to propose something beyond straightforward processes of value creation and propertization. But we couldn't ignore that these gestures, perhaps once an idealistic disruption to the status quo, might today be read as increasingly close to capitalism's own hegemonic forms. Finance, social media, real estate, to name a few, were prime contemporary examples wherein enormous private wealth seemed to be generated through taking up the spirit of art's once-oppositional experimentations.

It was in this complex shadow that *Undoing Property?* developed. The book is a careful look at contested relationships between culture, political economy, immaterial production, and the public realm. In its pages, artists and theorists address aspects of computing, curating, economy, ecology, images, music, publishing, piracy, and much more. Essays and artworks investigate diverse sites, from the body, to the courtroom, to the server, to the museum; revealing nuanced ways that propertization itself has changed significantly over the last few decades.

OWNERSHIP IN QUESTION

Property shapes all social relations. Its invisible lines force separations and create power relations felt through the unequal distribution of what is otherwise collectively produced value. The city is a prime site of such relations; we are unable to decipher how what we encounter physically translates into legal ownership. The contemporary life of the city, as well as our lives, is threatened by unprecedented financial speculation. Such speculation breaks up many aspects of public life, replacing them with more private aspirations. Introducing this set of concerns writer Matteo Pasquinelli asks if punk culture and the political movements of 1977 anticipated cognitive capitalism, and, if they did, how we are now projecting ourselves beyond the current crisis. In sounding the "ruins" that knowledge society and financial capitalism are leaving behind, and examining the crumbling topography of the postindustrial metropolis and the sabotage of debt, Pasquinelli connects interactions between art and gentrification, art and modes of production, as well as art and financial crises.

Some of these proposals resonate with ideas that circulated at a conference titled "The Labour of the Multitude? The Political Economy of Social Creativity" held in Warsaw in 2011, which sociologist and curator Kuba Szreder addresses. In his text, Szreder examines reputational economies through the example of authorial attribution in publishing and what he refers to as "project making" inside the art world. He dissects the wide varieties of labor present in the creative economy, identifying its structural inconsistencies while sketching some future prospects. By shifting the focus from the author's oeuvre, he considers the apparatus as a site that enables production, dissemination, and ownership of artifacts. In doing so, he raises a fundamental problem with attribution—that a distributed "labor of pollination" remains unrecognized and unrewarded. This lack of visibility results in deprivation. How do we recover and account for collective investment beyond the authorial announcement?

If we look more closely at performance, music, and the live event—where communication between performer and audience is often blurred—we witness examples of collaborative authorship. What is owned, embedded, and activated in a shared moment? This question is explored by artist and musician Mattin, who makes connections between improvisation and communization, drawing vivid examples from jazz, the Situationists, Théorie Communiste, and Tiqqun/The Invisible Committee. He suggests that "negative improvisation" offers a method to work against the pervasiveness of capitalism, engaging examples from his own work as well as Tony Conrad's *Dream Syndicate*, Bruce Russell's *Improvised Sound Work*, Cornelius Cardew's writings, and Jarrod Fowler's activities at Arika's festival in Scotland. His essay investigates instability as one possible escape from deeply inscribed property regimes. The way forward, Mattin stresses, emerges when authorship becomes distributed throughout a participating community.

Growing engagement with distributed authorship online marks a shift articulated by historian and journalist Rasmus Fleischer, who charts a history of Sweden's Internet culture since early 2001. He recalls a time when the merging of digital communication with politics and activism opened up new forms of protest and civil disobedience, resulting in groups such as Piratbyrån, and later, the infamous file-sharing website, Pirate Bay. He also invokes the loose philosophy of "kopimi," an idea that points to distinctions between producing and consuming culture in favor of copying as something that is *always* transformative. Initiatives and movements, such as those that Fleischer took part in, concerned with nourishing the public domain, often suffer from a marginalized status. They lack proper understanding in mainstream culture and are often dismissed as a tension between activism and art.

How might an alternative system of artistic validation flourish when artists leverage their symbolic power in tune with growing social movements? Artist Claire Pentecost leads us to this question through a discussion of agriculture and its forms of enclosure that carry dire implications for our existence. Using the seed as a symbol of a certain kind of knowledge, Pentecost writes about forms of privatization related to food production. She examines destructive practices like those of Monsanto, positioning them against projects where community-based initiatives seek to follow a different logic of knowledge distribution and conservation. Ultimately relating these examples to contemporary art, Pentecost asks: What is the credibility of art as an autonomous practice? How will it survive and adapt?

What might a true negation of property or a practice of the commons look like today? Marina Vishmidt, whose writing often explores issues around art, labor, and the value-form discusses our shifting notions of production, ownership, and exchange. Touching on everything from social media to alternative forms of currency to social practice art, she analyzes the abstract conditions of our experience in relationship to the digital, the financial, as well as the artistic.

The act of publishing, with its inbuilt capacity for reciprocity, reminds us of the importance of keeping things public. Publication Studio, as an experiment in book publishing that, according to its founders, "beckons a public into being" through acts of writing, book making, dinners, and discussions, provides a compelling model of publishing. One of its initiators, writer and publisher Matthew Stadler leads us through the "unique political space" that is the complex, mutually negotiated world of literature. What does a commons reading of literature offer for our notions of property and public resources? Stadler's text asks how we can ensure that art and literature are sustainable. What are our contributions, as readers, to the common-pool resources from which we all sustain intellectual life? Stadler proposes a different perspective and argues for a paradigm shift from ownership to belonging—creating an inviting conceptual space of engagement.

With his essay, artist Sean Dockray considers the life of files as they are published online, lost in the digital commons, and locked out through the enclosure of code. Some of the most challenging and complex new property relations to emerge relate to so-called immaterial production. His essay tells the story of "the cloud," which he describes as an ambiguous space that sucks up property, labor, and free time, asking what these blank superstructures in fact are. Dockray's contribution makes a sharp incision into our all-too-cooperative minds, prompting us to pay attention to "openings that might circumvent the logic of access" in our contemporary moment. He scrutinizes our computational and digital practices—from buying products on Amazon, to utilizing interfaces like Facebook and Google. Are these the manufactories of the twenty-first century? How do we riot on such an ethereal factory floor, and from whom do we claim back our investment of creative time?

But perhaps to even start to riot we must first depart from normative concepts of property relations altogether. To this end, artist and filmmaker Florian Schneider introduces of a new lexicon of "imaginary property," bypassing the dialectics of the very idea of the private. Inside networked digital technologies, he problematizes new hybrid divisions of labor that combine algorithmic and poetic work, disciplined and undisciplined activities, deterministic and precarious states, and paid and unpaid labor. Schneider shifts the discussion to relations of production, which, he argues, are primarily speculative. The notion of property is no longer the mirror image of the self, but instead an illusionary character of property released as a specter, a force that seems to mirror everything in everything.

How are property relations embedded in the very reproduction of life itself? Anthropologist Marilyn Strathern extends questions of property into the contested terrain of the body and gender. What is at stake when bioethics is exposed to commercially-driven interests, and when DNA sequences are privately owned? What are the consequences for our definitions of ownership, belonging, and artifacts? By drawing on her fieldwork, Strathern confronts the concerns of property within the context of reproductive technologies.

Moving away from the body, Antonia Hirsch's contribution lifts us up to the stars and makes compelling parallels between the sun and the logic of capital. As the earth's most important star, the sun divides our existence into night and day, and so does money. Utilizing the writings of Nicolaus Copernicus, Hirsch questions circulation and reflects on how representation itself alters value. She proposes a parallel between a monetary economy and an economy of ideas. It is, she argues, in the sharing and transacting of money or ideas that realities are created, allowing culture itself to be made possible.

Alongside these texts, artists' projects are also featured—all of which explore questions of property and test their boundaries from other angles. Public Access by David Horvitz urges us to reconsider Wikipedia, the infamous online encyclopedia of collectively produced knowledge editable by anyone, as a digital space that radically challenges yet, oddly, reproduces dominant property relations. During a two-week drive, the artist stopped and photographed himself on the beaches of California's coastline, all of which are legally protected to ensure public accessibility. Horvitz then uploaded these photos to the Wikipedia entries for each beach he visited, introducing them into the public domain. This act of generosity unleashed a surprising backlash by Wikipedia, as its members started a witch hunt to uncover his identity and the purpose of the photographs, criticizing, editing, and deleting them out of unfounded suspicion. Commissioned specifically for the pages of this book, Horvitz repeats this exercise and introduces a new set of concerns with *Private Access*, photographing privatized beaches along the east coast of America. Both projects' engagement with rights of access, knowledge, and ownership reveal to us the fragility of these constructs.

From a legal vantage point, Agency's *Thing 001895 (playing cards)* examines the subjects of copying and ownership. As one "thing" in a much larger project initiated by artist Kobe Matthys in 1992 devoted to collecting examples of legal disputes involving copyright, this case animates a long history of monopolization. In 1463, King Edward IV banned the import of playing cards in England to encourage their domestic production. In 1576, Elizabeth I granted a single person the rights to manufacture, sell, and license them. In 1602, a court case challenging this monopoly took place. This work details its fascinating and tedious legal intricacies—revealing deep historical and cultural roots for current conflicts relating to property.

The contribution by Open Music Archive, a collaboration between London-based artists Eileen Simpson and Ben White, reminds us that the public domain is not a safe zone, and that the potential and limits of the public as a site of political intervention must constantly be tested. Their project, *The Edges of Public Domain*, considers intellectual property law, identifying a gap in the present legal reality and allowing brief public access to sonic materials before they are privatized through impending changes to legislation. Their ongoing project is committed to collecting and freely distributing copyright-expired music and creating platforms for its discussion and dissemination. Considering the context of *Undoing Property?* as a specific site of engagement and distribution, they offer a collection of eighteen new recordings, made available inside this publication. Each track is generated as its own QR code, accessed through scanning with a smartphone, which in turn allows the mp3 file to play online—turning the book into a music box.

A drawing submitted to the United States Patent Office succinctly sums up an act of generosity that has meant the difference between life and death for many. Designer and engineer Nils Bohlin working for car company Volvo in 1962 openly released his invention, the three-point safety belt. His decision to make the seat belt's design free to all other car manufacturers, despite owning its patent, is a powerful example of attending to a public good over potential profit.

How and why do art's institutional structures end up reproducing property relations? Researching inside the Van Abbemuseum's publicly accessible archive led to a little known exchange of letters between the artist Michael Asher and the museum from 1975 to 1986. Through a third person account, the reader learns of the fate of two of Asher's fascinating, unrealized projects. The first proposal to the museum invokes a landlord–tenant relation between the artist and the institution, and tests the notion of permanence as embodied in *Permanent Collection*. The second proposal suggests establishing *The Michael Asher Trust Fund*, introducing and complicating financial and cultural exchanges controlling the purchases of art for the museum's collection. Asher demonstrates, with patience and wit, and through his heightened awareness of the existing conditions and internal mechanisms of the art world, how a work is constituted and validated by the museum. However, his determination and graceful insistence yields no return, as the director and curators, while willing and committed, were ultimately unable to bring either project to fruition. In a final turn, while all correspondence written by the museum is made publicly available and could be reproduced in the pages of this book, the permission to print the letters by Asher was declined by the trustees of his Estate.

The book finishes with a pooling of common resources collectively generated by the contributors, creating an inventory of artists' projects, urban initiatives, media archives, books, and websites that resonate with the themes explored throughout its pages. This not only marks the book as a repository of ideas, texts, artworks, and images, but suggests further proliferation. Throughout *Undoing Property?* we have argued for art as an embedded social practice, exposing its many points of connection with a wider world. Looking realistically at where we are today, and acknowledging that much still needs to change, we aspire to a more equitable system, with a well-nourished commons and public domain, where the making of a collective culture is encouraged, acknowledged, rewarded, and protected. The undoing in *Undoing Property?* begins with recognition that something else is possible.

The Sabotage of Debt

Matteo Pasquinelli

27

> Coming of age in the heyday of punk, it was clear were living at the end of something—of modernism, of the American dream, of the industrial economy, of a certain kind of urbanism. The evidence was all around us in the ruins of the cities. [...] Urban ruins were the emblematic places for this era, the places that gave punk part of its aesthetic, and like most aesthetics this one contained an ethic, a worldview with a mandate on how to act, how to live. [...]
>
> A city is built to resemble a conscious mind, a network that can calculate, administrate, manufacture. Ruins become the unconscious of a city, its memory, unknown, darkness, lost lands, and in this truly bring it to life. [...] An urban ruin is a place that has fallen outside the economic life of the city, and it is in some way an ideal home for the art that also falls outside the ordinary production and consumption of the city.
>
> —Rebecca Solnit, *A Field Guide to Getting Lost*

WELCOMING THE RUINS OF A KNOWLEDGE SOCIETY

Rebecca Solnit's words resound today like an endearing lament out of time, not because punk is gone for good with all its vinyl memories and suburban ruins—no! Punk and, more generally art are very alive today, though in their petit bourgeois caricature, they have turned into the current mode of production. It is untimely to romanticize punk and underground art as the drive toward a space "outside the economic life of the city." Quite the opposite: growing on the ruins of the Fordist regime, they anticipated *from within* the spectacular, biopolitical, cognitive turn of today's economy. Punk accelerated the tendency of cognitive capitalism like an ischemic spasm.

Indeed faster than any other form of art, music is said to incarnate the unconscious of technology and dominant means of production, and in particular their crises, the shift from paradigm to paradigm. Repeating the history of experimental music is a useful exercise of political economy. Whereas Futurism, for example, welcomed the age of machines for the masses, punk and postindustrial music, in contrast, paid tribute to the disintegration of Fordism. Beyond the surface of their industrial fetish, Throbbing Gristle, the most experimental and filthy of UK punk bands, declared as early as 1976 their drive for "information war,"[1] while in Germany computer-made music was already becoming popular thanks to Kraftwerk (literally, power station). In the late '80s, techno music appeared in Detroit: the original soundtrack of Motor City started to incorporate the synthetic presentiment of coming digital machines. The term "techno" was in fact inspired by Juan Atkins's reading of Alvin Toffler's book *The Third Wave*, in which the first "techno-rebels" were described as the pioneers of information age.[2] These few examples show how art avant-gardes look *against*, precisely because they grow *within* the ontology of the present, and never *outside*. Punk music started to play information, right when information started to become value. Paolo Virno designates the rise of post-Fordism and the subject of the multitude in Italy to the same period, specifically "with the social unrest which is generally remembered as the movement of 1977," and was centered around the rise of so-called creative autonomy in Bologna.[3]

Today, we find ourselves at the very end of the parable of the information age: we are witness to the sunset of the political paradigm of knowledge society, the policies of cultural industries, and the easy dreams of "creative cities." In 2012, the financial crisis has become a global hurricane hitting all the cities in Europe, the destruction of which includes arts funding. These are the very ruins of post-Fordism on which the art world is called to work and which a contemporary punk wave would be asked to "occupy." Here the old political coordinates and artistic concepts no longer function. Indeed, the nostalgic notion of *underground* belongs to the age of industrialism—when society had a sharp class division and was not yet atomized into a multitude of precarious workers and freelancers.[4] What, then, is the form of resistance specific to the current age of financial capitalism?

If punk and the political movements of 1977 anticipated cognitive capitalism, where is today's movement that crosses the very crisis of cognitive capitalism and projects itself beyond the financial crisis? In which innervations can new artistic and political avant-gardes be found at work? Here, I will sound the "ruins" that a knowledge society and financial capitalism are leaving behind. Not surprisingly, the economy of ruins—inaugurated by punk—will be found introjected within the general gears of cognitive capitalism, and exploited by a general process of financial speculation.

THE INVISIBLE SKYLINE OF THE POSTINDUSTRIAL METROPOLIS

There is a red line connecting the art world's colonization of urban spaces, the mode of production specific to knowledge society, and the financial tricks of speculative capitalism. This text tries to connect these three interactions experimentally: art and metropolis, art and mode of production, art and financial crisis.

The relation between the spaces of the metropolis and artistic and cultural production is today an apparent one. The city of Berlin could be taken as the most notorious example within Europe. Especially in East Berlin, the art colonization of urban and industrial relics of Fordism is still an ongoing affair—not only the vestiges of previous totalitarian regimes, but also the stratification of failed urban plans form the geology and humus of the cultural world. This stratification includes a thick immaterial layer of cultural and symbolic capital, which has catalyzed the "creative city" buzz and well-known processes of gentrification. There is an immaterial architecture that was fed unconsciously by Berlin's art world and underground subcultures until a few years ago. Today, this mechanism is debated by politicans and within local media, and is openly recognized by inhabitants of certain districts undergoing heavy gentrification (such as Prenzlauer Berg, Kreuzberg, and Neukölln). The capitalism of speculative rent, which started with the first pension funds on the New York stock market at the end of the '70s, had to intervene in the rent prices of Berlin to be finally understood and discussed in plain words within the art world. It is common sense nowadays to recognize that the good old art underground has become one the main engines of real estate business, as our lives have been incorporated within a more general biopolitical production (that is, the whole of our social life being put to work to produce of value).

The relation between cultural production and real estate speculation was less obvious when the discourse on creative economy was booming. Time has past, and the literature that pushed the hype of "creative cities" (such as Richard Florida),[5] or denounced their hidden neoliberal agendas and social costs, has become extensive.

Usually both radical critics and liberal partisans of "creative economies" were used to employ a symmetrical paradigm, where material and immaterial domains were defended in their autonomy and hegemony against each other. Therefore, the metropolis was respectively described in terms of urbanism *or* symbolic capital, material economy *or* the supposedly virtuous economy of creativity. Opposing this, a new link between material and immaterial domains became manifest in the processes of gentrification. The processes of gentrification show new forms of conflicts, frictions, and value asymmetries that can no longer be described with the grammar of the industrial political economy—not even with the cheap political economy of the supporters of the new creative commons.

THE ARTISTIC MODE OF PRODUCTION AND THE NEW TOPOLOGY OF RENT

The paradigm shift from Fordism to post-Fordism has been described by Carlo Vercellone as the passage from the regime of profit to the regime of economic rent. He penned a slogan: "Rent is the new profit."[6] Indeed, economic rent is the only model to describe the form of valorization behind gentrification, as real estate business just exploits the common resources of land and cultural capital without producing anything in exchange—this is the typical position of a rentier. Economic rent is the paradigm of the so-called FIRE economy (Finance, Insurance, and Real Estate), not to mention the global oligarchies of oil and natural resources. However, dynamic forms of economic rent can be defined also as the monopolies over software patents, communication protocols, and network infrastructures, as they exploit a dominant position (Microsoft's operative system, Google's datacenters, and Facebook's social network are examples from the digital sphere). If profits and wages were the main vectors of capitalist accumulation under industrialism, monopoly rent and expropriation of the common appear to be the business models specific to the age of cognitive capitalism.[7] But once again, it is only thanks to the more recent phenomena of gentrification that this link between speculative rent and immaterial production became materially clearer.

In his seminal book *The New Urban Frontier*, Neil Smith introduced gentrification as the new fault line between social classes within the contemporary metropolis.[8] In his model, the gentrification of New York City is described through the notion of a "rent gap": the circulation of a differential of ground value across the city triggers gentrification when such a value gap is profitable enough in a specific area.[9] David Harvey further expanded such a theory of rent to include the collective production of culture as an asset that the market exploits to find new "marks of distinction" for its urban territories. In his essay about the gentrification of Barcelona, "The Art of Rent," Harvey introduces the notion of "collective symbolic capital": real estate business works by exploiting old and new cultural capital, which has gradually sedimented in a given city (as forms of sociality, quality of life, art production, gastronomic tradition, and so on).[10] Harvey's essay is one of the few analyses useful to unveil the political asymmetries that can be found within the much-celebrated cultural commons. Harvey links intangible production and money accumulation not via the regime of intellectual property but along a parasitic exploitation of the immaterial domain by the material one. Collective symbolic capital is but another name for the expropriation of the common—a form of exploitation that in these cases completely skip the regime of intellectual property and its battles.

The notion of collective symbolic capital is crucial to reveal the intimate link between cultural production and less obvious parasitic economies. Collective symbolic capital can be accumulated in different ways: in a traditional way, by exploiting the historical and social memory of a given locale, like in the case of Barcelona covered by Harvey; in a contemporary way, by exploiting new urban subcultures and art scenes, like in the case of Berlin; or, in an artificial way, by engineering a city marketing campaign, like in the case of Amsterdam and its new brand "I-am-sterdam." Rosalyn Deutsche and Cara Gendel Ryan explained similar techniques of urban regeneration in their essay "The Fine Art of Gentrification," which described the renovation of the Lower East Side of Manhattan in the early '80s, where artistic development was fundamental in attracting business developers.[11] It was Sharon Zukin who, in 1982, named this specific artistic mode of production, and connected it directly to the financial sphere: "By an adroit manipulation of urban forms, the AMP

[Artistic Mode of Production] transfers urban space from the 'old' world of industry to the 'new' world of finance, or from the realm of productive economy to that of nonproductive economic activity."[12]

Today, the AMP has become an extended immaterial factory throughout the whole of Europe. The trick is now very well known, and the real estate business has established a perverse machinery in an explicit alliance with the art world. If, for decades it was renown that counterculture was just feeding culture industries with fresh ideas, now, for the first time, the current generation of artists have to face the immediate ambivalence of their symbolic labor or biopolitical production—that is, the valorization of their social relations. The ambivalence of contemporary art and culture toward these forms of speculation is never discussed properly because of silent opportunism—but also because of a lack of a new political grammar.

The concept of AMP should be further articulated and opposed to neoliberal notions such creative industries and creative cities.[13] In this sense, a new conceptualization of the "culture factory" should include those forms of antagonism and crisis that other models overlook. The old idea of subculture, for instance, was developed within early Cultural Studies as a conflictive alternative to the paradigm of dominant culture. Postmodernism then intervened to destroy the reassuring dialectics between highbrow and lowbrow culture, but failed at developing a new value theory. Contrary to the most recent interpretation of the free culture movement by apostles like Lawrence Lessig and Yochai Benkler, the commons of culture are not an independent domain of pure freedom, cooperation, and autonomy, but they are constantly subjected to the force field of capitalism.[14]

THE SABOTAGE OF DEBT

Financial capitalism emerged from the ruins of knowledge society simply because the business models of knowledge society reached the limit of accumulation too quickly, and the process of valorization fatally stopped. Right after the dot-com crash in United States, investors went desperately back to real estate speculation and the new derivative market was established "artificially" on subprime mortgages. The following subprime bubble then came to affect major national banks, and a private credit crisis turned into a public debt collapse. Two coincidences are found here. In New York, financial speculation began with the introduction of pension funds into the New York Stock Exchange in the late '70s, which aligned with the first case studies of gentrification. Today, Berlin, as political capital, is the center of the new financial governance of Europe (based on the exploitation of national public debts by "virtuous" countries), and its hosts the most turbulent debates and cases of gentrification.

A purely imaginary fabrication of value is a key component of both financial games and gentrification processes. Since the "creative destruction" of value characteristic of stock markets has become the political issue of current times, a political recomposition of the cultural commons and artistic agency in this direction is needed too. What might occur if the urban multitudes and the art world enter this valorization game and recover a common power over the chain of value production in which they are completely absorbed, but that reveals its inherent fragility in these very days? From students in the United States and Canada protesting university debt to the multitude dissenting around the Greek parliament's austerity measures, the new vector of conflict is debt. As Maurizio Lazzarato put it: "the class struggle is today unfolding and intensifying in Europe around the issue of debt."[15]

Stock markets were the first to teach everybody the sabotage of value: no wonder in Berlin and all over Europe urban activism is targeting gentrification with symbolic and less symbolic attacks against the expropriation of that collective symbolic capital described by Harvey. The new regime of economic rent, from digital networks' monopolies to real estate monopolies, is pushing toward a polarized and neo-feudal society. The new coordinates of the art underground in the age of financial capitalism can then be only found along the new vectors of debt that are growing on the "ruins" of the previous knowledge society. As much as the new political forms surrounding it, the sabotage of debt is the general form of the art of the multitude in late capitalism.

Notes

1 V. Vale and Andrea Juno, eds., *RE/Search 6–7, Industrial Culture Handbook* (San Francisco: RE/Search, 1983), n.p.

2 Alvin Toffler, *The Third Wave* (New York: Bantam Books, 1980). "The techno-rebels are, whether they recognize it or not, agents of the Third Wave. They will not vanish but multiply in the years ahead."

3 Paolo Virno, *A Grammar of the Multitude*, trans. Isabella Bertoletti, James Cascaito and Andrea Casson (Los Angeles: Semiotext(e), 2004), 98.

4 See Rosalind Williams, *Notes on the Underground: An Essay on Technology, Society, and Imagination* (Cambridge, MA: MIT Press, 1990).

5 Richard Florida, *The Rise of the Creative Class* (New York: Basic Books, 2002); and *The Flight of the Creative Class* (New York: HarperCollins, 2005).

6 See Carlo Vercellone, "La nuova articolazione salario, rendita, profitto nel capitalismo cognitive," in *Posse: Potere Precario*, ed. Tarì M (Rome: Manifestolibri, 2006); my translation.

7 See Michael Hardt and Antonio Negri, *Commonwealth* (Cambridge, MA: Belknap Press, 2009).

8 Neil Smith, *The New Urban Frontier: Gentrification and the Revanchist City* (London: Routledge, 1996).

9 Ibid., 67. "The rent gap is the disparity between the potential ground rent level and the actual ground rent capitalized under the present land use. [...] Once the rent gap is wide enough, gentrification may be initiated in a given neighborhood by any of the several different actors in the land and housing market."

10 David Harvey, "The Art of Rent: Globabalization and the Commodification of Culture," in *Spaces of Capital: Towards a Critical Geography* (London: Routledge, 2001).

11 Rosalyn Deutsche and Cara Gendel Ryan, "The Fine Art of Gentrification," *October* 31 (Winter 1984).

12 Sharon Zukin, *Loft Living: Culture and Capital in Urban Change* (Baltimore, MD: Johns Hopkins University Press, 1982), 178.

13 These two notions have different genealogies: the definition of creative industries was introduced by the UK Government Department for Culture, Media and Sport, with a focus on intellectual property; creative cities is a concept invented by Richard Florida that focuses on cultural capital.

14 See Lawrence Lessig, *Free Culture* (New York: Penguin Books, 2004); and Yochai Benkler, *The Wealth of Networks: How Social Production Transforms Markets and Freedom* (New Haven, CT: Yale University Press, 2006).

15 Maurizio Lazzarato, *The Making of the Indebted Man*, trans. Joshua David Jordan (Los Angeles: Semiotext(e), 2012), 7.

Cruel Economy of Authorship

Kuba Szreder

37

Let me start this reflection about reputational economies with a telling example. In 2011, together with my fellow collaborators from the Free/Slow University of Warsaw (F/SUW),[1] I organized a conference titled "The Labour of the Multitude? The Political Economy of Social Creativity." Afterward, F/SUW published a post-conference publication, which was coedited by the core group of conveners.[2] The book's editors are named and listed, every published paper is clearly authorized, all the quotations are attributed, and the credits due are paid. All the customary publishing rules were followed and all the editorial boxes were ticked. And yet doubt lingers. During the conference we discussed the "labor of the multitude" as creativity that is diffused throughout the social—in art scenes, intellectual circuits, and creative milieus. But when it comes to the moment of publishing, all those multitudes vanish from the list of contents. There are listed only clearly identified names of individuals.

A vast majority of books, texts, or art pieces that are published have clearly identified authors. In the current state of publishing, the act of authorial attribution is self-evident. That's what we do when we publish: we authorize. It does not matter if we are critical practitioners, established academics, or commercially oriented artists. We all follow similar patterns. Authorial attribution saturates all sectors of the contemporary art world. It underlines the operations of the competitive art market, public institutions, and the small, informal, critical art initiatives—despite their seemingly opposite stances toward intellectual property.

As I will argue here, authorial attribution is one of the fundamental mechanisms underlying the cruel economy of the arts, to use Hans Abbing's framework.[3] The problem is located in the structural injustice of reputational economies that perpetuate contemporary symbolic production. They are founded on the invisibility of the labor of the multitudes.

As critical cultural producers, many of us lean on and frequently refer to the notions of diffused creativity. But our own acts of publishing rest on a lack of recognition of the plethora of inputs that thrive beyond narrowly understood authorial or artistic attribution. Our stance toward intellectual property plays only a secondary role. It counts less whether we use creative commons or other public licenses. What matters most is the fundamental act of individual appropriation.

Licensing and limiting copyrights might, but does not have to, be used as a way of safeguarding previously acquired privileges. But the efficacy of authorial attribution derives partially from its wide acknowledgment as a customary way of doing things, entrenched in worldviews, habits, and values, rather than in legal formulas.

Let me make a short methodological note. My understanding of cultural production relies on the legacy of a materialistic analysis of the art apparatus. Among many others my method is intellectually indebted to Walter Benjamin. In his seminal essay "The Author as Producer," he shifted the focus from the author and his oeuvre to the social totality of the apparatus of symbolic production. Following Benjamin, I reject the notion that the apparatus is a neutral infrastructure, a form of institutionalized enablement that simply facilitates production, dissemination, and ownership of artifacts. On the contrary, in my opinion, the main function of the apparatus is to produce and reproduce social conceptions that define artwork, author, public, act of reception, or intellectual property.

From this perspective, I will attempt to disentangle this problematic bundle, dissect the creative economy, identify its structural inconsistencies, and even risk sketching some future prospects. At first, though, let me briefly introduce some of innovative business models developed recently in the creative industries, as they cast interesting light on reputational economies in the arts.

PROPERTY MODELS IN LATE CAPITALISM

The commonly recognized form of profiteering in cultural industries is based on aggressive copyrighting and safeguarding of intellectual property through rigid licensing. This practice is founded on a fundamental contradiction. The innovation and creation of symbolic contents derives from an unhampered flow of ideas. But if they are to generate profit, the ideas become, by definition, scarcities, and are transformed into commodities through copyright. However, where every symbol has an owner, the creation of new content simply becomes too expensive.[4] For this reason, intellectual property owners exploit the "tragedy of the commons"[5] for their own advantage. They need to appropriate and exploit the non-copyrighted reservoirs of symbolic imagination that can be sourced at small costs.[6]

Another business strategy is adopted by service providers in information-technology (IT) sectors: Tiziana Terranova refers to specialized programming enterprises for which replenishing intellectual commons enables their commercial operations.[7] They participate in open coding to secure access to common pools of knowledge. Their profits are made by providing highly sophisticated programming services. They lower their research and development expenditures by sharing the costs of pooling knowledge with the open source programming community. Moreover, through working for the common benefit, those enterprises establish their reputations, which later attract commercial clients.

Other models characteristic of late capitalism depend on what Yann Moulier Boutang calls the "work of pollination."[8] To explain, Boutang provides the following example: a majority of people believes that the main economic function of bees is to produce honey. But this conviction is misleading, as the true role of bees in an economic cycle is to pollinate orchards and plantations. Honey is only a byproduct of an economically much more significant process. Similarly in cognitive capitalism, the symbolic product emerges only as a result of long and demanding processes of multifaceted exchange—as an effect of a socially dispersed "work of pollination." The ideas and symbols have to be carried, exchanged, reworked, undone, redone, spoken over, and discussed. In this business model, characteristic for Web 2.0, getting a grasp on a product is much less important than capturing socially produced values "on the move." What matters is a control over the social processes of valorization and distributed symbolic production. The main mode of profit making is crowdsourcing: attracting communities of users who do unpaid work. They pollinate portals, web pages, blogs, and search engines, creating values harvested by their owners and administrators.

PROJECT MAKING AS DOMINANT MODE OF PRODUCTION IN CONTEMPORARY CULTURE

The models that I outlined above respond to the demands set by the mechanisms of flexible accumulation in late capitalism. These transformations are mirrored by the changes in the art world, and, more generally, in the changes that cultural production has gone through in recent decades. To understand them, one needs to dissect the apparatus of project making and its impact on the reputational economies perpetuating the contemporary art world. In this regard I follow sociological analysis of Pascal Gielen,[9] who points out how the art world was reconfigured by following the mechanisms, patterns, and ways of doing things characteristic to what Luc Boltanski calls a projective city.[10]

The theoretical model of the projective city was introduced by Boltanski and Ève Chiapello in their seminal study, *The New Spirit of Capitalism*.[11] Historically speaking, the projective order of worth emerged between the 1970s and 1990s as the result of tectonic shifts in Western societies. According to Boltanski and Chiapello, it originated in the new management discourses accompanying the rise of neoliberalism, the spread of globalization, the crisis of Fordism, and the financialization of the economy.[12]

The implications of these transformations are felt across the whole art field, as the general conditions of cultural production have shifted according to the specific logic of the projective city. They unfolded not only in the metropolises of the art world, but also in its peripheries, impacting equally major institutions, biennales, art fairs, independent cultural initiatives, and critical practitioners.

Apparently, the core element of the projective value regime is the very project itself.

A project is a temporary undertaking. Generally speaking, projects emerge and recede. As managerial formats, projects enable flexibility and adaptability, while maintaining a satisfying level of efficiency, accountability, and control. Every project is always a projective endeavor; it projects itself into the future. Due to their short-term character, projects favor tactics over strategies, affairs over relationships, loose ties over friendships, migrations over stiff arrangements.

Projects bind together agents, institutions, things, spaces, pools of resources, channels of distributions, and audiences. A project is an efficient way of investing resources by concentrating them on those undertakings that promise the highest rate of symbolic or economic returns. The resources and agents are assembled on a temporary basis, just to leave and migrate to another node of the network after the project is done.

Projects partially level professional hierarchies, as they have to constitute temporary cooperative environments. The success of any project-based undertaking demands full and creative involvement of its participants. They are encouraged to contribute to a collective brainstorming regardless of their specializations or positions. As a managerial tool, projects have been invented to crisscross corporate bureaucracies and stimulate the flow of previously compartmented knowledge. The aim of a project is to release potentials otherwise contained by rigid divisions between sectors, disciplines, or branches.

Every project provides only temporary employment, which wanes after the task is executed. Projects are always collective undertakings, but their teams often dissolve afterward. Every project maker moves between projects as an individual whose ability to conduct new promising projects is tested when the previous project is already executed, but a new one has yet to begin.[13]

The majority of project makers work as freelancers, and are involved and engaged in such projects for a limited period of time. In the ideal scenario, cultural producers behave like global "joyful riders" migrating from one project to another, roaming the globe in search of new exciting opportunities.[14]

Existential and professional precarity is the reverse side of flexibility, freelancing, and "independency." Cultural producers as project makers are free to take individualized risks, but their main responsibility is to remain employable. They need to be always ready for new challenges, constantly searching for new opportunities.

In the projective city, the network provides a particular kind of flexible security. It fills the gaps between projects. The network connects together institutions, agents, pools of resources, and audiences. It is a reservoir of latent power. As a hub of communication, it secures conditions for new projects to emerge. The network provides access to accumulated opportunities and stored resources. It endows selected cultural producers with a raw potency, a power to change reality without even "owning" anything. The power of every project maker is to command, assemble, and mobilize resources depends on his position in the network. For this reason, property issues are of secondary importance in projective polity. What matters is the access to opportunities, as mediated by the network. But as the access is limited, the network is a field of fierce competition and intensive struggles.

THE COOPETITION If we compare business models in late capitalism with the structural tendencies of the projective city, it becomes quite clear that contemporary cultural producers resemble rather innovative IT service providers rather than intellectual property holders. They simultaneously participate in a collective production of common values, and need to capture a creative flow for individual benefit. The essential mechanism of the projective apparatus is a cooperative competition—a "coopetition." Projects are successful only if they stimulate the extended cooperation of an engaged collective. The network operates based on intensive, multifaceted, and cooperative exchange. But the success of every project maker is accounted on an individual basis, which encourages fierce competition.

The basic principle of the project economy results from this paradox: though concepts are created collectively, eventually they have to be attributed to individuals. This is the way to guarantee individual motivation, create competitive advantages, reproduce hierarchies, secure the fluidity and continuation of the network, and enable new projects to emerge.

The ability to link seemingly contradictory strategies of cooperation and competition constitutes the backbone of any successful career in an art field dominated by the "new spirit of capitalism." Cultural producers, willingly or not, have to capture, reformulate, and publicize "good ideas."[15] They are generated and accessed through cooperative exchange and intensive communication—in which cultural producers need to partake. Additionally, they hone their personal skill sets by exercising on collective training grounds and participating in an extended social collaboration.

But despite their participation in a cooperative nexus, cultural producers are eventually obliged to build their own reputations. Being individually recognized (for abilities or "good ideas") is the main way to move between consecutive projects and secure access to opportunities.

To illustrate this, it let me come back to Free/Slow University of Warsaw. F/SUW is not an exception to this coopetative economy. Every project of F/SUW is the result of extensive cooperation and an intensive flow of ideas. Simultaneously, though, everyone from our team follows individual careers and strives to secure personal stability. In the context of our individual professional tracks, we are assessed according to specific and differing sets of criteria. Something else counts for academics (quantifiable peer reviewed publishing), other factors matter for careers of curators or artists (less tangible, but not less important reputational gains). What links us all is that unless we want to cease to be cultural producers, we are assessed on an individual basis, whether we like it or not.

AUTHORIAL ATTRIBUTION AND "BEING SEEN ON THE SCENE"

The access to opportunities depends on one's position in a reputational economy. Every cultural producer needs to be recognized and is ranked according to his own individual reputation.[16] A "good idea" has to be attributed to an individual, regardless of its collective origins. In this way, the cultural producer is able to secure future remuneration and professional progress. It is important to note that in order to establish reputations, ideas do not need to become anybody's property—much less do they need to be copyrighted. The networked acknowledgment of an authorial link is much more important.

The process of authorial attribution is not a smooth operation. It is based on a structural inconsistency between demands for extended cooperation and individualized competition for access. Moreover it is underpinned by symbolic violence between (unrecognized) exploited and (celebrated) exploiters of symbolic production.

The network secures authorial attribution by linking it with the specific regime of visibility. As Gielen says, individual authorial rights are secured by "being seen on the scene."[17] Only communicating openly and announcing ideas in public, in front of a peer group, secures recognition. In this way, ideas become more or less formally attached to their *announcers*, prompting and propelling their reputational advances. The louder the announcement is, the more people hear it, and the greater the chances are that the act of attribution will be appreciated. Some project makers have fewer opportunities to properly announce their ideas. The ones who occupy central positions and are already recognized as authors are much more eligible to promote "their" "good ideas"; moreover, they cherish access to publishing channels that grant global recognition of their proliferation.

In this system, gatekeepers are able to extract their toll by regulating the flow of communication. Global institutions, publishers, or electronic communication providers guarantee the public staging of ideas, rubberstamping authorial assertions and personal reputations. For this reason, they are able to either charge directly for their services or exhort free contributions from project makers. As this model depends on a skillful capture of a commonly created value, it resembles strategies of Web 2.0 giants, but I will not dwell on this in detail, as it needs another study.

The gains are never distributed equally. They do not directly relate to the workload, but rather to a professional profile in the network, which is reciprocally based on access and visibility. This structural tendency of the projective city prompts the reoccurrence of the freeloader syndrome and of the "tragedy of the commons." From the individual's point of view, instead of being involved in the long process of a demanding collaboration, it is more essential to indulge in self-promotion and extensive self-attribution. Of course, such individualization of gains is possible as long as there is a cooperatively constituted resource to be exploited, directly depending on the constant and hidden labor of the multitudes.

The hanging on to the authorial figure results in an automatic feedback loop. If we think about the art scene, it is almost impossible to spot unattributed ideas, though every concept originates in primarily cooperative circumstances. To illustrate how fundamental and unavoidable this mechanism is, I refer again to the example of F/SUW's publication. In response to attributive demands and customs, we coauthored our book. This, in my opinion, was done for good reasons: if we named ourselves as a collective entity and remained individually anonymous, none of us would receive any credit. Even more importantly, if, as a collective of editors and conveners we remained anonymous, the credits would have been distributed anyway—we simply would lose any remaining control over the process of attribution. The symbolic capital would be spread through informal channels, and would go to either a charismatic leader, to a "face" of the collective, or to those from our group who travel most extensively and cherish access to a larger network.

CRUEL ECONOMY OF ATTENTION

"Being seen on the scene" is perpetuated by the cruel economy of attention. It is a winner-takes-all economy, founded on an unequal distribution of links and visibility.[18] In the same moment as a tiny minority of globalized "joyful riders" flourish due their reputational gains, the vast majority of artists and cultural producers remain not only poor, but also invisible. According to Abbing, the level of poverty in the arts is astonishing—as much as 40 to 60 percent of artists live below the poverty line.[19] The projective city reinforces the causal link between poverty and a lack of recognition, which has traditionally haunted artistic careers. Currently, the projective apparatus utilizes the labor of "unsuccessful" (or simply unrecognized) cultural producers for the benefit of a few and for the sake of its own social reproduction.

Due to this cruel economy of attention, a majority of cultural producers find themselves below the radar, trapped in what Gregory Sholette calls "the dark matter of the art world," which "includes [...] all work made and circulated in the shadows of the formal art world, some of which might be said to emulate cultural dark matter by rejecting art world demands of visibility, and much of which has no choice but to be invisible."[20] Moreover, it is based on a "structural invisibility of most professionally trained artists whose very underdevelopment is essential to normal art. Without this obscure mass of 'failed' artists the small cadre of successful artists would find it difficult, if not impossible, to sustain the global art world as it appears today."[21] Furthermore, as Sholette points out, "while astrophysicists are eager to know what dark matter is, the denizens of the art world largely ignore the unseen accretion of creativity they nevertheless remain dependent upon."[22]

In my opinion, dark matter is a repository of dispersed labor of pollination, indispensable for the reproduction of a project-based art world. It holds the art world together by maintaining its social gravity, symbolic economy, and creative ecology. Still, it hovers below the threshold of authorial attribution and remuneration. Dark matter perpetuates the same economy that robs it of the fruits of its own creative toil.

LABOR OF POLLINATION AND LABOR OF LOVE

Generally speaking, multifaceted, frenetic, and informal exchanges constitute the core of cultural activities or intellectual research. At F/SUW we team up, pool our knowledge, and create collective surplus value—for our existential satisfaction, research interests, and professional progress. What is essential is that we do not do it in the closed team, but in the more diffused networks. This labor of pollination exceeds what can be formalized and attributed to the group of identifiable individuals. The flow of inspirations that allows us to define the field of research and pose sensible questions never happen on the lonely island—be it in the mind of genius or in the collective of supremely talented creatives. We need a variety of situated exchanges, links, contacts, relations, flows, chats, readings, seminars, summer camps—formal and informal, authored and anonymous. And yet when it comes to the moment of publishing, as I have already hinted in the introduction, the obvious challenge is to decide who is named and who is not. A text (and, much more rarely, an artwork) can have two, three, even five authors. There are always limits to the amount of individuals to whom any work can be attributed. Attribution loses its main social function when it ceases to distinguish between authors and others. Loose networks of cooperators and their labor of pollination are simply not accounted for. Those contributions are possibly individually less significant. But taken together, they constitute an enormous body of creative input, indispensable for the formulation of any sensible project or idea.

The situation is even more nuanced, as the majority of those exchanges are not stereotypically accounted for as "creative." George Yúdice provides the following account of the role played by support personnel of large-scale art event: "staff members also make an enormous personal investment into the projects and the artists, including ferrying them to sites and suppliers, having long discussions with them into the wee hours, and investing the unmeasurable labor of love (of art) and the labor of producing process. This investment includes critical work that does not always surface in the exhibition materials like the catalogue and guide."[23]

More often than not, as the reputational economy grows, enthusiastic engagement and under- or unpaid labor (especially the one of interns or assistants) is shamelessly exploited. In any case, no authorial credits are attributed to the support personnel. The complete disregard of the input of all the non-authorial contributions to creative processes has a long tradition in the art world, as convincingly presented by Howard S. Becker.[24] But in the project-based production, like site-specific commissions, public art projects or any new artistic endeavors, support personnel do not only organize and support, but also participate in the creative exchange. They engage in all those "long discussions [...] into the wee hours," crucially impacting the artistic success of any project, which is rarely accounted for.

Moreover, the labor of love is not limited to the inside of any particular project. It is an anonymous work of "significant others" (often female) that keeps projects intact. They labor on the margins of a project, maintaining its context. They emotionally stabilize otherwise disruptive working patterns, and are the first ones with whom "good ideas" are exchanged, edited, and formulated.

To reiterate and summarize: the artistic economy recognizes neither the socially diffused and distributed labor of pollination, nor the labor of love. Resources flow only to those who are successful in their reputational attributions. The collective toil remains both invisible and unpaid.

WHAT IS TO BE DONE?

The question remains: how to recognize, evaluate, and reimburse the dispersed laborers of pollination and love? My argument up to this this moment might seem rather pessimistic, continuing the general feeling of entrapment, compromised agency, and lack of possibilities. Yet I have not referenced Benjamin in vain. According to his argument from "The Author as Producer," one needs to first position the author in relation to the products of his period in order to overcome them in later stages. For Benjamin, the author needs to abandon his own privileges and turn from "reproducer of the apparatus of production into an engineer who sees his task as the effort of adapting that apparatus to the aims of the proletarian revolution."[25] Such a revolutionary task would consist of the "socialization of the intellectual means of production," the "organization of production process" by the "intellectual worker himself," and of "transforming the function" of literature.[26] The process of sublation, encompassing all those revolutionary transformations, needs to start with thorough dissection of the apparatus and its position in relations of production, which, here, means an understanding of the apparatus of project making and a "new spirit of capitalism."

Zygmunt Bauman compares our confused period with the beginnings of modernity. Following Reinhart Koselleck, Bauman calls our period a "threshold time" or a "saddle time."[27] That is, it is the epochal moment when humanity, after a long climb, begins to reach a mountain pass—here it is already too late for us to turn back, but we still are not able to glimpse beyond the narrow line of the horizon. The threshold is the time of rapid change and profound confusion, or, to use Immanuel Wallerstein's notion, of "systemic bifurcation."[28] It is when old solutions are not able to contain new dynamics; institutions of the past are faced with problems of the future. We reiterate already tested solutions while facing different challenges. But we spot the glimpses of what might be in what already is, inventing responses on the move and testing them in action, without relying on existing manuals.

Taking this into consideration: could the labor of pollination and the labor of love be better accommodated in other apparatuses? Or, rather, how do we reinvent and revolutionize the current one?

I believe that the process of sublation is already deep in historical (re)shaping, consisting of a multiplicity of struggles. They constitute a "chain of equivalence"[29] informed by the acceptance of basic principles, such as the promotion of expanded models of authorization, the appreciation of the structural role of invisible labor in the arts-based economies, and the equalization of gains for a multiplicity of cooperators. They all repose the postulates of justice, sustainability, and equality in relation to the specificities of coopetative economy.

This is not only a theoretical endeavor, as there are plenty individuals and collectives (F/SUW among them) that identify these problems, develop solutions, and test them in practice.[30] They exercise expanded authorship, balance the division of socially necessary labor, struggle for recognition of invisible work—of love or of pollination—and institute mechanisms against exploitation. All utilize the structural inconsistencies of projective apparatuses, reframing coopetition for the benefit of the multitudes and not only for the gain of the few.

Notes

1 As I will lean on the example of F/SUW, it is important to present it briefly. F/SUW is a project-based mock institution. It came into being as a result of a cooperation with Bęc Zmiana Foundation, a small but vibrant NGO in Warsaw. F/SUW's program consists mainly of research-oriented activities, both publically funded or not funded at all. F/SUW is run by a collective of fellow cultural producers, of whom it is important to mention Michał Kozłowski, Janek Sowa, Bogna Świątkowska, Szymon Żydek, Agnieszka Kurant, and Krystian Szadkowski, among many others.

2 The book was coedited by Michał Kozłowski, Janek Sowa, Agnieszka Kurant, Krystian Szadkowski, and Kuba Szreder. See Michał Kozłowski et al., eds., *Wieczna radość: Ekonomia polityczna społecznej kreatywności* (Warsaw: Bęc Zmiana, 2011).

3 Hans Abbing, *Why Are Artists Poor? The Exceptional Economy of the Arts* (Amsterdam: Amsterdam University Press, 2002).

4 Marion von Osten, "Such Views Miss the Decisive Point... The Dilemma of Knowledge-Based Economy and its Opponents," in *On Knowledge Production: A Critical Reader In Contemporary Art*, eds. Binna Choi, Maria Hlavajova, and Jill Winder (Utrecht: BAK, basis voor actuele kunst, 2008), 120–32.

5 Garrett Hardin, "The Tragedy of the Commons," *Science* 162 (1968): 1243–8.

6 For more general view on capturing of socially produced values see Christian Marazzi, *The Violence of Financial Capitalism*, trans. Kristina Lebedeva (Los Angeles: Semiotext(e), 2010); on specific enterprise strategies related to culture see George Yúdice, *The Expediency of Culture: Uses of Culture in the Global Era* (Durham, NC: Duke University Press, 2003).

7 See Tiziana Terranova, "Free Labor: Producing Culture for the Digital Economy," *Social Text* 18, no. 2 63 (2000): 33–58.

8 Yann Moulier Boutang, *Cognitive Capitalism*, trans. Ed Emery (Cambridge: Polity Press, 2011), 117.

9 See Pascal Gielen, *The Murmuring of the Artistic Multitude: Global Art, Memory and Post-Fordism* (Amsterdam: Valiz, 2010).

10 Luc Boltanski uses a couple of synonyms for the concept of the "city," by which he means a "polity," a social "order of worth." The projective city is one of the several orders of worth that perpetuates social (like inspirational, domestic, industrial, civic, and reputational) polities. See Luc Boltanski and Laurent Thévenot, *On Justification: Economies of Worth*, trans. Catherine Porter (Princeton, NJ: Princeton University Press, 2006).

11 See Luc Boltanski and Ève Chiapello, *The New Spirit of Capitalism*, trans. Gregory Elliott (London: Verso, 2006).

12 Ibid.

13 See ibid., 161.

14 Gielen, *The Murmuring of the Artistic Multitude*, 36–38.
15 Pascal Gielen writes about "good ideas" in the following way: "A good idea in today's art world should still be understood according to the axioms of modernity, as a new or innovative thought [... it] constantly renews itself [... and] responds to the geographic or social context, the client, the artistic setting. [...] The point is that today a good idea has to be appropriate as well as innovative: it takes into account the local artistic, economic and/or political circumstances. A good idea, in other words, is opportunistic." Ibid., 38–39.
16 Rankings can be formal like already mentioned academic assessments, market ratings, formalized accounts of professional carriers (like www.artfacts.net), or results of Google searches; they can be based on more subjective accounts like various "Top One Hundred" or "The Best Exhibition of the Year" rankings published by art media—or they can be totally informal and based on a networked understanding of someone's position in the art world.
17 Gielen, *The Murmuring of the Artistic Multitude*, 50–54.
18 See Abbing, *Why Are Artists Poor?*.
19 Ibid.
20 Gregory Sholette, *Dark Matter: Art and Politics in the Age of Enterprise Culture* (London: Pluto Press, 2011), 1.
21 Ibid., 2.
22 Ibid., 1.
23 Yúdice, *The Expediency of Culture*, 327–28.
24 See Howard S. Becker, *Art Worlds* (Berkeley: University of California Press, 1984).
25 Walter Benjamin, "The Author as Producer," *New Left Review* 1, no. 62 July–August 1970), www.newleftreview.org/?view=135.
26 Ibid.
27 See Zygmunt Bauman, "Pięć przewidywań i mnóstwo zastrzeżeń," in *Futuryzm miast przemysłowych: 100 lat Wolfsburga i Nowej Huty*, eds. Martin Kaltwasser, Ewa Majewska, and Kuba Szreder (Krakow: Korporacja "Ha!art," 2007), 74–85.
28 See Immanuel Wallerstein, *Utopistics: Or Historical Choices of the Twenty-First Century* (New York: New Press, 1998).
29 Chantal Mouffe, "Artistic Activism and Antagonistic Space," *Art & Research* 1, no. 2 (2007), www.artandresearch.org.uk/v1n2/mouffe.html.
30 The list is included in the collective bibliography of the book.

Improvisation and Communization

Mattin

53

> To speak of the product is to suppose that a result of human activity appears as finished in relation to another result, or amongst other results. We should not proceed from the product, but from activity. In communism, human activity is infinite because it is indivisible. It has concrete or abstract results, but these results are never "products," for that would raise the question of their appropriation or of their transfer under some given mode.
> —Théorie Communiste, *Self-Organisation Is the First Act of the Revolution; It Then Becomes an Obstacle Which the Revolution Has to Overcome*

We could see improvisation as a type of music making that takes activity as a starting point rather than focusing on a final product. Improvised practices anticipate some of the problems in regard to their appropriation—especially if we take into account improvisation's collaborative nature and the way it deals with the relationship between the self and the collective. With this text I intend to look at specific connections between improvisation and communization in order to reconsider the notion of freedom in improvisation today and its potential to generate a collective agency beyond individual expressions. How can improvisation be a "praxis of freedom" in conditions of unfreedom?

Currently, improvisation and the type of subjectivity it proposes has more in common with contemporary capitalism than ever before, through its emphasis on risk taking, adapting quickly to unexpected situations, self-assurance in difficult situations, and coming up with different approaches and embracing a constant sense of fragility and crisis.[1] Free improvisation emerged in the '60s in Europe and the United States out of free jazz and modern classical music and is supposed to be without idioms, rules, or hierarchies between the players, as opposed to the relationship between performer and composer. Its production and reception happen simultaneously without any preparation phase. Because of this, it was thought that improvisation could challenge its own commodification more than any other type of music making. In those times, culture was breaking away from bourgeois values and there was the possibility of a revolution in the atmosphere. In the '60s improvisers linked these qualities to a radical political potential,[2] but at some point, the limited political potential of a niche practice linked to the avant-garde tradition became clear. This was one of the key elements for the dissolution of the Scratch Orchestra,[3] and why people like Cornelius Cardew stopped improvising and became members of the Communist Party of England.[4]

Let's take a look at some of the similarities between the communization discussed by Théorie Communiste and improvisation: for both are against the notion of prescriptive programs, emphasize activity rather than product, question representation, and strive toward unmediated social relations. Both perspectives challenge property relations by proposing a collective human activity beyond the capitalist subject–object relationship. I am aware of the problems of bringing together an artistic practice and a revolutionary theoretical work, but we also have to take into account the kind of political questions and engagements that improvisation has been going through since the '60s. Théorie Communiste's theories around communization resonate with certain aspects of improvisation, while also problematizing and questioning improvisation's agency today. By learning from these theories we could reinject the political awareness that was once more present around improvisation, but this time without its utopian connotations. Communization, as used here, is the production of communism by the abolition of all capitalist social relations and the mediations that they entail: commodity, exchange, class, property, divisions of labor, the State, wage labor, and gender relations, as we understand them today. Communization is the revolutionary process that abolishes these forms as part of the logic of the revolutionary process and the expansion of the revolution. To take into account the ideas of communization would mean to understand improvisation neither as a form of prescription or prefiguration, nor as an exemplary vanguard of activity in the present. This is precisely the opposite of improvisation as it is historically understood by the people who have theorized it as the praxis of freedom in the present.

> If we can speak of infinite human activity in communism, it is because the capitalist mode of production already allows us to see—albeit contradictorily and not as a "good side"—human activity as a continuous global social flux, and the "general intellect" or the "collective worker" as the dominant force of production.
> —Théorie Communiste, "Communization in the Present Tense"

THE INSTABILITY OF IMPROVISATION

Improvisation by itself might not directly question property relations but it does pose some crucial problems—for example, with regard to intellectual property. In the United States, if you want to copyright an improvisation with the American Society of Composers, Authors, and Publishers (ASCAP) you have to transcribe all the material to music scores (keep in mind the level of abstraction in improvised music) and divide up the ascription of authorship. For example, if the group is a trio, you have to credit 33.3 percent to each member. This conceptual problem points out the contradictions behind intellectual property and its necessity for authorship and the divisions of labor. Improvisation takes activity as its starting point, but it is a self-negating activity in that it tries to constantly undermine its own conventions. The language of improvisation is also different from other art practices that need to rely on terms such as stability, fixity, artwork, piece, and project—all of which inevitably presuppose an author behind the work, and a product of the work, however elusive these might be. These terms envisage an enclosed framework where there is a projection of what the work will look like, or become. This resembles a transitional mode of production, which communization is opposed to. Instead, improvisation tries to abolish hierarchies and divisions by repudiating scores and the notion of the composer. Tony Conrad has written about his collaborative improvisations with Marian Zazeela, La Monte Young, and John Cale, between 1963 and 1965—particularly that in contrast to other types of music, what they wanted to do "was to dispense with the score, and thereby with the authoritarian trappings of composition, but to retain cultural production in music as an activity."[5] Improvisation, by emphasizing activity as radical performativity—as collective extreme attention to the last instance in which every moment can change the state of things—also proposes an anti-programmatic approach that questions moments of mediation. It does not have any transitional moment before its realization (rehearsal, composition, or preparation); its realization is immanent to its production, and there are no distinct stages in between the two. Historically, improvisation has also been very conscious about its own commodification. At the beginning of the 1970s, Cornelius Cardew talked about the impossibility of improvisation being recorded: "Improvisation is in the present, its effects might live on the souls of the participants, both active and passive (i.e. audience) but in its concrete form it is gone forever from the moment that it occurs, nor did it have any previous existence before the moment that it occurred, so neither is there any historical reference available."[6] What one hears about most in improvisation is an implied sense of agency and self-containment, which is extremely questionable today as an alternativist perspective. For example, Conrad, with *Dream Syndicate*, conceived of what they were doing as a pragmatic activity that gives gratification in the realization of the moment.[7] From a contemporary perspective, Bruce Russell goes much further when he frames his Improvised Sound Work (ISW) as an autonomous creative praxis that could generate forms of consciousness that are counter-ideological and anticapitalist.[8] Writing on the Situationist practices of the *dérive* and *détournement*, he explains: "The virtue of these practices depends on the form of consciousness that they engender; the aim was to produce a new type of person to inhabit a new society. I believe that these same subjective effects might follow from the audio art practices of ISW, arising from the invention of a new medium. In particular these practices are anti-hierarchical, networked, improvised and limited to the field of restricted production, acting like Debord's anti-Spectacular cinema as an immanent critique of culture itself."[9]

Under today's conditions, the claim that improvisation has a critical purchase over capitalism and can produce autonomous moments that are counter-ideological not only seems to feed the idea of this practice as a self-satisfying avant-garde niche, but could also be seen an act of self-investment in the form of cultural capital. We have to take into account that improvisation is also complicit with the culture industry like any other type of music making, through concerts, records, festivals, and magazines. Rather than fetishizing its claims on producing unmediated experiences, improvisation should question its own mediations both by looking at the informal habits and rules that it has developed through the years and their relations to present material conditions.

> There is nothing to affirm in the capitalist class relation; no autonomy, no alternative, no outside, no secession.
> —Endnotes, "What Are We to Do?"

COMMUNIZATION Today, ultra-left political groups have diverse ways of dealing with the notion of communization. The term has been around for a very long time and has become more developed by ultra-leftist French political groups in the wake of May '68. There are two main strands that take the politics of the Situationist groups as a starting point but then diverge greatly. One perspective is theorized by the poststructuralist influenced milieu around Tiqqun and the Invisible Committee: they strive toward direct action and exodus, and want to start the process of communization right now by seceding from society. Their insurrectionist approach contains residues of the post-Heideggerian critique of technology. This strand is strongly criticized by groups like Théorie Communiste, Endnotes, Blaumachen and Riff Raff,[10] who deem this approach to be, what they call, an "alternativist perspective." Théorie Communiste's emergence in the 1970s in France showed the influence of Louis Althusser, and thus are more structuralist and less utopian and moralistic than Tiqqun and the Invisible Committee. With a refreshing dose of antihumanism, they strongly question the possibility of subjective agency and do not claim that secession from society is possible. Théorie Communiste take a close look at the different changes in capitalism, as well as the struggles against it, and make assessments in understanding what the revolution of today could be. Less suggestive and more descriptive, Théorie Communiste are very careful to not to prescribe how the revolution should proceed as this would bring back "programmatism."

In their analysis of the failures of previous revolutions, Théorie Communiste has come to the realization that previous working-class movements did not abolish themselves as workers nor did they destroy the value-form,[11] because their agenda was to affirm labor, not to abolish it along with capital. Théorie Communiste calls this kind of politics programmatism.[12] They claim that capitalism was never seriously challenged by it, and that the historical moment of programmatism has long since passed. For them, programmatism refers to any ideology that proposes measures to be taken for and after the revolution. Here you can think of unions, parties, and organizations that embrace the identity of the workers. It also refers to ideologies that prescribe a transitional program, such as first getting the means of production, then taking the State, and gradually achieving the results of the revolution, or those ideologies that put forward demands for better wages and work conditions.

According to Théorie Communiste, the end of programmatism came about with the capitalist recuperation of the struggles of the '60s and '70s, especially when some of the demands made by the Autonomia movement in Italy (like breaking away from Fordist rigidity) helped to shape the strain of neoliberalism we have today. "Self-organisation is the first act of the revolution; it then becomes an obstacle which the revolution has to overcome": this subtitle from their booklet synthesizes the problem neatly. Any prefiguration of how a postcapitalist society might look gets neutralized, absorbed, and valorized, thus helping capitalism to overcome its own internal contradictions. This is even more acute for artists when we have internalized the law of value in our brains to such a point that even if we do not know exactly what we are doing; we can already speculate on potential value in its different forms (cultural, experiential, economical). By now it is clear that we cannot anticipate the revolution by having an agenda. We will have to improvise, as we really do not know what the world would look like without value-form.

Under today's financial capital, the role of the worker is losing prominence. As Michael Hudson argues, the circuit no longer appears as money-commodity-money but money-money,[13] which means that that the proletariat is no longer as important for the creation of value as it once was. We also have the production of a surplus population, which cannot be integrated into the circuit of commodity production. The process of individuation and fragmentation that capitalism is generating through debt also helps to annul the programmatist view that we can strive toward the revolution (and ultimately communism) through a process of the appropriation of the means of production. Under this rubric we can also take Théorie Communiste's theory as a strong critique of the notion of the commons. Often, the discussion of the commons resembles the alternativist perspective, as if it was a possible to have an ongoing balance between private property and the commons. As Karl Marx, after David Ricardo, shows us: "The subjective essence of private property, private property as activity for itself, as subject, as person, is labor."[14] Following this, Théorie Communiste's reply to the commonsargumentwouldbethatunlessyouabolishlaborandthevalue-form of capitalism completely, they will keep reproducing themselves. The abolition of the value-form would also imply a process of self-abolition, as our subjectivity—as we conceive it today—is, to a great degree, produced by capitalism. This is not pessimism or a catastrophic perspective, but a realist one that comes from an analysis of the failures of previous class struggles. There is no ethical or responsible way of dealing with capitalism. Taking into account Endnote's quote above, we cannot assert ourselves positively under today's conditions, and, without abolishing the value-form, we cannot abolish property.

PERIODIZATION

Another key term to understanding Théorie Communiste's work is their use of the notion of periodization.[15] According to them we are living in specific historical times in capitalism, which makes the alternativist and programmatist position obsolete. This historical rupture emerges from the distinctions between what Marx called "formal and real subsumption," and, more specifically, what they term the "second-phase of real subsumption" in the '60s and '70s. In his drafts for *Capital*, Marx differentiates formal subsumption, in which capitalism appropriates old forms of production and integrates them into the circuits of capital, from real subsumption, which no longer relies solely on labor processes but also produces the conditions for it through technological innovation and the social organization of labor. In real subsumption, capital no longer formally subsumes labor into its valorization process, but reshapes the whole process entirely for its own interests. In this process, the reproduction of the proletariat and the reproduction of capital become increasingly interlocked. Through real subsumption, capital "integrates the two circuits (of the reproduction of labour-power and the reproduction of capital) as the self-reproduction (and self-presupposition) of the class relation itself."[16] Debt accelerates this process in a feedback loop, a cannibalizing un-reproductive process where "we only create value for capital through the extraction of our debt (which is to say, we create no value—not because of massive, if unorganized, waves of defaults and bubble deflations, but because that's not where value comes from)."[17] Currently, this never-ending abstraction of capitalism is reaching a universality that we have never seen before. However, today this is done negatively through the increase of debt, which is shaking the labor theory of value. That is, labor is expressed in value, and the measurement of labor duration is expressed in the magnitude of the value of the product.

The traditional understanding of commodity fetishism—as the inversion where humans are dominated by the results of their own activity—might well be translated today as the notion that humans are dominated by the needs of their own self-investment. This clearly goes in hand with Théorie Communiste's understanding of real subsumption as ever-evolving and always in crisis: "The real subsumption of labour (and thus of society) under capital is by its nature *always unfinished*. It is in the nature of real subsumption to reach points of rupture because real subsumption overdetermines the crisis of capital as an unfinished quality of capitalist society."[18]

These are two key assertions: (1) that the reproduction of the proletariat is linked increasingly with the reproduction of capitalism, and, (2) the unfinished quality of real subsumption, which constantly pushes the expansion of capitalism, questions our personal and collective agency more than ever.

Our own commodification is not only happening at the supra-personal level (sociocultural and economical), but also at the infra-personal level. As with the commodification of consciousness, historical materialism meets eliminative materialism.

However, the philosopher Ray Brassier makes urgent the necessity of agency, even if we would need to reconsider what the self is. Brassier expands on private conversation: "The point is that the manufacturing of consciousness and hence of selfhood—i.e. the objectivization of subjectivity—can only be challenged via a correlative objectivation of subjectivity; one that reinscribes the latter in the objective realm but as a pivot between reason-less processes and conceptual norms: rationality is a collectively instantiated and distributed capacity which can be funneled into agential vectors at crucial sensitive points—the point at which an intervention is required—only insofar the constitution of an agent is not subordinated to the activity of a self or group of selves."[19]

NEGATIVE IMPROVISATION

Arika, an organization in Scotland that has been producing experimental music, film, and art events since 2001, has become increasingly wary of the supposedly self-inherent critical potential of improvisation and experimental music in general. They rightly claim that music is not just music and that is always a product of rich and complex social, philosophical, political, and economic factors. Some of their ideas point toward this negative improvisation in the sense that they not only question how the notion of value has produced a specific context, but also how our own process of subjectification is part of this valorization. In order to counter this, they suggest artists should "cultivate processes of uncreativity so as to guard against the production of selves as commodities. [...] Actions that seem to lack in any artistry whatsoever: uncreativity, unoriginality, illegibility, appropriation, plagiarism, fraud, theft, and falsification as your art or your own province and precepts; information management, databasing, and extreme process as methodologies; and boredom, valuelessness, and nutritionlessness as an ethos."[20]

Jarrod Fowler is a musician and artist who took these suggestions the furthest, even before they were formulated.[21] He was due to participate at the final night of Arika's Kill Your Timid Notion, a festival in Dundee in 2009. Fowler, previous to and throughout the festival, did not disclose what he would do, and on the last day he decided that his contribution would be a non-contribution, in the sense that he would not use any performance space or time—he announced that he would just be in the space like any other member of the audience. My guess is that many in the audience were not aware of his contribution at all. However, for the people who knew what was going on, it opened a can of worms. It was a drastic undermining not only of the concert conventions but also of himself as a performer—he did not provide the festival-goers with any of his qualities apart from a blank refusal and his presence. In terms of improvisation from a traditional perspective, this does not give much to hold on to: only the sounds of his voice (if you were talking to him), and an anecdote that you could tell a couple of friends. However, it links improvisation to its wider context, and directly and radically questions equivalent forms of value.[22] While Fowler's performance is problematic in its accessibility and could easily fall into obscurantism, it challenged established roles of performer and audience, and brought fragility to the situation—both in terms of the organizers and the people who knew what was going on—and proposed a different understanding of what experimental music production might mean today.

Artists or musicians engaged in negative improvisation deal in the dialectical process between being human capital on the one hand, and being a subject on the other. This functions in a similar way to communization's insistence on abolishing identities in the world of capital instead of refining them. This negative improvisation is no longer based on individual freedom, rather it is based on a questioning of freedom while also reconsidering what individuality and collectivity could be. All this is being done while subverting the artist's role as a musician or improviser (i.e., no longer being a specialist). Following Brassier, if improvisation wants to claim some agency it will need to: (1) distinguish agency from selfhood; (2) distinguish rational "hetero-autonomy" from freedom in the spontaneist/libertarian sense; (3) materialize cognitive labor in such a way as to expose the commodification of immaterial labor.[23]

Improvisers embody the precarious qualities of contemporary labor—both in their practice and in their everyday life. The question would be how to incorporate them into a practice of improvisation that could materialize our anxieties. Today, our crisis is not only an economic one but also a cultural one. If there is a practice that should acknowledge this, and be able to take this crisis as potential in its extreme fragility, it is improvisation. Out of this it will need to generate a form of agency that goes beyond the improviser's self. It could resemble the general intellect that Théorie Communiste mentions, one that constantly questions its own parameters and undermines its own conventions without shying away from confrontation. Rather than experimenting with instruments it would be experimenting with our own selves, material conditions and broader social relations. This negative improvisation would accelerate situations to the point of mirroring our impossibilities and our limitations by producing situations where one is confronted with the negativity of our times. Out of this negativity this improvisation will try to generate a form of agency that would link freedom with collective rationality rather than with individual expression.

Thanks to Marina Vishmidt, Anthony Iles, Ray Brassier, Liam Sprod, Marysia Lewandowska, and Laurel Ptak for their comments and suggestions.

Notes

1 For a detailed argument on the connections between improvisation and contemporary capitalism see Matthieu Saladin, "Points of Resistance and Criticism in Free Improvisation: Remarks on a Musical Practice and Some Economic Transformations," in *Noise & Capitalism*, eds. Anthony Iles and Mattin (Donostia: Arteleku Audiolab, 2009), available for download at www.arteleku.net/audiolab/noise_capitalism.pdf.

2 Frederic Rzewski, a member of Musica Elettronica Viva (a group formed in Rome in 1966 that conceived music as a collective, collaborative process, with improvisation and live electronic instruments), puts it neatly: "Free music was not merely a fashion of the times, and not merely a form of entertainment. It was also felt to be connected with the many political movements that at that time set out to change the world—in this case, to free the world from the tyranny of outdated traditional forms." Frederic Rzewski, "Little Bangs: A Nihilist Theory of Improvisation," in *Audio Culture: Readings in Modern Music*, eds. Christoph Cox and Daniel Warner (New York: Continuum, 2004), 268.

3 The Scratch Orchestra was an experimental music ensemble with an emphasis on improvisation. No musicianship was necessary and anybody could join. It was formed in 1969 by Cornelius Cardew, Michael Parsons, and Howard Skempton, and ended in 1974 mainly because of political disagreements between different factions that developed in the group. The Cardew's Ideological Group was more inclined toward party politics, while the Slippery Merchants had more of an artistic and anarchic approach. Hanne Boenisch's 1971 film *Journey to the North Pole* documents some of the discussions and tensions that emerged in the orchestra.

4 As Anthony Iles mentioned to me while reading this text, they did not want to be thought as "softies" or "hippies," so they went for the most authoritarian branch of leftist politics at the time!

5 Tony Conrad, "LYssophobia: On Four Violins," in *Audio Culture*, 316.

6 Cornelius Cardew, "Towards an Ethic of Improvisation" (1971), in *Cornelius Cardew (1936–1981): A Reader*, ed. Edwin Prévost (Harlow: Copula Press, 2008), 126.

7 Conrad, "LYssophobia."

8 Bruce Russell, "Exploding the Atmosphere: Realizing the Revolutionary Potential of 'the Last Street Song,'" in *Reverberations: The Philosophy, Aesthetics and Politics of Noise*, eds. Michael Goddard, Benjamin Halligan, and Paul Hegarty (London: Continuum, 2012), 245.

9 Ibid., 252.

10 Théorie Communiste, Endnotes, Riff Raff, and Blaumachen publish *Sic – International Journal for Communisation*. See sic.communisation.net.

11 "For Marx, the value-form is an expression of the dual character of labour in capitalism—its character as concrete labour appearing in the use-value of the commodity, and its character as abstract labour appearing in the

value-form." "Communization and Value-Form Theory," *Endnotes* 2 (April 2010), www.endnotes.org.uk/articles/4.

12 For a detailed explanation of programatism see Théorie Communiste, "Much Ado About Nothing," *Endnotes* 1 (October 2008), www.endnotes.org.uk/articles/13.

13 Michael Hudson, "From Marx to Goldman Sachs: The Fictions of Fictitious Capital, and the Financialization of Industry," *Critique* 38, no. 3 (2010), available at www.michael-hudson.com/2010/07/from-marx-to-goldman-sachs-the-fictions-of-fictitious-capital1/.

14 Karl Marx, "Third Manuscript: Private Property and Labor," available from www.marxists.org/archive/marx/works/1844/epm/3rd.htm.

15 For a critical account on periodization see "The History of Subsumption," *Endnotes* 2 (April 2010), www.endnotes.org.uk/articles/6.

16 Ibid.

17 Marina Vishmidt in exchange with Neil Gray, "The Economy of Abolition/Abolition of the Economy," *Variant* 42 (Winter 2011), www.variant.org.uk/42texts/EconomyofAbolition.html.

18 Théorie Communiste, "Théorie Communiste Responds," *Aufheben* 13 (2005).

19 Ray Brassier in an e-mail to the author, February 2013.

20 Arika and Glasgow Open School, "Collective Manifesto Attempt 1," handed out at Instal 10 in Glasgow, 2010.

21 Fowler runs the website www.nonmusicology.com.

22 Benedict Seymour points out the connections between these types of practices and fictitious capital. In opposition to previous improvisational practices, Fowler makes you aware of today's crisis. The point then would be how to take it further in a collective way. See Benedict Seymour, "Short Circuits: Finance, Feedback, and Culture," *Mute* 3, no. 1 (July 2011), www.metamute.org/editorial/articles/short-circuits-finance-feedback-and-culture.

23 In an e-mail to the author from February 2013, Brassier expanded on this: "Cognitive labour retains the capacity to expose its own commodifying mediation. This is not to say it can miraculously undo it; but if the necessity of linking theory to practice means anything it means that the need to understand and explain capitalism already presupposes a crucial link between cognitive and practical efficacy."

Copying Is Always Transformative

Rasmus Fleischer in conversation with Laurel Ptak

69

In November 2012, I sat down with Rasmus Fleischer, a writer and historian who has published widely in Sweden on issues of copyright, network culture, and the political economy of publishing. We conversed about the legacy of online file sharing culture in Sweden in the 2000s that gave rise to Piratbyrån—an infamous pro-piracy group that Fleischer helped to cofound. Equally influenced by technology, activism, and philosophy the group was in search of ways to abolish existing notions of property in tandem with the rise of the Internet as mass medium. Piratbyrån's activities spawned everything from an intervention at the 2009 Venice Biennale's Internet Pavilion known as the Embassy of Piracy, to an informal philosophy of copy culture called "kopimi," to creation of the legendary peep-to-peer file sharing website, the Pirate Bay.

Laurel Ptak: Tell us about the history of Piratbyrån and the context in which it emerged in Sweden in the 2000s.

Rasmus Fleischer: Piratbyrån was a project with three different phases between 2003 and 2010. I've become a historian of the group, but this is a subjective telling of the story. By the late 1990s, Sweden was focused on becoming a network society. The state paid for this infrastructure. They allowed union members to buy cheap computers though credit unions. At that time, it was the country with the fastest bandwidth in the world. After the dot-com crash we had lots of unused bandwidth.

The bubble left highly skilled people unemployed after its crash. Many of them were hackers but there were also graphic designers and copywriters, people working inside advertising—an industry that was sucking up young people and spitting them back out. Some people didn't need unemployment because they managed to get out of the bubble with some money.

There was a parallel situation with politics. There was a vacancy after the momentum from the anti-globalization movement. In Sweden it escalated until 2001. That year, in Gothenburg, there was a big EU summit that mobilized activists of all kinds. There were several protests in the name of social justice, but there was direct repression and police shot people. The same summer there was a protest in Genoa where police killed people. By September, there was a very different situation in the world given 9/11.

For left-wing activists, this left a couple of ways to go. Many friends and I were thinking that we had to do something else besides taking part in the big mobilizations. How to change everyday life and find new forms of political activism? We wanted to try and get away from a model of protest we thought was failing.

LP What new forms of protest emerged form this thinking?

RF We started a campaign called planka.nu in 2001 when the authorities wanted to raise the cost of public transportation. *Planka* means "free riding" in Swedish. Inspired by the Italian autonomists of the 1970s, we tried to politicize and encourage the free riding of subways. In the beginning we sent out warnings by text message so that people knew exactly where the subway controllers were and could avoid being caught. Later members paid a modest 100 kronor per month for "insurance" and planka.nu would then pay your penalty fees if you got caught. Today the situation is harder as the subway system has put a lot of money into erecting barriers that you can't jump, unlike the older turnstiles, but planka.nu still has many members. The insurance fund actually runs a surplus, which gets put into political campaigning. Planka.nu began affirming ideas of mobility and speed, but later became critical of it.

LP It was also under these conditions that Swedish file-sharing culture began, correct?

RF This was 2001/2; a time of an economic crisis. The world economy was threating to unravel. We had bandwidth, people with amazing skills that could code, and no employment. This combination is really what started Swedish file-sharing culture.

A group of us emerged; it was hard to tell exactly how many. We hung out in chat rooms online and used Internet radio a lot. Many of us were at university studying philosophy. But it was pretty diverse—for instance, there was an Evangelical Christian in the mix for a while. We were thinking hard about piracy and file sharing; having political and philosophical conversations all night in chat rooms.

Some of us were from the radical activist side and others of us were from the hacker side. Both were looking for ways to act but from different perspectives. For those of us that came from the political side we questioned everything. Maybe we didn't call it politics, but we definitely wanted to find ways to abolish the commodity form. We found two parallel ways to practice this in free transport and file sharing. Both were opposed to critical ways of thinking on the Left. We were criticized for privileging the individual and basically saying, "I just take what I want." Ultimately it was affirmation of speed and access to digital information.

LP How did debates around intellectual property at the time shape your thinking?

RF By 2002/3 intellectual property was not just an issue inside digital culture, it was also newly associated with South Africa and access to HIV medicine. At the very same time, the pharmaceutical companies went after medicine and the music industry went after Napster, the pioneering peer-to-peer file sharing website. This was not officially reported as related, but we thought it was. We saw it as a sign of things to come. The copyright industries of Sweden set up an anti-piracy bureau, so in response we decided to found our own pro-piracy bureau—hence the name Piratbyrån.

In September 2003 we sent out a press release that Piratbyrån had a website and a week later we were on television. It happened to be me. I was on primetime television, on a news debate program with someone from the punk band Refused. On the other side there were the anti-pirates, saying that our piracy was funding terrorism. We laughed at them on television, saying, "Well, then its great if you don't have to pay for it, then it can't fund anything!"

LP You first announced yourself on the Internet, a form of self-broadcast. How did you adapt to this engagement with mass media—a very different kind of broadcast?

RF We thought we could play the media. And it wasn't that hard to do. The mass media had our phone number and would call us whenever they wanted a point of view against the anti-pirates. We never wanted to be that. We made it clear that we were not representing the people who were file sharing. But at the same time this representation was going on, and we were using that.

LP Who was the group comprised of? How did you organize and make decisions together?

RF Though based on online communication, we often met face to face. We were self-reflexive about decision making, though undemocratic. There were no majority decisions, rather people who happened to be there at the moment made them. Overall, it was dominated by twenty-somethings, but you could also find people who were younger and older. And it was not as male-dominated as it might have seemed. There were numerous pubic appearances by men in the group. Only two or three women were very public. We tried in some ways to counteract that.

LP How did you frame and think about the ideas behind what you were doing?

RF I would use the term "accelerationism" to describe Piratbyrån's general approach by 2003/4—though the term appears later in philosophy. Benjamin Noys wrote the great book, *The Persistence of the Negative,* criticizing Gilles Deleuze, Antonio Negri, and Bruno Latour. It connects to a 1970s ultra-Left Marxian standpoint. It's trying to cope with a new situation by going for an acceleration of everything, exacerbating capital to show its contradictions. In every case it did not succeed, but it produced very interesting philosophy.

We were looking at the free circulation of culture in a very accelerationist way—ultimately saying this will be driven by us and not by the corporations. For May Day one year we organized a celebration with the slogan, "Welfare starts at 100 megabytes." We positioned ourselves in a race to get to the future first. Many of us at the time were living on student loans and did not work. We were opposed to wage labor. There was an unspoken radical consensus. We were driven by an anti-capitalist idea of acceleration. We thought: capital might make us desire Hollywood movies, but instead of working to have the money to watch them, let's just download them at a speed beyond capital.

LP How was Pirate Bay started and how does it fit into the story?

RF In late 2003, the infamous Swedish file-sharing site Pirate Bay was founded. At the time, BitTorrent was a new technology, a protocol for transferring files in peer-to-peer networks that some wanted to try it out. I was skeptical, I felt it only facilitated the transfer and was missing a curatorial aspect where you could see how people organize information. Pirate Bay was started by members of our group, but later it became more independent.

By 2005/6 we were feeling that we had to level up. It's hard to describe this feeling. In terms of a conceptual foundation we wanted more or better theories. Though we had reached out with a pro-piracy message, we also had a feeling that this could get stuck in a narrowly political copyright reformism, or simply in some kind of technological optimism of a liberal kind. This was not enough for us, so we had serious discussions about how to go on with our positioning and what we could say.

LP What happened next?

RF In early 2005 we came up with the concept of "kopimi." The phrase was distorted English for "copy me." It became a guiding concept and is still alive today with certain groups. Kopimi marks a shift away from affirming speed, access, and sharing to copying: an affirmation of copying *as* practice. To really think of it not in a strictly digital way, but in the broadest sense—copying as a basis for everything.

We were trying to get out of our role as digital natives or pirates and move towards something we thought was more interesting. One member of the group had a two-year-old kid who copied a dance from the Internet and then wanted his father to copy him. We were like, "Wow, that is kopimi." It transgressed the digital.

At the same time, the Swedish government was about to decide on stricter copyright laws. The discussion about copyright was taken to another level in Sweden. People seemed to be interested in talking about anti-copyright and pro-piracy. We tried to plant our message everywhere: on the Left, on the Right. And it was kind of successful. Copyright has always been a consensus in Sweden—neither right nor left wing, historically.

Around the same time, the social democrats lost in elections. We were angry with them because they had introduced a super-surveillance FRA law that granted governmental authority to copy all Internet traffic going in and out of the country. At that time it was not common and seemed extreme. People began to approach us and asked us to start a political party. We had made a lot of comments about FRA law but we didn't propose what copyright law we wanted or didn't want. We didn't want to join or support any party. Suddenly, one day there was a party called the Pirate Party and we didn't know where they came from. They explained to the world that they had copied us. We stuck to our own ethics; we want to be copied. They copied us into party politics.

Copying is always transformative, that is part of the radical idea of it. You are copying and something is transferred along the way. It will of course not be the same thing. They had a more fundamental and open critique of copyright. We never felt that close to them, though we were not opposed in the sense of rivalry, and we did cooperate with them in some ways. Next, the Swedish Pirate Party began to be copied by other countries—for instance the German Pirate Party copied the Swedish one.

When they talk about copyright, the German pirates are not very radical at all. The Swedish party started thinking about anti-surveillance and insisting on a strict division between public and private spheres. In contrast, we rather wanted to question that very divide. Maybe it was a consequence of our group coming from a chat room and later moving into people's living rooms.

LP It's interesting to think about this questioning of the public/private divide in terms of undoing property.

RF Classic file-sharing networks used to be less defined around this question of public/private. With the change of Swedish law in 2005, one important aspect to note was the shrinking of the allowed size of a private sphere. In all kinds of law it is legal to copy inside a private setting. Before 2005 you were allowed to copy at work, in school, and share files freely as long as you had an existing social relation. But that changed: the law shrank the definition of private to mean only a household. It shows how as a legal practice intellectual property always exists in relationship to social norms.

We were questioning not only the pubic/private but also consumer/producer and idea/expression divides. We began early on to talk about the gray zones of copyright. The very idea of kopimi is a way of questioning the distinction between producing and consuming culture in favor of copying as something that is always transformative. At this time we had thousands of people following us on the Internet. We tried to fight the predominate ideas in the group of passive consumption. We wanted to do something to make them question why they were hanging out on our forum and what consumption was.

This was 2005/6—also the time of the rise of YouTube. We were not affirming YouTube at all—not by refusing to use it, but by questioning what kind of archives we relied on. We clearly preferred distributed archives like BitTorrent—not centralized ones like YouTube. For instance, the content you share on YouTube can disappear and you can't do anything about it. Whereas in the kind of file-sharing culture we were engaged in, you distribute and archive on your computer and also keep it open to sharing. It's not possible for it to be taken away for legal or political reasons.

LP There is redundancy and multiplicity in distributed sharing. How does this affect the notion of property itself?

RF This is interesting. A file in a digital network has properties in a digital manner. If you ask a technician they will not understand the file as being the property of someone, but rather as having properties. We saw the file as an alternative to property instead of shared property. Take the example of the record industry who was selling a physical object and that was property. We engaged in the sharing of music files but did not think we were sharing property. The one good thing about it was that we did not have to engage with property! The industry itself eventually began to understand files not as property but as being in illegal competition with property—something that affected how property existed.

Gradually, the music industry began to look at new business models. That is when they began to think about files as property. And they began to try and sell files by including digital restrictions that acknowledged distinctions between pubic and private. Customers soon realized that they could not do with files what they could do with CDs—for instance, if you buy a CD you can sell it to someone else afterwards. But buying a file is really rent and not property. You don't own it, but rather enter into an agreement to use it. An expiry date isn't necessarily in the agreement, but one day you update your hardware and the file can be gone or unusable. An acceleration of the lifecycle of the commodity. Next came Web 2.0, the cloud, and, by 2007/8, social media. Apple established the iPhone, and Facebook's popularity hit big time in Sweden. I call it a counterrevolution.

By now we were bored of the so-called file-sharing debate, which came up every three months or so in Sweden—is it good or is it bad? We were always trying to get out of these dichotomies but never quite succeeding in changing the terms of the mass media debate. So we decided to leave it behind. We became interested instead in what to do with files after they are downloaded. We don't lack files, but how do we use them? They have to be materialized in a certain way to be meaningful.

We felt a need to create communal forms for selecting files to use. We already had too many. It was a shift toward being selective, editorial, and post-digital.

LP How did you proceed?

RF We climbed to the top of a mountain in a Stockholm suburb and burned all the early texts we wrote. It was not a turn away from politics, but rather a turn back to politics and to build certain kinds of community and collectivity.

In the beginning we were activists and hackers, and by now more people from the art context had joined in. The last activity of Piratbyrån really happened at the Venice Biennale in 2009. There we had a project called the Embassy of Piracy. It provoked the official leadership of the biennial. This was the Berlusconi state, which had blocked access to Pirate Bay. Military police came, searching for the Pirate Bay server. They shut down the exhibition for a while. But all we had were balloons and papier-mâché and mash-ups of the logotype from the Venice Biennale with the Pirate Bay logo. We cooperated with a local group who held demonstrations of precarious workers from the biennial. The curator that year was Daniel Birnbaum; he didn't comment.

After that, Piratbyrån dissolved into many different groups organically. Some went into Telecomix, a chaotic activist group based online that was related to Anonymous before it became everything and nothing. They played an important role when Internet access was taken away in Egypt and Africa. Many people also went into the emerging hackerspace movement, which has been growing since 2007. In Stockholm, a social center called the Secret Garden was created. I see this ending as an acknowledgment that we need physical space—not just online space—in order to make political change.

Fields of Zombies: Biotech Agriculture and the Privatization of Knowledge

Claire Pentecost

81

We begin with the seed. In this case, a very particular cache of seeds banked in a remote and barren location: Svalbard, Norway, 620 miles from the North Pole. The Svalbard Global Seed Vault functions as a backup depository to a network of official seed banks worldwide. Boasting dual blast proof doors with motion sensors, two airlocks, and walls of steel-reinforced concrete one meter thick, the so-called doomsday seed vault is advertised as a kind of insurance "against both incremental and catastrophic loss of crop diversity held in genebanks around the world."[1]

In the history of agriculture, seeds represent a kind of knowledge. I'm interested in the doomsday seed vault as a model of knowledge, the idea that if you lock up the world's library on a given subject and consign its administration to a few powerful people, it will be safe—it will ultimately be available to the people who know best how to use it. Technically owned by the Norwegian government, the doomsday seed vault is administered by Nordgen, the regional seed bank of the Nordic countries, and an advisory council called the Global Crop Diversity Trust. Major donors to the Global Crop Diversity Trust include the Bill and Melinda Gates Foundation, the Rockefeller Foundation, Dupont subsidiary Pioneer Hi-Bred (the second largest seed company in the world), Syngenta Corporation (the third largest seed company), the Consultive Group on International Agricultural Research (CGIAR), and several national governments.

There are no permanent staff persons on-site at the doomsday seed vault, as it is monitored by electronic surveillance. Indeed, one of the curious things about Svalbard is how far it is from the people who might actually use the material in the vault. It presents an idea of knowledge as an object that can be kept secure without people. What does this imply about who is going to use the material and how? Remember that CGIAR and the Rockefeller Foundation were responsible for the "green revolution," which brought industrial monoculture to the Third World, making it dependent on expensive seeds and chemical inputs from the First World. Both parties are presently collaborating with the Gates Foundation to bring a new green revolution to Africa and all three are strong advocates of biotechnology as a solution to world hunger.

Halfway across the globe, we have a counter-model of knowledge: Navdanya, a program of the Research Foundation for Science, Technology and Ecology (RFSTE). Navdanya is a seed savers cooperative and exchange system in India, which was started by scientist and environmental activist Vandana Shiva.[2] In this system, seeds can be borrowed by any farmer who consents to use them by planting and then returning a portion of seeds from their harvest to the collective. Other farmers can then continue to cultivate them. This model follows a different logic of knowledge distribution and conservation in which the knowledge is distributed in a system of reciprocity and kept in active practice and development. It proposes that the best security for plant diversity is a widely distributed practice of actually using, planting, developing, and exchanging the seeds freely. The development and exchange of genetic plant material in the form of seeds is perhaps the longest running open-source knowledge network in human history. Navdanya is only one, well-publicized example—there are countless official and unofficial seed savers' exchanges operating in the world, practicing open-source cultivation and simultaneously providing security of food, genetic material, and working knowledge of the materials.

Given the continued robustness of this system, what are the threats to global genetic diversity? According to the Global Crop Diversity Trust, these threats include natural disasters, poor management and lack of infrastructure, and war (such as the reckless occupation of Iraq and Afghanistan, which allowed their national seed banks to be destroyed).

But there are other threats to crop, seed, and genetic diversity that the Svalbard website fails to mention. The most pressing threat to the flourishing of agricultural biodiversity supported by farmer-driven, open-source seed research is the monocultural industrial agriculture system, long dominated by patented hybrid seeds and increasingly dominated by the makers and marketers of transgenic crops, popularly known as GMOs (genetically modified organisms). It's important to understand the extent to which GMOs are designed to consolidate monocultural industrial agriculture and what that system does to the kind of food security provided by having a large and diverse population of small farmers practicing agricultural knowledge and research on the ground.

Genetically modified seeds represent some of the most assiduously protected kinds of knowledge ever produced. However, there are no plans to store GMO seeds in the doomsday seed vault. Though widely distributed, they are maintained in another kind of vault, one constructed through legal and policing systems. On February 19, 2009, the *New York Times* published an article by Andrew Pollack, in which he reported on a statement submitted to the EPA by twenty-six corn-insect specialists on the impossibility of conducting independent research on GMO crops. "The problem, the scientists say, is that farmers and other buyers of genetically engineered seeds have to sign an agreement meant to ensure that growers honor company patent rights and environmental regulations. But the agreements also prohibit growing the crops for research purposes."[3]

Contracts restricting buyers are not the only problem for these scientists. As the article relates, the scientists who wrote the complaint to the EPA withheld their names for fear of being blacklisted by the corporations against whom the complaint is lodged.

"Dr. Shields of Cornell said financing for agricultural research had gradually shifted from the public sector to the private sector. That makes many scientists at universities dependent on financing or technical cooperation from the big seed companies."[4] Independent science has long been one of the casualties of corporate intellectual patents and the privatization of our university system. But the larger part of our agricultural heritage is the outcome of science in the field, practiced by farmers. Like the scientists, farmers who buy GMO seeds sign contracts agreeing, among other things, that they will not save the seed from one harvest to the next, much less exchange them or practice the kind of open-source knowledge development and sharing that has informed agricultural practice for millennia. The knowledge and skill that was once securely distributed in the heads and hands of millions of farmers worldwide is rapidly being transferred to vaults controlled by a few private interests.

Despite all this protection from independent research, a shoddy kind of science is being practiced via GMOs in large, uncontrolled, and sketchily documented experiments. Despite the efforts of the seed companies to obscure it, the evidence of the effects of the GMO system is mounting. Take the case of Argentina. Up until the 1980s, Argentina's agriculture system was dominated by small family farms growing a wide variety of crops, with small-scale animal husbandry in the same locations, where animal manure could be used as fertilizer. The productivity of Argentina's farmers contributed to one of the highest standards of living in Latin America, feeding the country with a diverse diet and producing surpluses for export. The ravaging of Argentina's economy by a US-backed military dictatorship and other corrupt regimes, years of IMF austerity plans, structural adjustment, privatization, liberalization, and fire sales to foreign investors is a long sad tale, but it made the country particularly ripe for the promises of the latest imported cure-all: GMO agriculture for export cash. Between 1997 and 2003 more than half of Argentina's arable land was converted to host Monsanto's Roundup Ready transgenic soy. Roundup Ready crops are engineered to resist Monsanto's blockbuster glyphosate-based herbicide, Roundup. They are designed to be part of a system that relies on expensive petroleum-based inputs of pesticide, herbicide, and artificial fertilizers, and the labor-cutting machinery that makes the system turn a profit. Since the capital-intensive outlay to run such a system is very expensive, it results in larger, but fewer farms and the inevitable concentration of wealth in the hands of a much smaller proportion of large corporate landholders. Since the introduction of GMO soy monoculture in Argentina, upwards of 200,000 peasants and small farmers have been driven off the land and into the poverty cycle of large cities and unemployment.

The environmental and health hazards have been monumental. Initially captured by the promise of requiring less herbicide than conventional agriculture, over time farmers use much more due to the naturally evolving resistance in the weeds repeatedly doused with the same herbicide. Glyphosate usage in Argentina skyrocketed from 13.9 million liters in 1997 to 150 million in 2003. What we have learned from such intensive use is that Roundup destroys the beneficial microbes that break down organic matter and nourish the soil to produce nutritious food. Meanwhile the spread of resistant weeds and unwanted GMO soy is so pernicious that, in an effort to control it, farmers are using other, even more virulent herbicides like atrazine, paraquat, metsulfuron, and clopyralid, marketed by other multinational chemical companies like Dow, Dupont, and Syngenta. In this mammoth uncontrolled experiment, we have also learned that large dosages of glyphosate produce birth defects in humans and livestock, and skin, respiratory, and neurological diseases in people unlucky enough to live in the vicinity.

Where is all this soy going? To the confined animal feeding operations mostly in the north, and to provide meat for the increasingly unhealthy people of richer nations. In Argentina itself, hunger has risen over 13 percent in the period that saw the first wave of transgenic monoculture.

One of the curious things about the case of Argentina is that Monsanto marketed its Roundup Ready system there without having obtained a protection for its patent. This meant that early adaptors to the technology paid no royalty fees and did not sign the usual contract forbidding them to save, share, exchange, or sell the seed produced in the harvest. Was this a bad calculation on Monsanto's part? Or a ruse to have the seed spread rapidly to the entire southern cone? Brazil, which initially outlawed GMO technology, finally threw in the towel and legalized it in 2005. By then, so much transgenic seed had crossed the border from its neighbor that this other agricultural giant decided it was better to legalize and try to regulate it than try to enforce laws against it. Whatever Monsanto's original plan, by 2004 they stopped selling their seeds to Argentinian farmers and pressured their government into creating a "Technology Compensation Fund" by imposing an extra tax when they sold their soy to the multinational grain exporters.

What's so striking about this case is that even without initial patent protection, the introduction of transgenic seeds was used to transform a system into industrial monoculture, effectively eradicating small farmers and the practices that safeguard genetic diversity and distribution. Along with agricultural biodiversity, subsistence agriculture, food security, nutrition, and autonomy all go down the tubes. These risks are real.

But there is another risk growing here and that is to the credibility of science itself. In the words of sociologist Ulrich Beck, "the sciences' monopoly on rationality is broken."[5] In his 1986 book *Risk Society*, Beck describes what he calls a second or "reflexive" modernity, which applies to affluent, industrialized, "post-scarcity" economies. In this phase, society becomes more significantly characterized by the risks posed by industrialization than by its achievements. Beck elucidates several distinguishing features of risk society: (1) the risks are invisible and difficult to analyze by conventional scientific methods of singly located cause and effect; (2) the risks extend in space so that any national or constructed boundaries do not contain them; (3) they extend in time so that no one knows exactly when or how they will actually jeopardize health and well being; (4) new players arise whose very business is risk, exploiting it as another frontier for profit; (5) expertise loses credibility, compromised by exaggerated claims that rarely turn out to be as advertised or have produced security and wealth for only a privileged few, compromised also by their own internal contradictions and increasingly by the mounting evidence of complicity with predatory commercial interests; (6) society becomes most critically organized around risk positions, and individuals and groups are defined by degrees of vulnerability to various threats; and (7) knowledge becomes a key factor: the more you know about the dangers, the better equipped you are to avoid them, provided of course, that you have the means.[6]

In the 1980s, Beck was particularly concerned with nuclear war, nuclear waste, and environmental toxins. To those dangers we can now add climate change and the global economic crisis. Unfortunately, still mired in false controversies, overwhelming scale, and incalculable futurity on the level of perception, climate change persists—misleadingly—in the realm of invisible, vague threats. But the financial break down is all too present. Because it is undeniably upon us, transforming daily life into an unrelenting episode of high anxiety, the global financial crisis is particularly illustrative. At its core is a collapse of risk evaluation, a case of colossal risk profiteering and mismanagement. Expertise, through ineptitude or corruption, is seen to have masked a failure to estimate the risks involved for all of us. What we have is a crisis of legitimation for the entire neoliberal system and ideology.

Beck reminds us that simultaneous to the growing centrality of risk, we have developed the technologies for unprecedented reflexivity. More than ever, we have the tools for populations to educate themselves widely and deeply on the nature of our risks and on the authorities we may have once trusted to protect us. We have the tools to develop, share, and enhance knowledge about the state of our world and our options. As authority breaks down, more of us realize that what we need is simply not going to be provided for us by experts. We embark on a path of massive collective self-education.

The question is: how we are going to confront the terrors now breaking through the long running, lopsided fantasy of progress through technology? How will we understand and respond to the risks that can no longer be ignored? I have highlighted two models of the risk of biodiversity devastation, designating them as the "doomsday vault model" and the "Navdanya model." The doomsday vault consolidates old arrangements—the management of risk by select authorities whose interests have proven to be self-preservation. It doesn't acknowledge monocultural industrial agriculture as a threat but rather presumes it as a given. It doesn't acknowledge the question of who is going to activate the knowledge inherent in a seed bank because it presumes the condition of zombies in the field; humans emptied of volition, following remote instructions from labs, markets, and legal teams. The Navdanya model cannot be actualized by zombies. It presumes that knowledge *and* its materials will thrive when implemented by populations invested fully in agency and responsibility. This is a model that presents a different engagement with the risks involved in its deployment, an engagement shared by the people who must bear the responsibility for that knowledge and also the consequences of choices made about it.

How do artists fit into this scenario? The practice of art can also be seen as a model of knowledge production, conservation, and distribution. Artists are particularly well suited to a practice of public amateurism, a kind of experimental and experiential learning in an affective sphere of open exchange. Most are able to garner some scale of a public, they generally have access to cognitive resources, their work is open to scrutiny, and they are accorded the freedom to experiment. Scientists' freedom is increasingly constrained by a dependence on large market players and the rules they enforce through both funding and legal imbalances.

The freedom of artists is primarily limited by self-constraint, by careerist accommodation to the vault constructed by the major legitimizing institutions of museums, commercial galleries, mainstream art magazines, and ultimately the art market. Let's call it the "boomsday vault model": millions of artists betting on the advance of their individual careers in the hands of a market-oriented validation authority. But it's not the only model. Just as vernacular seed exchanges are not waiting for the catastrophe that will send us begging to the doomsday bosses, alternative systems of artistic validation are flourishing. They are building a living, open core where artists leverage their symbolic power in concert with growing social movements.

Art by itself is not going to change fundamental social conditions, not only because that takes broad social movements, but also because, when detached from collective social demand for change, the critical power of art is so easily turned to the service of masking the contradiction between inequitable arrangements of power and the rhetoric of liberal democracies. Almost a century of both internal and external critique—from the Dadaists to the Situationists, from Antonio Gramsci to Herbert Marcuse—should have taught us something by now: art repeatedly forfeits the power to leverage its critical play toward real social change, serving instead as an aestheticized zombie in the latest field of capitalist exploitation and inequality. The world capitalist system that has brought us to the brink of meltdown is currently undergoing the gravest legitimation crisis of our lifetime and we have to ask ourselves how our agency will fare in that crisis. As the art market rises and falls with capitalism's fortunes, so, inversely, does the credibility of art as an autonomous practice.

Artists' desire to cross disciplinary boundaries (like those guarding the sciences) is an expression of a desire to be part of something larger than art. If we want to do more than supply diverse novelties to the boomsday vault, we need to tune our efforts to the resonance of collective movements.

Notes

1 See "Structure," Global Crop Diversity Trust, www.croptrust.org/content/structure.

2 The Navdanya website does not include details on funding sources for RFSTE. In a conversation with the author, Dr. Shiva explained that this information is not publicized because of the frequent threats from the industry to donors. The fees from her many speaking engagements provide a substantial portion of support for the organization. RFSTE accepts no corporate donations.

3 Andrew Pollack, "Crop Scientists Say Biotechnology Seed Companies Are Thwarting Research," February 19, 2009, *New York Times*, www.nytimes.com/2009/02/20/business/20crop.html.

4 Ibid.

5 Ulrich Beck, *Risk Society: Towards a New Modernity*, trans. Mark Ritter (London: Sage Publications, 1992), 29.

6 See ibid.

Public Access
Private Access

David Horvitz

93

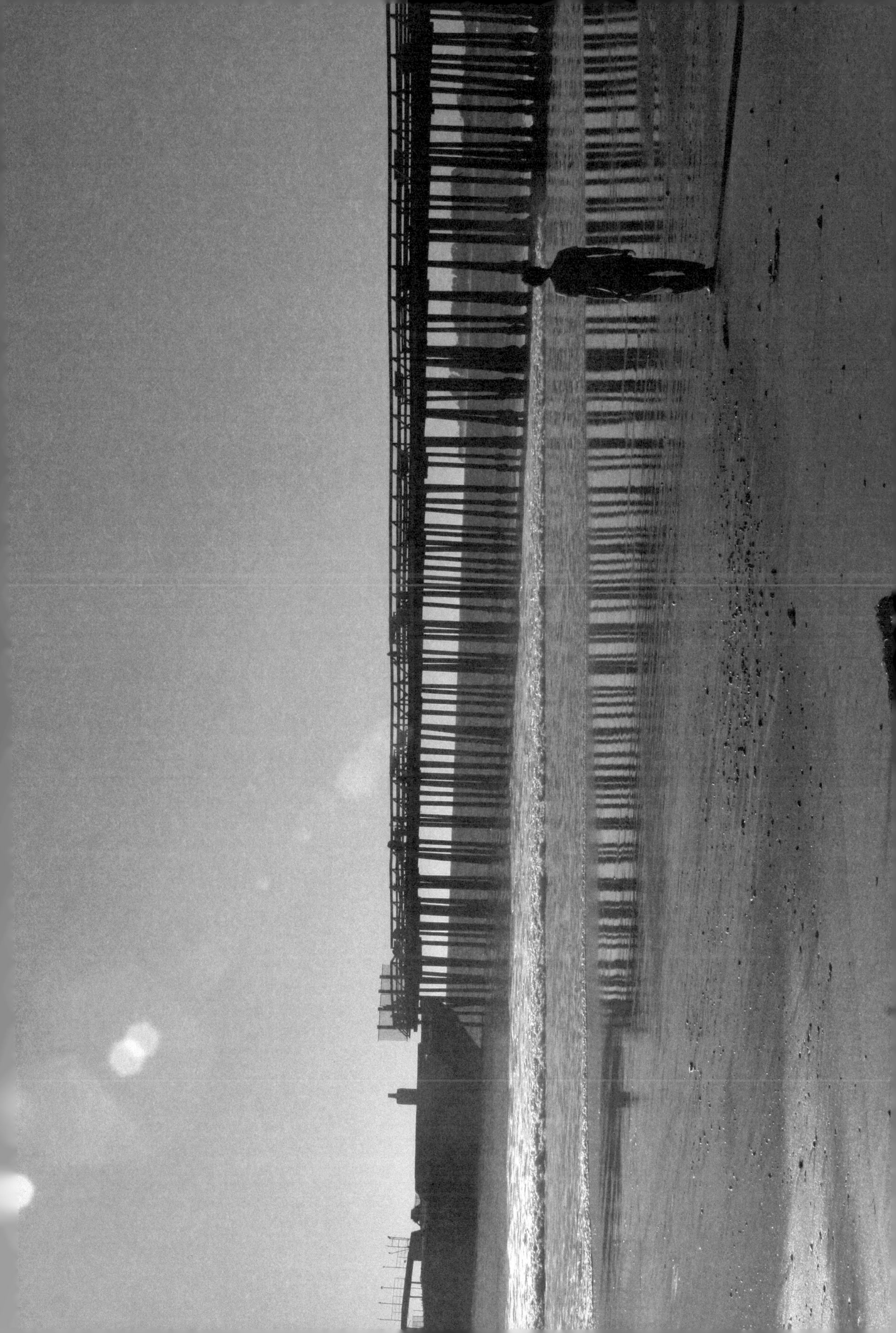

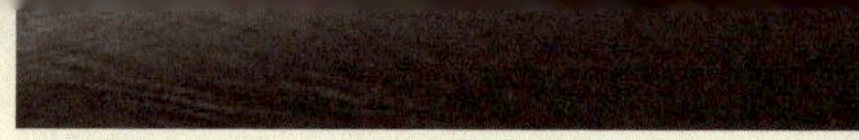

Location	Aptos, California
Coordinates	36°58′20″N 121°54′50″W
Established	1931[1]
Governing body	California Department of Parks and Recreation
	Official website

History [edit]

The beach was originally home to the Ohlone people.[1] Spanish missionaries established the Mission Santa Cruz here. In 1821, when Mexico broke away from Spain the land was divided up into land grants.[2] The area of the beach was a part the Rancho Aptos grant to Rafael Castro in 1833.[3] Castro worked with Claus Spreckels to establis Castro-Spreckels wharf. The beach soon became a successful shipping port. The logging industry a thrived here with the local redwood trees.

The port facilitated major trade with the Kingdom of Hawai'i. In 1838, King Kamehameha III request that Mexican vaqueros from California travel to Hawai'i to teach Hawaiians how to manage herds of cattle. Seacliff became a popular place to recruit vaqueros, who were known as paniolos by the Hawaiians.

In the 1850s, Thomas Fallon acquired part of beach and turned it into a resort. He named this new "New Brighton", in honor of his favorite seaside resort in England.

In the 1920s, after Claus Spreckels' death, sections of the beach were developed into the Seacliff F and the Rio Del Mar Country Club.[4]

In 1930, the first California state grant for preserving land was granted for the beach and, in 1931, it became a state beach.

SS *Palo Alto*

The beach's most notable feature is the concrete ship SS *Palo Alto* lying at the end of a pier. The ship was hauled to Seacliff Beach in 1929 and sank and turned into an amusement center complete with a dance floor, cafe, pool, and carnival booths.[5] The Cal-Nevada Company constructed a dance floor on the main deck, a cafe in the superstructure of the ship, a 4-foot heated swimming pool and a series of carnival type concessions on the aft-deck. The Cal-Nevada Company went bankrupt after only two seasons and the ship was stripped. This left the pier and the ship used only for fishing.[6] It is now permanently closed to the public.

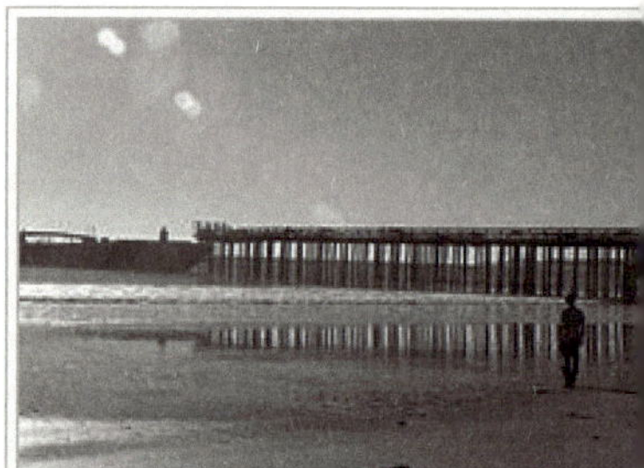

The fishing pier leading to SS Palo Alto at Seacliff State Beach.

Animal and plant life

The beach is home to many types of birds and marine life, including mussels, ocean worms, sea s sea anemones, barnacles, rock crabs, harbor seals, anglers, flounder, mackerel, halibut, lingcod, p cabezon, jacksmelt, steelhead, anchovy, bocaccio (tomcod), kingfish, dark seabirds, sea lions, dolphins, harbor seals, sea otters and whales. The Palo Alto serves as a main place for marine life

Recreation

Seacliff includes RV facilities, picnic tables, and fire pits. It is also a popular place for surfing and fishing.

See also

- List of California state parks
- California State Beaches

External links

- California parks department

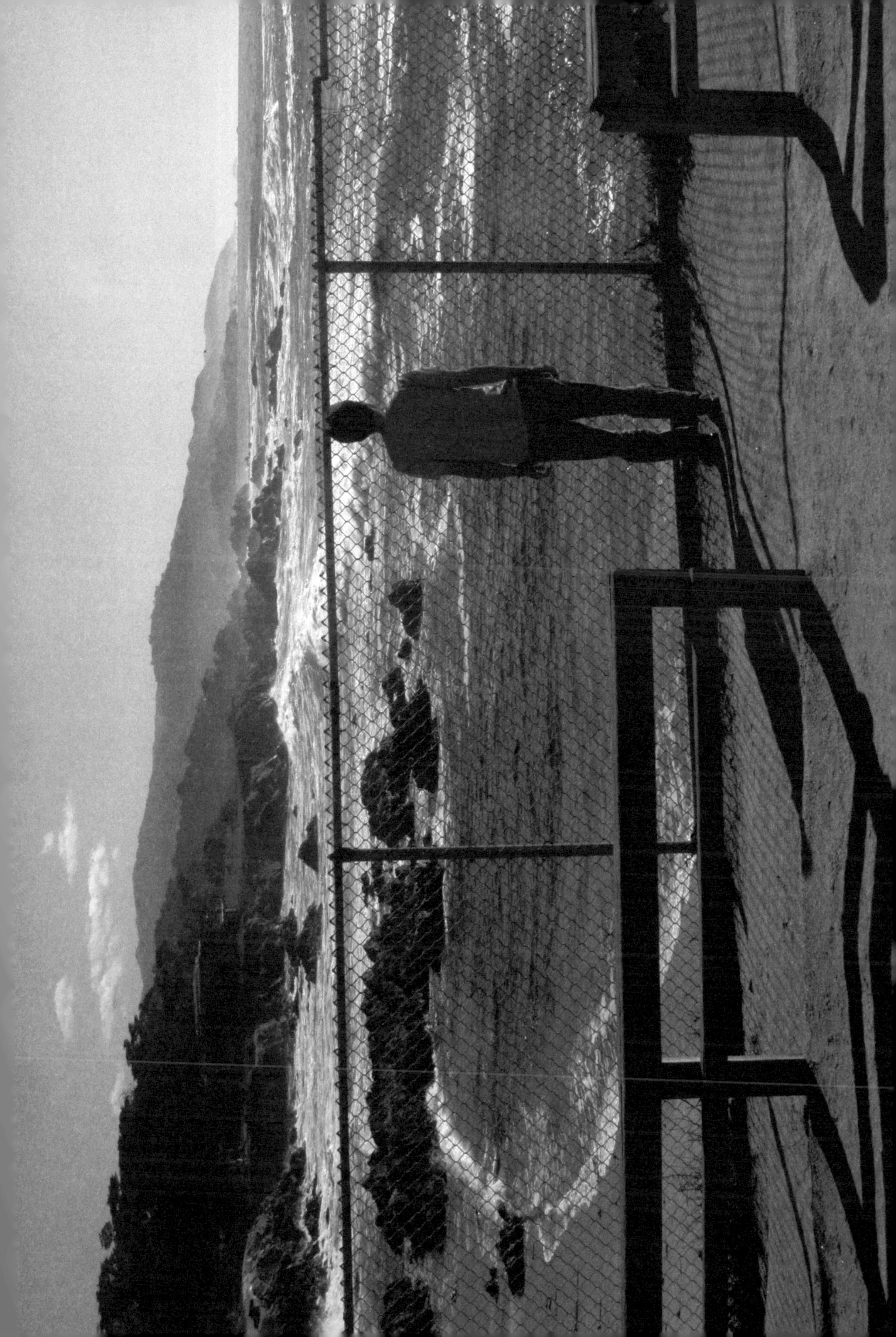

of it serves as the main road through the gated community of Pebble Beach. Inside this community, nonresidents have to pay a toll to use the road.[1] Like the community, the majority of 17-Mile Drive is owned and operated by the Pebble Beach Corporation. The 17-Mile Drive is a 17-mile (27 km)-long scenic loop having five entrances, including one at California State Route 1 and one at Pacific Grove off Sunset Drive.

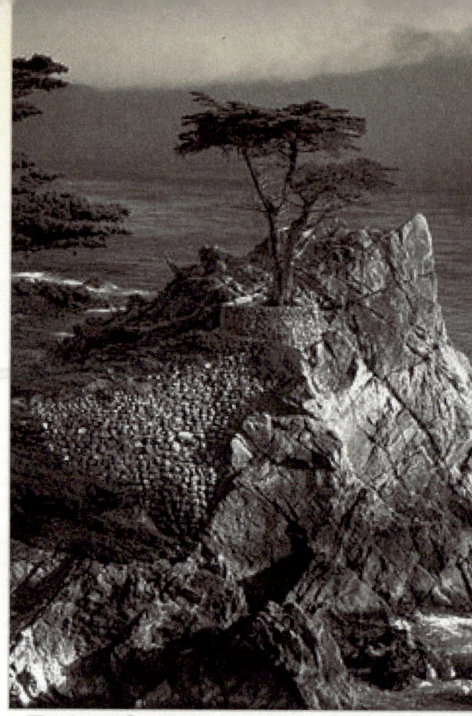

The Lone Cypress, a prominent landmark along road

Maintained by	Pebble Beach Company
From	Del Monte Blvd in Pacific Grove
Major junctions	SR 68 / Sunset Dr Carmel Way
To	SR 68 / SR 1

Contents [hide]

Route description [edit]

At the north end, a portion of the early route through Pacific Grove begins at the intersection of Del Monte Blvd and Esplanade Street. The famous portion of 17-Mile Drive then begins a few miles south of this point. The crossing of Highway 68 (Holman Highway/Sunset Drive) and 17-Mile Drive marks the entrance to Pebble Beach.

From the Sunset Drive/Pacific Grove gate, the drive runs inland past Spanish Bay, then adjacent to beaches and up into the coastal hills, providing sce viewpoints. The route allows for self-directed travel and stopping, with frequent turnouts along the roadway in many locations along the route. Without stops, it takes a minimum of 20 minutes to rea Carmel. The numerous turnouts allow stopping to take pictures, or getting out to stroll along the oce among the trees. Visitors receive a map that points out some of the more scenic spots. In addition red-dashed line is marked in the center of the main road to guide visitors, and help prevent them fr venturing into the adjacent neighborhood streets.[2]

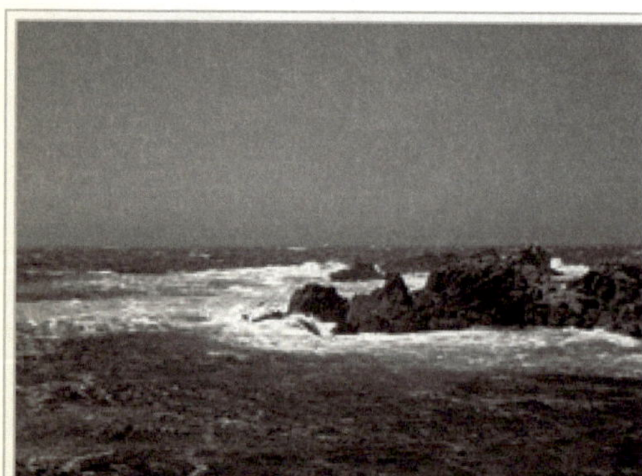

The turbulent coastline

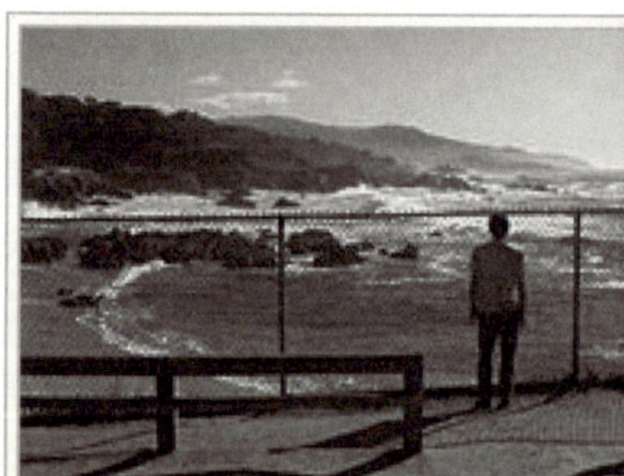

A view from Sunset Point on 17 Mile Drive

The road provides vistas of golf courses including Spyglass Hill, Cypress Point and Pebble Beach. After reaching Carmel Way, and the exit to Carmel, the 17-Mile Drive then heads northeast to Highway 68/Highway 1 interchange, where one can exit, or continue to loop along the higher vistas

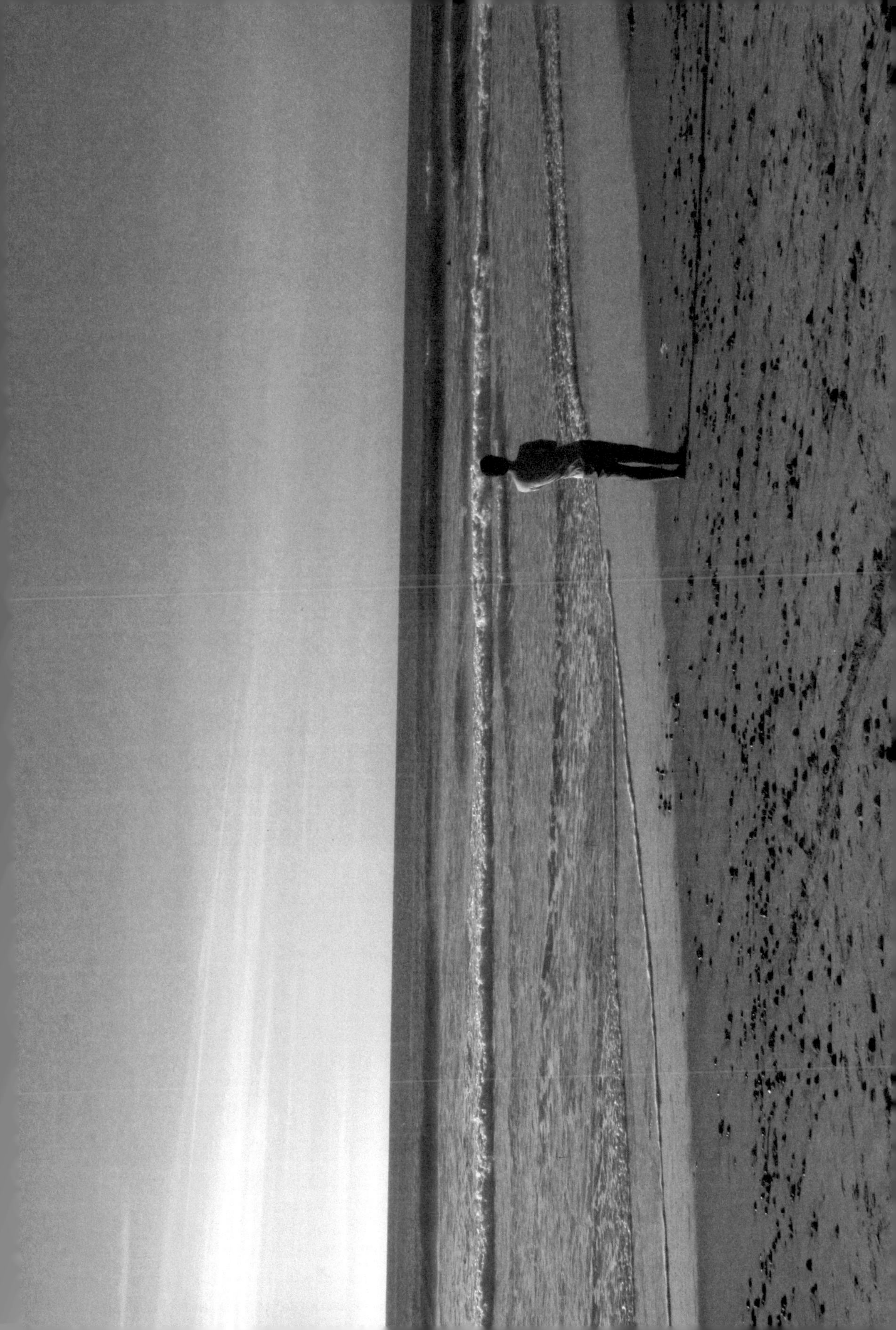

IPEDIA
Encyclopedia

e

content
vents
article
Wikipedia
ion

Wikipedia
unity portal
changes
t Wikipedia
x
port

Create account

Article Talk Read Edit View history Search

South Carlsbad State Beach

From Wikipedia, the free encyclopedia

Coordinates: 33°06′14″N 117°19′

South Carlsbad State Beach is a beach located in Carlsbad, California.

Known for being a place for swimming, surfing, skin diving, fishing, and picnicking, the campground, which is led by the stairway from the beach, is very popular during the summer.[1]

This beach is located immediately south of Carlsbad State Beach.

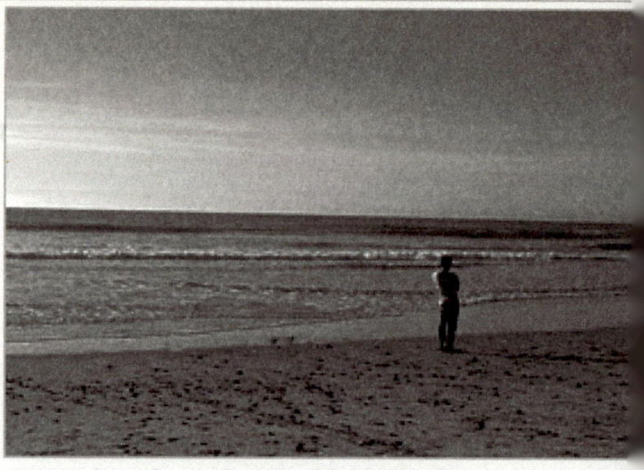
A view from South Carlsbad State Beach.

References [edit]

1. ^ South Carlsbad SB, accessed March 5, 2010

External links

- official **South Carlsbad State Beach** website

V·T·E **Protected areas of California** [sh

This California-related article is a stub. You can help Wikipedia by expanding it.

Categories: Beaches of Southern California | Parks in San Diego County, California | California State Beaches | Landforms of San Diego County, California | Carlsbad, California | California stubs

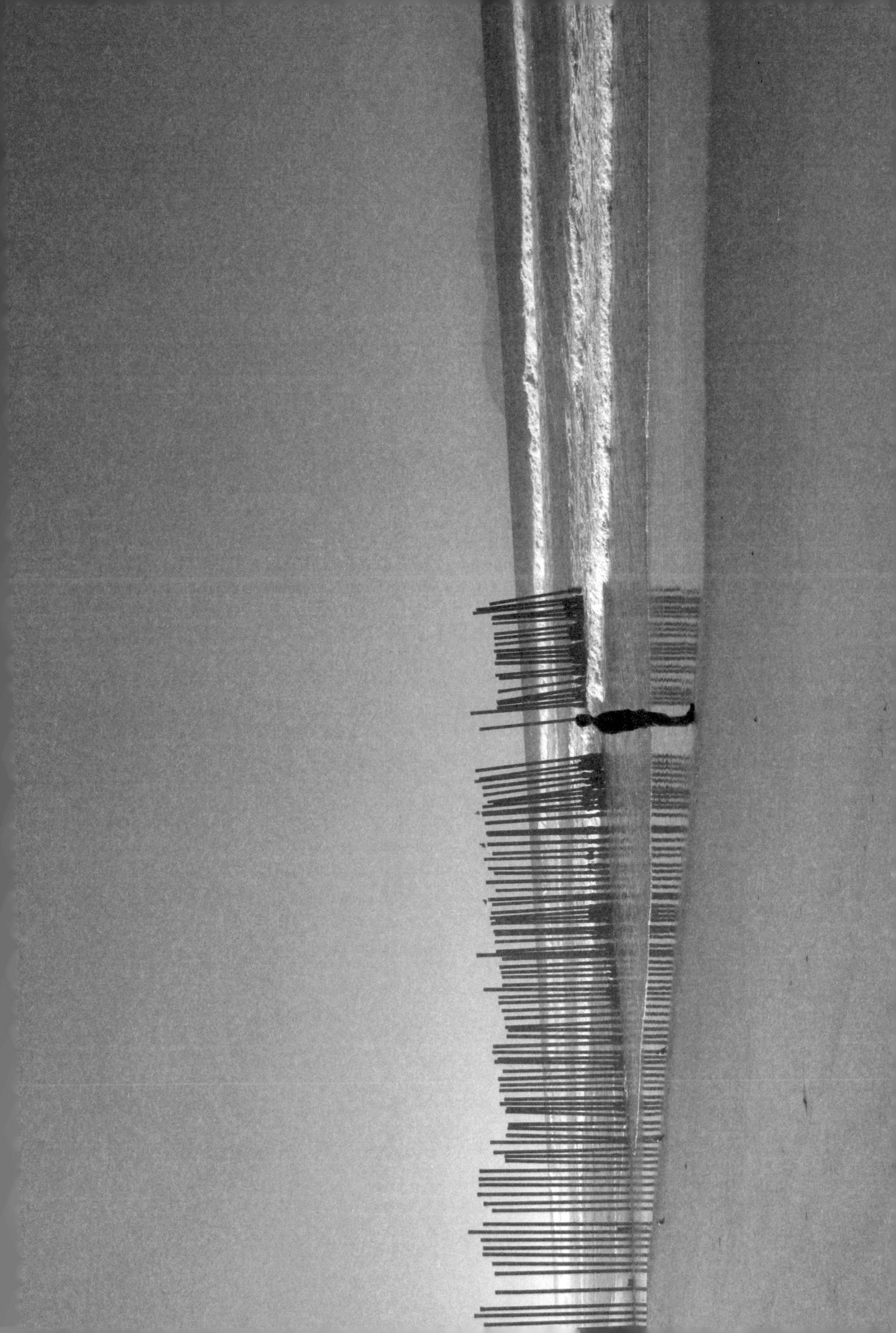

Border Field State Park

From Wikipedia, the free encyclopedia

Coordinates: 32°32′4″N 117°7′22

Border Field State Park is a state park of California, USA, containing beach and coastal habitat on the Mexico – United States border. The park is located within the city limits of Imperial Beach in San Diego County, adjacent to the suburb of Playas de Tijuana in Mexico. It is the southwesternmost point of the contiguous United States and is also the southernmost point in the state of California.[1]

The Tijuana River National Estuarine Research Reserve contains much of Border Field State Park and is an important wildlife habitat. The salt and freshwater marshes give refuge to migrating waterfowl and resident wading birds, such as Black-necked Stilt, American Avocet, Green-winged Teal, American Wigeon and pelicans. The park offers hiking, horse trails, surf fishing and birding.[1]

The Treaty of Guadalupe Hidalgo was concluded on February 2, 1848, officially ending the war between the United States and Mexico. It provided that the new international border between the two countries be established by a joint United States and Mexican Boundary Survey. The commission began its survey at Border Field.[1]

Approximately 53,000 people visit the Tijuana River National Estuarine Research Reserve and Border Field State Park each year.[*citation needed*]

Small portions of the park often become flooded and are inaccessible to the public. New border fences have also taken small portions of the park away.

Border Field State Park

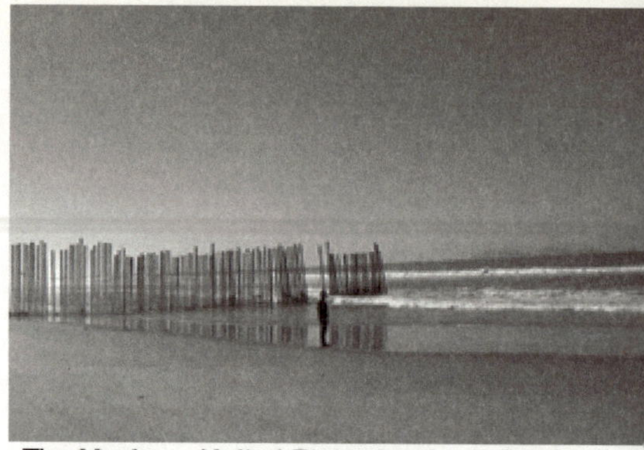

The Mexico – United States border at Border Fiel
State Park

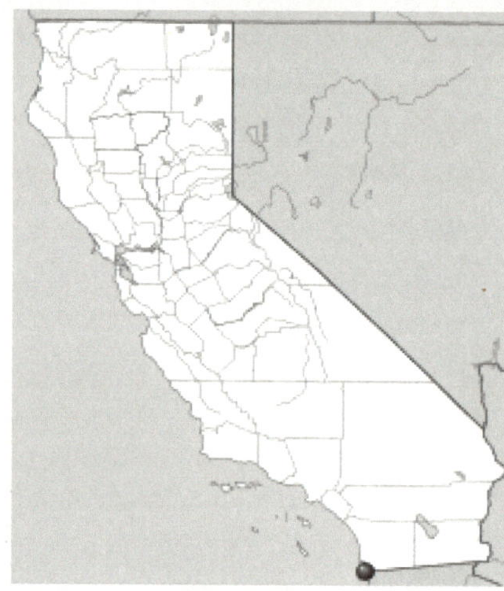

Location	San Diego County, California, USA
Nearest city	Imperial Beach, California
Coordinates	32°32′4″N 117°7′22″W
Area	1,316 acres (533 ha)
Established	1972
Governing body	California Department of Parks and Recreation

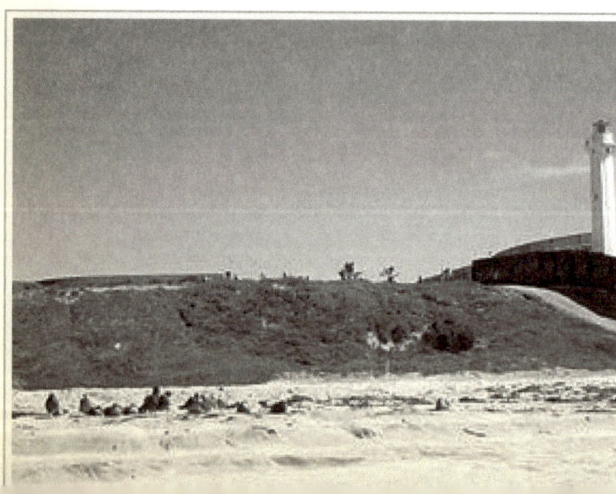

Article Talk Read Edit View history Search

WIKIPEDIA
The Free Encyclopedia

Main page
Contents
Featured content
Current events
Random article
Donate to Wikipedia

Interaction
Help
About Wikipedia
Community portal
Recent changes
Contact Wikipedia

Toolbox

Print/export

Languages
Français
Edit links

Silver Strand (San Diego)

From Wikipedia, the free encyclopedia
(Redirected from Silver Strand State Beach)

Coordinates: 32.64660°N 117.14

Silver Strand, or simply **The Strand**, is a low, narrow, sandy isthmus 7 miles (11 km) long in San Diego County, California partially within the Silver Strand State Beach. It connects Coronado "Island" (actually not an island but the northern end of the Silver Strand) with Imperial Beach. Together with the Point Loma peninsula it shelters and defines San Diego Bay. State highway 75 runs the length of the strand and is a popular site for jogging and bicycling. The Silver Strand Half Marathon is run along the route each November.[1]

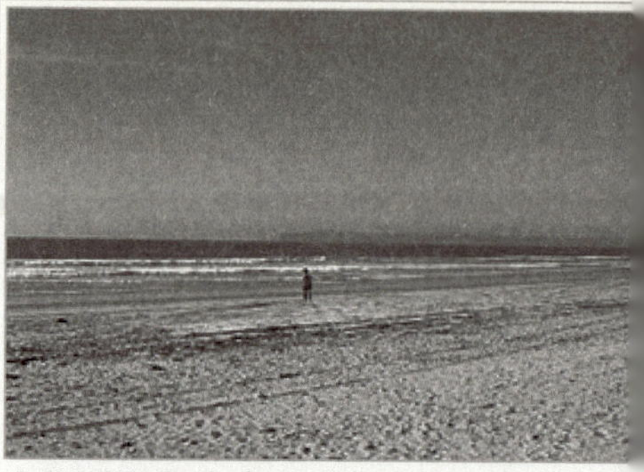

A view of the Pacific Ocean at Silver Strand Beach.

Silver Strand State Beach, which encompasses both the San Diego Bay and Pacific Ocean sides of the strand, is a little farther off the beaten path the highly popular beaches in Ocean Beach and Mission Beach, offering more solitude for those wh wish to get away from the beach crowds. The ocean side of the strand features 2.5 miles (4.0 km) coastline trimmed with silver shells (thus named Silver Strand).

Contents [hide]

Beach

The Silver Strand State Beach is just 4.5 miles (7.2 km) south of Coronado on California State Rou The beach offers many activities including camping, surfing, swimming, body boarding, jet skiing, sailing, and water skiing, as well as fishing and beach volleyball. [2] There are approximately 130 fir come, first serve campsites. Park facilities include four large parking lots, which can accommodate to 1,000 vehicles. This recreational destination features camping, fishing, swimming, surfing, boatir water-skiing, volleyball, and picnicking are popular activities. Anglers can fish for perch, corbina, gr and yellow-fin croaker. [3]

Military Bases

The beaches north and south of the state beach are military property. North of it is Naval Amphibio Base Coronado and south of it is Silver Strand Training Complex. Much of the SEALs' training take place on the beaches.

References

1. ^ "Silver Strand Half Marathon & 5K". Retrieved March 7, 2013.
2. ^ California State Parks
3. ^ California Resort Life

External links

- official **Silver Strand State Beach** website

Categories: Beaches of Southern California | California State Beaches | Parks in San Diego County, California | Peninsulas of California

PUBLIC ACCESS

Between late December, 2010, and early January, 2011, I drove the entire California Coast. The trip started at the Mexican border at Border Field State Park and ended at Pelican State Beach on the Oregon border. The drive covered the entirety of California's Highway 1, also known as the Pacific Coast Highway. I made photographs of the view of the Pacific Ocean at over fifty different coastal access points along the trip. In each photograph I stood somewhere in the frame. My back was always facing the camera as I looked toward the horizon.

All of the photographs were placed onto the Wikipedia articles about the specific coastal points. Here, the title, *Public Access*, plays on both the public nature of the Internet (more specifically the 2.0 nature of Wikipedia) and California's coast as public property. I added new photographs to articles that had preexisting images. But for many coasts, whose locations were remote, these images became the first visual data for the articles. In one case, I had to create the Wikipedia entry for the location. Lacking an article, I created the Wikipedia entry for Oakland's Radio Beach near the Bay Bridge.

Each photograph depicts a kind of looking that is impossible online. One in which you stare out at the horizon, out into the distance. There is no distance online. Vision is mediated by a flickering screen only inches away from your eyes. The Internet also produces an imagined space in which the faraway no longer seems far away. The instantaneous movement of information makes everywhere seem right here. What is longed for is not only the faraway, but also a right here that your presence can fully occupy.

The intent of the project was to create a body of photographs that would circulate as a kind of meta-data for these locations. The photos would be hosted on Wikipedia, but could recirculate outside of Wikipedia, as they are sourced and re-hosted as free information. My image, standing anonymously and staring out into the distance, would be carried with this movement. I wanted to be the anonymous person who you happen to find in a snapshot whose existence is caught in the split second of time it takes to make a photograph.

The project essentially never really has an end. There is the moment of inception, the posting of the photographs, which puts them into motion. What happens in this movement can be repackaged into the project. Any future exhibition or publication would inevitably contain new activity.

After I posted the first batch of photographs (from Border Field State Park to San Francisco), discussions began to emerge in the background of Wikipedia. Wikipedia users had noticed the same IP address tinkering with articles about California beaches. I tried to hide my IP address by creating multiple usernames when posting the next set of photographs (San Francisco to Pelican State Beach). But, I was noticed again and accused of sock puppetry (creating multiple usernames for purposes of deception). The reason I was using multiple usernames was an attempt to make my actions untraceable. If one user (or a single IP address) is discovered, all of their actions, linked together, would be in plain sight. Wikipedia users discussed what to do with my photographs, and debated what, if anything, was actually wrong. Did the photographs violate something? Did they deviate from some unspoken photographic standard?

My favorite reaction was when a Wikipedia user decided that my photographs actually served a valuable purpose. However, following the discussions, this user decided that the best option was to remove the figure (me) from the photographs, and re-upload them. I was taken out of my own project. Isn't releasing something into a commons a gesture of removing oneself? These edited photographs were residue of the project. A trace without a trace.

Soon after the original postings, all but one image was removed. The lone standing image was for Bodega Head, the first California photograph that I had uploaded to Wikipedia, taken sometime before the road trip, and before I had even conceived of the project. This one photo was the seed to *Public Access*. It was not traceable since it was done at a different time, and could not be associated with the cluster of activity. The key to go unnoticed was time, not space. I originally thought I would be able to hide in the space of the image, in the margins, where the central subject does not occupy—like in the distance, in the shadows, or off to the side. Or, I thought I could hide through my own anonymity, by the fact that you could not see my face. But doing all the editing close together, the pattern of what seemed to be the same figure showing up on various California beaches became noticeable. Recently I began to re-upload the photographs slowly. Instead of hiding in space, I am trying to hide in time.

PRIVATE ACCESS

In the autumn of 2012 I made a few road trips up the Atlantic coast from my home in Brooklyn. Each drive I mapped out an itinerary of coastal locations that I found online using real estate and mapping websites. The sites were all privately owned beachfront properties: private clubs, hotels, individually owned property, land currently in development, and the like. At each location I made a photograph of the view of the ocean. I stood in the frame, with my back to the camera. In each photograph there are two views: the view that is visible (the camera's view), and the view from the position where I am standing. Both my location and the location of the camera were located within the property lines. In a sense, this very view, made possible from this specific point, is privately owned.

But the photographs are not just these private views. They are another possible way of looking. Each photograph also becomes evidence of an act of trespassing. This view also becomes the view of the trespasser. A view that is stolen.

A selection of these photographs were then uploaded to Wikipedia on the pages for the general locations of where I stood: West Bay Shore, New York; Branford, Connecticut; Truro, Massachusetts. And they were also uploaded to pages such as "Private beach" (which has since merged into a single article for "Beach") and "Private property." In a sense, these private views were taken, and placed back into a public space—the public space of a digital commons.

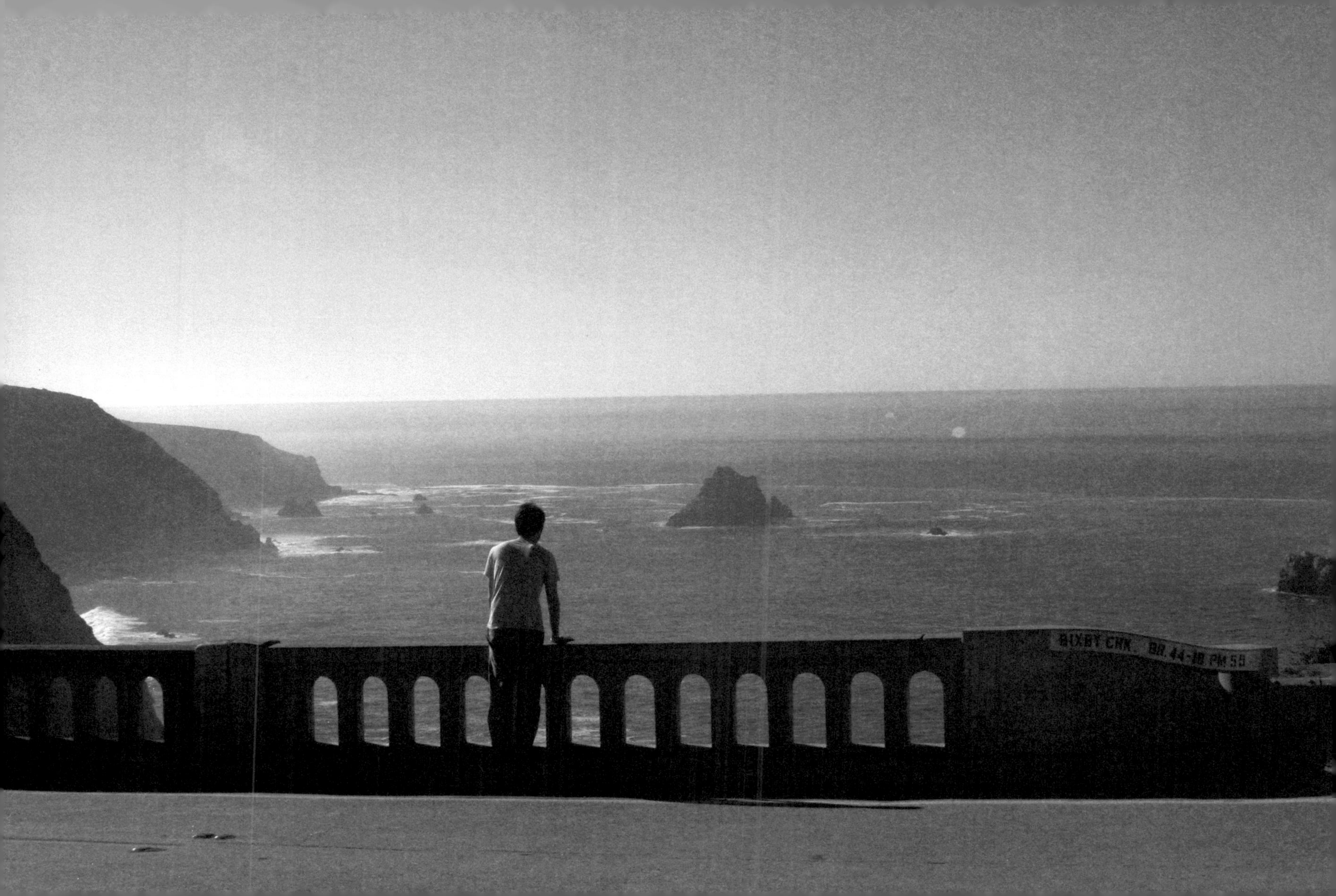
BIXBY CRK. BR. 44-18 PM 59

support the arch during construction was transported from the railroad terminal in Monterey over the narrow, one-way road to the bridge site. The falsework, built by crews led by E.C. Panton, the genera superintendent, and I.O. Jahlstrom, resident engineer of Ward Engineering Co., was difficult to raise because it was constantly exposed to high winds. Some of the falsework timbers were 10 by 10 feet (3.0 m × 3.0 m).[8] It took two months to construct the falsework alone. When high waves threatened falsework foundation, construction was halted for a short time until winter storms abated.[6]

The crews excavated 4,700 cubic yards (3,600 m^3) of earth and rock, and consumed 45,000 sacks c cement.[9] Eight hundred twenty-five trucks brought in 6,600 cubic yards (5,000 m^3) cubic yards of concrete and 600,000 pounds of reinforcing steel.[9] Sand and gravel was supplied from a plant in Bi Sur.

Crews began pouring concrete on November 27. The cement was transported from Davenport near S Cruz, and from San Andreas.[6] Material was transported across the canyon from platforms using sli suspended from a cable 300 feet (91 m) above the creek. The bridge was completed on October 15, 1932.[10] At its completion, the bridge cost $199,861 and was the longest concrete arch span at 320 (98 m) on the California State Highway System.[7]

Opening and dedication

In 1937, after 18 years of construction and aided by New Deal funds and the use of convict labor, th paved two-lane road now known as Highway 1 was completed.[11]

Seismic retrofitting

The bridge was retrofitted beginning in 1996 with an analysis by bridge engineering company Buckland & Taylor as part of the Caltrans Phase II seismic retrofit program.[12] In their detailed evaluation of the bridge's seismic vulnerabilities, they were challenged to find a solution that met several difficult challenges, including severe load factors, extremely limited physical access, maintaining the appearance of the existing historical structure, and a requirement by the State of California that at least one lane of the bridge remain open at all times. The crux of the design was the longitudinal posttensioning of the entire bridge deck from end to end.[13]

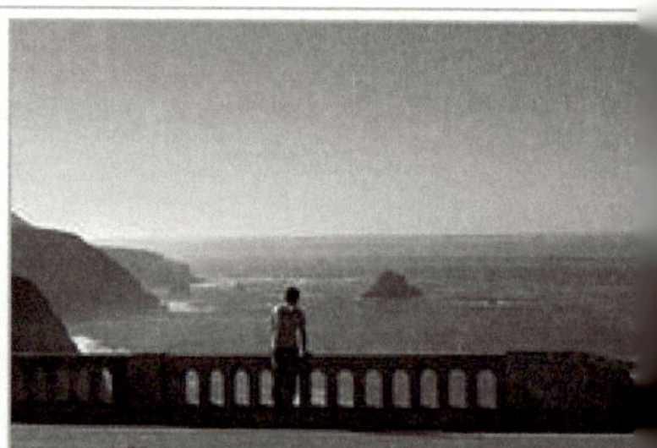

A view of the Pacific Ocean from the bridge.

The $20 million seismic retrofit began in May, 1998. The cost of the retrofit was considerably increa by the requirement to preserve the historical look of the bridge.[3] Prime contractor Vahani Construct of San Francisco was assisted by Faye Bernstein & Associates and Waldron Engineering. To supp the abutments, engineers put in place a floating slab, continuous with the deck, keyed into a massi pile cap with six 72 inches (1,800 mm) diameter cast-in-drilled-hole (CIDH) piles behind each abutm To support the towers, engineers designed a full height structural wall that was integrated within eac the two existing towers. During the retrofit, they removed the top portion of the towers, including the roadway, and replaced them with a prestressed diaphragm that anchors the full height of the vertica tower. The diaphragm simultaneously distributes the vertical prestressing forces uniformly to the ne concrete structural wall and the existing tower's concrete.[14]

The deck, which curves from one end to the other, was reinforced by adding heavily confined edge beams encasing high strength steel along the inside face of the exterior longitudinal girders underne These rods extended from one end of the roadway to the other. The reinforced edge beams ensure continuity across the many expansion joints and help distribute the bending strains due to lateral flexure.[14] In addition to the reinforced edge beam, four large prestressing tendons were installed th length of the bridge along the underside of the deck slab. These tendons are stressed to pre-compr the concrete deck to approximately 800 psi and also serve as flexural reinforcement along with the strength rods. Finally, engineers found a way to reinforce the bent columns attached to the arch, wh

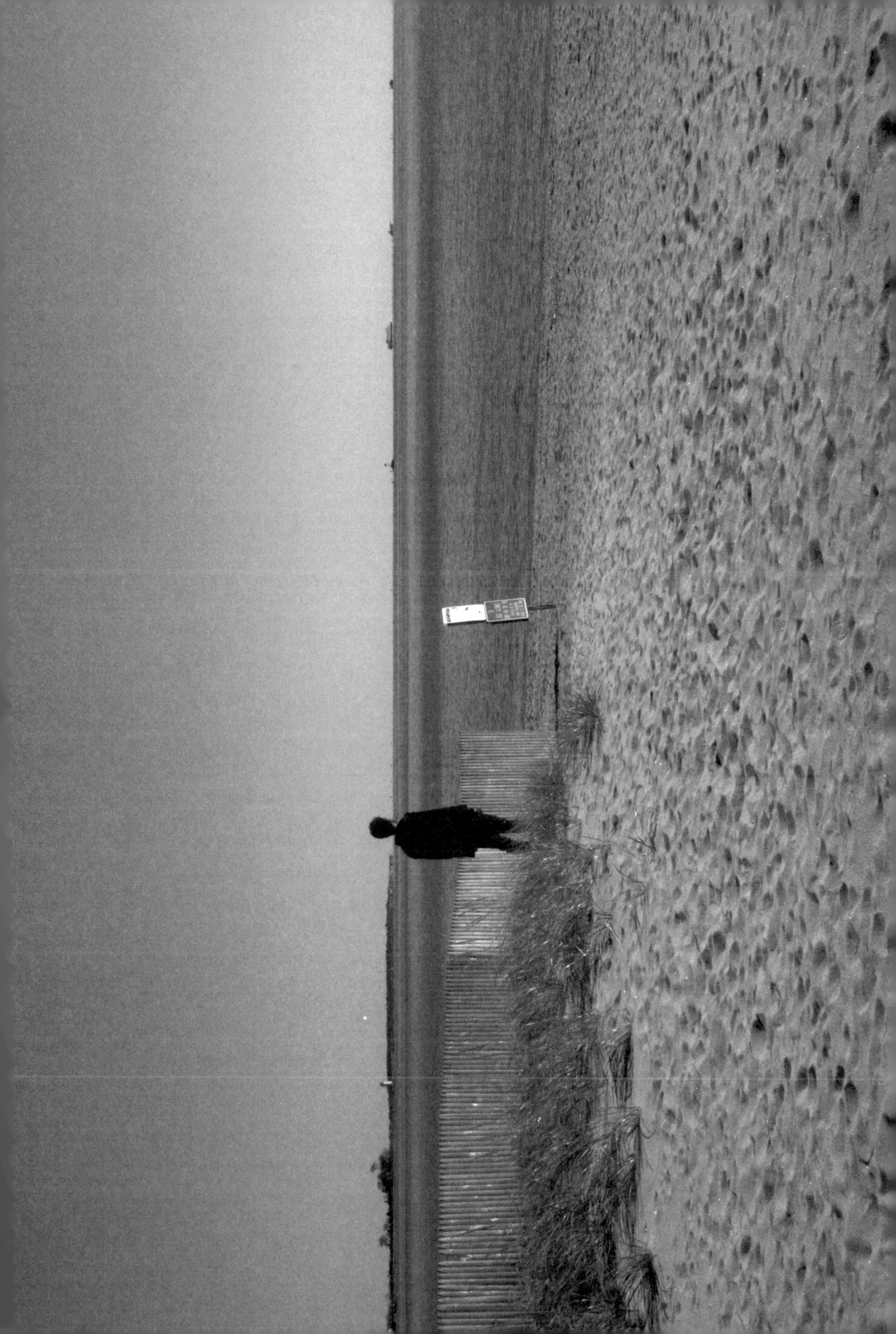

Create account

Article Talk Read Edit View history Search

Main page
Contents
Featured content
Current events
Random article
Donate to Wikipedia

Interaction
Help
About Wikipedia
Community portal
Recent changes
Contact Wikipedia

Toolbox

Print/export

Fairfield Beach (Fairfield)

From Wikipedia, the free encyclopedia

Coordinates: 41.1218°N 73.2

Fairfield Beach is a neighborhood of Fairfield, Connecticut.

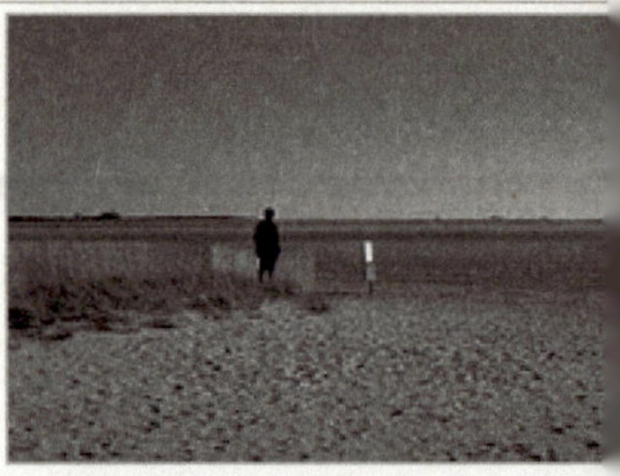
A view of the Long Island Sound from Fairfield Beach.

Contents [hide]

Location [edit]

Fairfield Beach is located to the south of downtown Fairfield, and the neighborhood extends south from Old Post Road to the Long Island Sound. neighborhood originally held a variety of income levels, with small family farms such as the Hauser farm on the corner of Reef Road and Charles Street on one end of the spectrum, and small summer cottages on the beach at the other. While only a few families lived there year in the early and mid-twentieth century, including the Barry, Flanagan, Hauser, Leverit and Lai families, the neighborhood began growing in popularity for year-round residents throughout th 1970s and 1980s.

Throughout the 1960s and 1970s the neighborhood was also known for its beach bars, includ the "Beachside" across from Penfield Beach, and "Flanagan's" on the corner of Reef and Fai Beach Road. Before Reef Road was widened, the corner of Reef and Fairfield Beach Road w home to several small stores, including "Danny's" and a fish-and-chips shop owned by Mayn Benson, called "Maynard's Reef." Flanagan's was originally owned by "Chippy" Flanagan but became the "Nautilus" under new ownership, and continued under this name until the 1980s, the bar was bought, renamed the "Seagrape," and remodeled to attract the student crowd fro Fairfield University.

Following the overwhelming onslaught of student renters from Fairfield University in the 197 and the aggressive expansion of the Seagrape's owners in the 1980s and 1990s, many origi residents of the neighborhood fled, driven out by the noise and overcrowding.

The neighborhood has more recently again become popular with year-round residents due to close proximity to the Long Island Sound beaches to the south and the downtown area with train station to the north. A recent surge in the neighborhood's popularity has led to a buildin boom as many of the smaller old homes have been torn down and replaced with the larger n homes. Many of the newer homes have been constructed in a distinctive architectural style known as "Nantucket" or "beach" style. [1]

Residents of the neighborhood are represented by several neighborhood organizations, inclu the Fairfield Beach Residents Association, which represents the entire beach area, and the Acres Association, which represents residents residing within the blocks between Rowland and Penfield Road.

Traditionally, many Fairfield University students have lived in the neighborhood, and althoug numbers have decreased in recent years as property values and rents have increased, ther continues to be a significant student presence, leading to occasional conflict between stude and permanent residents.[*citation needed*]

The area includes Jennings Beach and Penfield Beach; the Veterans Park; and the Fairfiel

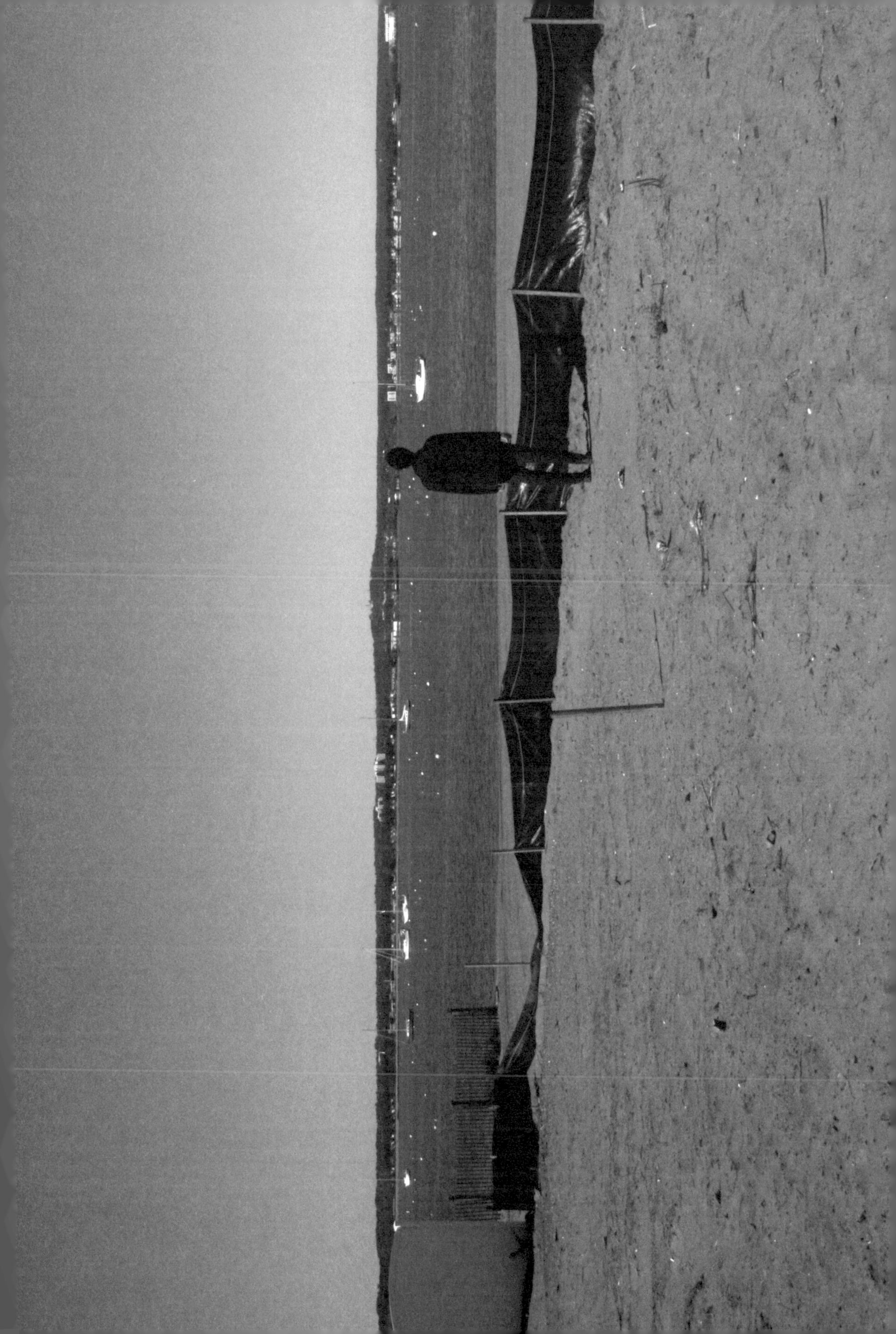

e Talk Read Edit View history Search

rivate property

n Wikipedia, the free encyclopedia

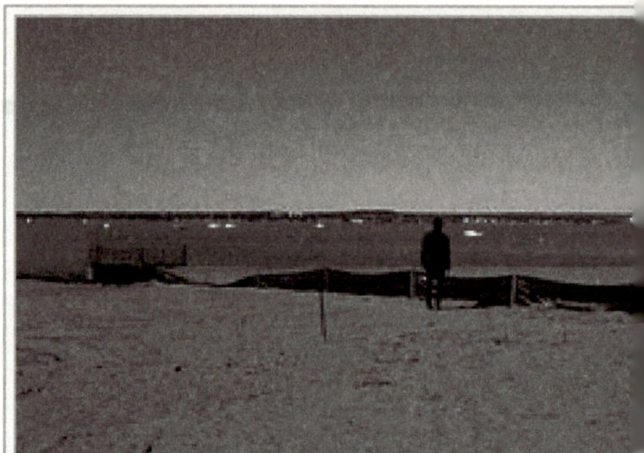

Privately owned coastal property in Connecticut under development.

vate property is the ownership of property by non-ernmental legal entities.[1] Private property is inguishable from public property which is owned by a ernmental entity and collective property, which is ned by a group of non-governmental entities [2] nership of collective property can be indeterminable, h as in a not-for-profit "private" university, or erminable, such as in a legal partnership.

Contents [hide]

story

This section requires expansion. *(November 2011)*

:onomic perspectives

This section requires expansion. *(February 2013)*

oeral perspectives

nomic liberals (defined as those who support a private sector-driven market economy) consider ate property to be essential for the construction of a prosperous society. They believe private ership of land ensures the land will be put to productive use and its value protected by the downer. If the owners must pay property taxes, this forces the owners to maintain a productive ou n the land to keep taxes current. Private property also attaches a monetary value to land, which c used to trade or as collateral. Private property thus is an important part of capitalization within the nomy.[3]

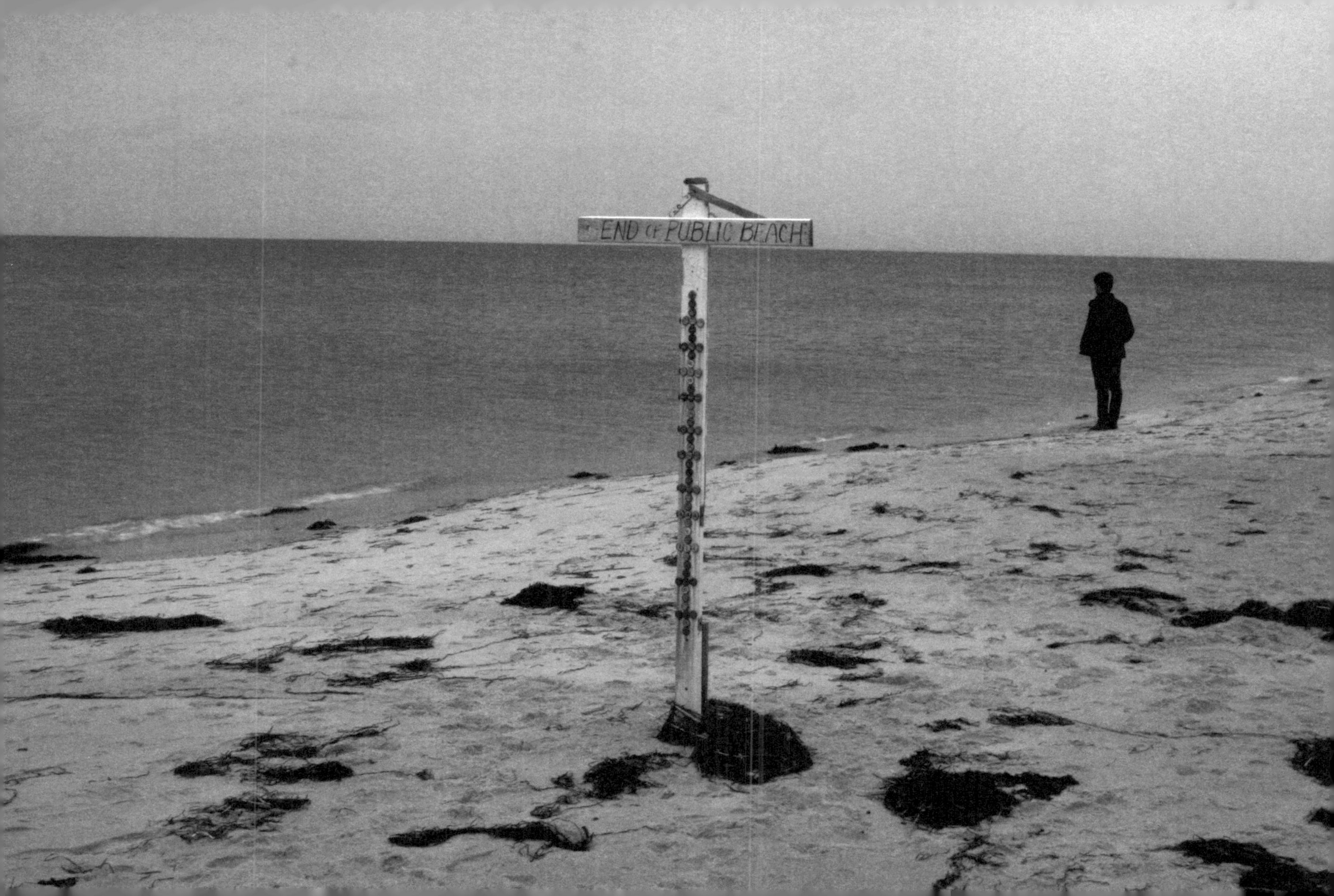
END of PUBLIC BEACH

covering beachwear of the period was considered immodest. This social standard still prevails in many Muslim countries. At the other end of the spectrum are topfree beaches and nude beaches where clothing is optional or not allowed. In most countries social norms are significantly different on a beach in hot weather, compared to adjacent areas where similar behaviour might not be tolerated and might even be prosecuted.

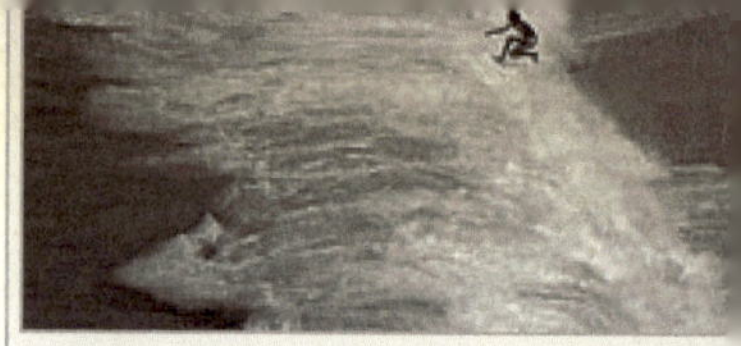

Playing in the surf is a favourite activity for many people. Porto Covo, west coas Portugal

In more than thirty countries in Europe, South Africa, New Zealand, Canada, Costa Rica, South America and the Caribbean, the best recreational beaches are awarded Blue Flag status, based on such criteria as water quality and safety provision. Subsequent loss of this status can have a severe effect on tourism revenues.

Beaches are often dumping grounds for waste and litter, necessitating the use of beach clear and other cleanup projects. More significantly, many beaches are a discharge zone for untrea sewage in most underdeveloped countries; even in developed countries beach closure is an occasional circumstance due to sanitary sewer overflow. In these cases of marine discharge, waterborne disease from fecal pathogens and contamination of certain marine species is a frequent outcome.

Artificial beaches

Some beaches are artificial; they are either permanent or temporary (For examples see Mona Paris, Copenhagen, Rotterdam, Nottingham, Toronto, Hong Kong, Singapore, and Tianjin).

The soothing qualities of a beach and the pleasant environment offered to the beachgoer are replicated in artificial beaches, such as "beach style" pools with zero-depth entry and wave p that recreate the natural waves pounding upon a beach. In a zero-depth entry pool, the bottor surface slopes gradually from above water down to depth. Another approach involves so-calle urban beaches, a form of public park becoming common in large cities. Urban beaches atter mimic natural beaches with fountains that imitate surf and mask city noises, and in some ca can be used as a play park.

Beach nourishment involves pumping sand onto beaches to improve their health. Beach nourishment is common for major beach cities around the world; however the beaches that h been nourished can still appear quite natural and often many visitors are unaware of the work undertaken to support the health of the beach. Such beaches are often not recognized (by consumers) as artificial. The Surfrider Foundation has debated the merits of artificial reefs w members torn between their desire to support natural coastal environments and opportunities enhance the quality of surfing waves. Similar debates surround beach nourishment and snow cannon in sensitive environments.

Restrictions on access [edit]

Public access to beaches is restricted in some parts of the world.[3][4] For example, most beaches on the Jersey Shore are restricted to people who can purchase beach tags.[5]

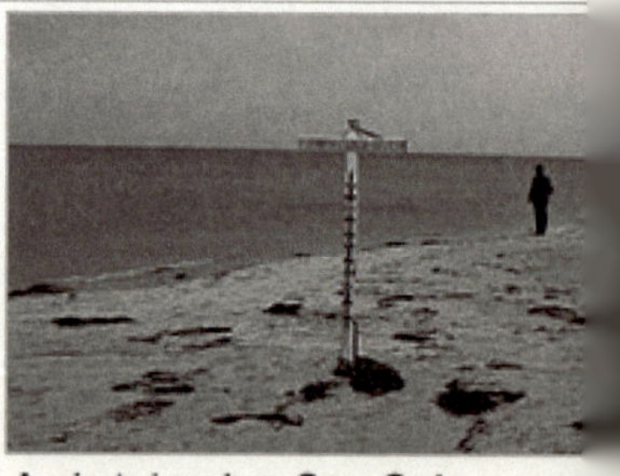

A private beach on Cape Cod.

See also [edit]

- Beach cleaner
- Beach evolution
- Coast
- List of beaches
- Sand art and play
- Shore

Thing 001895 (playing cards)

Agency

Thing 001895 (playing cards)

Since 1463, king Edward IV banned importation of playing cards in England in order to encourage domestic production. On June 13, 1576, queen Elizabeth I conferred by letters patent a monopoly to esquire Ralph Bowes to manufacture and sell playing cards, or to license others to sell them, for twelve years. Playing cards at the time relied upon print making developed for books. In 1588, Elizabeth I renewed this monopoly for twelve years. On August 11, 1598, after the death of the first patentee, Elizabeth I transfered the patent to groom Edward Darcy for twenty-one years for an annual rent of 100 pounds.

In 1600, Thomas Allin, a London haberdasher, sold 25920 sets of playing cards, without paying Darcy for the privilege or for the use of his stamp.

Darcy sued Allin alleging that Allin had imported 14400 and manufactured 11520 sets of playing cards in Westminster without his permission. In 1602, the court case *Darcy v. Allin* took place at Court of King's Bench.

Attorney Coke argued for Darcy:

> "*[...] Edward Darcy, esquire, a groom of the chamber to queen Elizabeth [...] declared, that Queen Elizabeth intending that her subjects being able men to exercise husbandry, should apply themselves there-unto, and that they should not employ themselves to the making of playing cards, which had not been any ancient manual occupation within this realm; and that the making of such a multitude of cards, card playing was become very frequent, and chiefly amongst servants and apprentices and poor artificers; and to the end her subjects might apply themselves to more faithful and necessary trades, by her letters patents under the great seal of the same did grant unto Ralph Bowes, esquire, full power, license and authority by himself, his servants, factors and deputies, to provide and buy in any parts beyond the sea, all such playing cards as he thought good, and to bring them within this realm; and to sell and utter them within the same, and that he, his servants, factors and deputies should have and enjoy the whole trade, traffic and merchandise of all playing cards. [...] And afterwards the queen [...] by her letters patents reciting the former grants made to Ralph Bowes, granted [Edward Darcy], his executors, administrators, and their deputies, the same privileges, authorities, and other the said premises for one and twenty years after the end of the former time, rendering to the queen hundred marks per annum; And further granted to him a seal for to mark the cards. And further declared [...] that [Allin] knowing the said grant and prohibition in the [Darcy]'s letters patents [...] without the queens license or [Darcy]'s at Westminster did cause eighty grosses of playing cards to be made and as well those, as 100 other grosses of playing cards, of which many were made within the realm, or brought within the realm by [Darcy], or his servants, factors or deputies, etc... nor marked with his seal; he had imported within the realm, and had sold and uttered them to sundry persons unknown, and shewed some in certain, for which [Darcy] could not utter his playing cards. "Contra formam praedict' literar' patentium, et in contemptum dictae Dominae Reginae" [Against the form of the aforesaid letters patent and in contempt of the said lady queen] [...]*"[1]

And attorney Fuller argued for Allin:

> "*[...] [Allin], besides to one half gross pleaded, not guilty; and as to that he pleaded, that the city of London is an ancient city, and within the same, time out of mind there hath been a society of haberdashers; and that within the said city there was a custom, "Quod quaelibet persona de societate illa, usus fuit et consuevit emere vendere, et libere merchandizare omnem rem et omnes res merchandizabiles infra hoc regnum Angliae de quocunque, vel quibuscunque personis" [That every person of that society has been used and accustomed to buy, sell, and trade freely all merchantable property within this realm of England from whatsoever person or persons, etc...]. And pleaded, that he was*

[1] *Darcy v. Allin*

> *"civis et liber homo de civitate et societate illa" [a citizen and free man of the city and of that society] and sold the said half gross of playing cards, being made within the realm as it was lawful from him to do; upon which the [Darcy] did demure in law. [...] Now therefore I will shew you how the judges have heretofore allowed of monopoly patents which is that where any man by his won charge and industry or by his own wit or invention doth bring any new trade into the realm of any engine tending to the furtherance of a trade that never was used before and that for the good of the realm; that in such cases the king may grant to him a monopoly patent for some reasonable time, until the subjects may learn the same, in consideration of the good that he doth bring by his invention to the commonwealth; otherwise not."*[2]

On the one hand judge Popham asked:

> *"[...] If the said grant to [Darcy] of the sole making of cards within the realm were good or not? [...] 1. Because the said playing cards were not any merchandise, or thing concerning trade of any necessary use, but things of vanity, and the occasion of expense of time, wasting of patrimonies, and of the livings of many, the loss of the service and work of servants, causes of want, which is the mother of wo and perdition, and therefore it belonged to the queen (who is "Parens patriae, paterfamilias totius regni" [Parent of the country, and the family head of the whole realm]), to take away the great abuse, and to take order for the moderate and convenient use of them. 2. In matters of recreation and pleasure the queen had a prerogative given her by the law to take such order for such moderate use of them as shall seem good to her. 3. The queen in regard of the great abuse of them, and of the deceit of the subjects by reason of them might utterly suppress them, and by consequence without injury to any one, she might moderate and suffer them at her pleasure. And the reason of the law which gave the king these prerogatives in matters of recreation and pleasure was, because the greatest part of men are ready to exceed in them. And upon these grounds diverse cases were put. That no subject can make a park, chase, or warren within his own land, for his recreation or pleasure without the kings grant or license; and if he do it of his own head in a "quo warranto", they shall be seized into the king's hands [...]. The king granted to another [a license for] all the wild swans between London bridge and Oxford. [...]"*[3]

On the other hand judge Popham asked:

> *"[...] If the license or dispensation to have the sole importation of foreign cards granted to [Darcy], were available or not in law. To the bar, no regard was had, because it was no more then the common law would have said, and then no such particular custom ought to have been alleged, for in his "quae de jure communi omnibus conceduntur, consuetudo alicujus patriae vel loci non est alleganda" [in those things that are granted by the common law to everyone, the custom of any region or place is not to be alleged], and there with agreed. [...] the said Grant to [Darcy] of the sole making of cards within the realm was void; and that for two reasons. The same is a monopoly, and against the common law. That it is against diverse acts of parliament.[...]"*[4]

First he stated it was against the common law, for four causes:

> *"[...] 1. All trades, as well mechanical, as others, which avoid idleness (the bane of the commonwealth) and exercise men and youths in labor for the maintenance of them and their families, and for the increase of their livings, to serve the queen if need be were profitable for the commonwealth; and therefore the grant to [Darcy] to have the sole making of them is against the common law, and the benefit and liberty of the subject; and there*

[2] *Darcy v. Allin*

[3] *Darcy v. Allin*

[4] *Darcy v. Allin*

with agreed "Fortescue in laudibus Legum Angliae" [chief justice of England]. And a case was adjudged in this court in an action of trespass between Davenant and Hurdis where the case was, that the company of merchant tailors in London having power by charter to make ordinances for the better rule and government of the company, made an ordinance, that every brother of the same society, who should put any cloth to be dressed by any cloth worker not being a brother of the same society, shall expose one half of his clothes to any brother of the same society, who exercised the art of a cloth worker, upon pain of forfeiting ten shillings, and to distrein for it, and it was adjudged, that the ordinance, although it had the countenance of a charter, was against the common law, because it was against the liberty of the subject; for every subject by the law hath freedom and liberty to put his cloths to be dressed by what cloth worker he pleased, and cannot be restrained to certain persons, for that in effect shall be a monopoly; and therefore such ordinance by color of a charter, or any grant by charter to such effect shall be void. [...]

[...] 2. The sole trade of any mechanical artifice, or any other monopoly is not only a damage and prejudice to those who exercise the same trade, but also to all other subjects, for the end of all these monopolies is for the private gain of the patentees; and although provisions and cautions be added to moderate them; yet "res profecto stulta est nequitiae modus" [it is indeed a useless thing to moderate wickedness]; it is mere folly to think that there is any measure in mischief or wickedness. And therefore there are three inseparable incidents to every monopoly against the commonwealth. [a.] That the price of the said commodity shall be raised, for he who had the sole selling of any commodity, may make the price as he pleased. And this word, monopoly, is said, "Cum unus solus aliquod genus mercaturae universum emit, pretium ad suum libitum statuens" [Monopoly is said when one single person buys the whole of any kind of merchandise and sets the price at his pleasure]. And the poet said, "Omnia Castor emit, sic fit ut omnia vendat" [Castor buys everything, so that he may sell everything]. And it appeared by the writ of "Ad quod damnum" [Writ directing the sheriff to determine what damage there would be if a Royal charter such as for a fair is granted]. That every gift or grant from the king had this condition, either expressly or tacitly annexed to it, "Illa quod patria per donationem illam magis solito non oneretur seu gravetur" [that the country should not be more burdened or vexed by that donation than is usual]. And therefore every grant made in grievance and prejudice of the subject is void; the kings grant which tended to the charge and prejudice of the subject is void. [b.] The second incident to a monopoly is, that after a monopoly granted, the commodity is not so good and merchantable as it was before; for the patentee having the sole trade, regarded only his private, and not the public wealth. [c.] This same leaded to the impoverishing of diverse artificers and others, who before by labor of their hands in their art or trade had kept themselves and their families, who now of necessity shall be constrained to live in idleness and beggary; "vide Fortescue ubi supra" [in the above passage]. And the common law in this point agreed with the equity of the law of god, [...] "Non accipies loco pignoris inferiorem et superiorem molam, quia animam suam apposuit tibi" [Do not take the lower and the upper millstone as a pledge, because that would take his life]; you shall not take in pledge the needed and upper milestone, for the same is his life; by which it appeared, that every mans trade doth maintains his life, and therefore he ought not to be deprived or dispossessed of it, no more than of his life. And the same also agreed with the civil law; "Apud Justinianum monopolia non esse intromittenda, quoniam non ad commodum reipublicae sed ad labem detrimentaque pertinent. Monopolia interdixerunt leges civiles, cap. De Monopoliis

lege unica. Zeno imperator statuit, ut exercentes monopolia bonis omnibus spoliarentur. Adjecit Zeno, ipsa rescripta imperialia non esse audienda, si cuiquam monopolia concedant" [For we read in Justinian that monopolies are not to be meddled with, because they do not conduce to the benefit of the common weal but to its ruin and damage. The civil laws forbid monopolies: in the chapter of monopolies, one and the same Law. The emperor Zeno ordained that those practising monopolies should be deprived of all their goods. Zeno added that even imperial rescripts were not to be accepted if they granted monopolies to anyone].[...]

[...] 3. The Queen was deceived in her grant, for the queen as by the preamble appears, intended the same to be for the wealth public, and it shall be employed for the private good of the patentee; [and for the prejudice of the wealth public]; Also the queen meant that the abuse should be taken away, which shall never be by this patent, but rather the abuse will be increased fort the private benefit of the patentee, and therefore, as it is said [...] in the earl of Kent's case, this grant is void "jure Regio" [by royal right]. [...]

[...] 4. This grant is of this first impression, for no such was ever seen to pass [by letters patent] under the great seal of England before this time, and therefore it is a dangerous innovation as well without any example as without authority of law, or reason. And it was observed that this grant to [Darcy] was made for twenty-one years, so that his executors, administrators, wife, or children, or others inexpert in the art and trade shall have this monopoly. And it cannot be intended, that Edward Darcy esquire, and groom of the queen's privy chamber had any skill in this mechanical trade in making of cards, and then it was said, that the patent made to him was void, for to forbid others to make cards who have the art and skill, and to give him the only making of them who had no skill to make them, shall make the patent utterly void [...]. And although the grant does extend to his deputies, and it may be said, he may appoint deputies who shall be expert; yet if the grantee himself be non-expert, and the grant be void as to him, he cannot make any deputy to supply his room, "quia quod per me non possum, nec per alium" [because what I cannot do by myself I cannot do through someone else]. And as to what had been said, that playing cards is a vanity, it is true, if it be abused, but the making of them is no pleasure, but labor and pains. And it is true that none can make a park, chase, or warren without the kings license, for that were "quodam modo" [in a certain manner] to appropriate those which are "ferae naturae, et nullius in bonis" [of a wild nature, and no one's property] to himself, and to restrain them of their natural liberty, which he cannot do without the kings license: but for hawking, hunting, etc... which are matters of pastime, pleasure, and recreation, there need no license, but every one may in his own land use them at his pleasure without any restraint to be made, if not by parliament, as appeared by the statutes [...]. And it is evident by the preamble of the said act of [king] Edward that the bringing in of foreign cards was forbidden at the grievous complaint of the poor artificers card makers, who were not able to live of their trades, if foreign cards should be brought in; as appeared by the preamble: by which it appeared, that the said act provides remedy for the maintenance of the trade of making cards, for as much as the same maintain diverse families by their labor and industry. [...] And therefore it was resolved, that the queen could not suppress the making of cards within the realm, no more than the making of dice, bowls, balls, hawks-hoods, bells, lewers, dog-couples, and other like, which are works of labor and art, although they shall be for pleasure, recreation and pastime, and they cannot be suppressed if not by parliament, nor a man restrained to use any trade but by parliament. [...] And the

playing at dice and cards is not forbidden by the common law, [...] is not "malum in se" [wrong in itself], for then the queen should not suffer, nor license the same to be done. And where king Edward the third in the 39 year of his reign commanded the exercise of shooting and artillery, and forbided the exercise of casting of stones and barres, and the hand and foot-balls, cock-fighting and "alios ludos vanos" [and other useless games] [...]"[5]

Second he stated that a monopoly is against diverse acts of parliament:

> *"[...] Which for the advancement of the freedom of trade and traffic extended to all vendible things, notwithstanding any charter of franchise granted to the contrary, or usage, or custom, or judgment given thereupon; which charters are adjudged by the same parliament to be of no force, or effect, and made at the request of prelates, barons, and grantees of the realm, to the oppression of the commons. [...] And it is further thereby enacted, that if any statute, charter, letters patents, proclamation, command, usage, allowance, or judgment be made to the contrary, that the same be utterly void, "vide Magna Charta" by Edward third [...]*
>
> *[...] It was resolved, that the dispensation or license to have the sole importation and merchandising of goods (without any limitation or stint) notwithstanding the said act of king Edward the third is utterly against law: For it is true, that for as much as an act of parliament which generally forbided a thing upon penalty which is popular, or only given to the king, may be inconvenient to diverse particular persons, in respect of person, place, time, etc... And for this cause the law had given power to the king, to dispense with particular persons; "Dispensatio mali prohibiti est de jure Domino Regi concessa, propter impossibilitat' praeviden' de omnibus particular', et dispensatio est mali prohib' provida relaxatio, utilitate seu necessitate pensata" [Dispensing with things that are wrong by prohibition (i.e. legislation) is rightfully granted to the king, on account of the impossibility of providing for every particular case; and a dispensation is a release of the prohibited wrong, or a measure of necessity]. But when the wisdom of the parliament had made an act to restrain "pro bono publico" [for the public good] the bringing in of many foreign manufactures, to the intent that the subjects of the realm might apply themselves to the making of the said manufactures, etc... and thereby maintain themselves and their family with their handy labor. Now for a private gain to grant the sole importation of them to one, or diverse (without any limitation) notwithstanding the said act is a monopoly against the common law, and against the end and scope of the same act; for the same is not to maintain and increase the labors of the poor card makers within the realm, at whose petition the act was made, but utterly to take away and overthrow their trade and labors, and that without any reason of necessity, or inconvenience in respect, place or time, and so much the rather because it was granted in reversion for years, as hath been said, but only for the benefit of a private man, his executors and administrators for his particular commodity, and in prejudice of the commonwealth. And king Edward the third by his letters patents, granted to one John Peche the sole importation of sweet-wine into London, and at a parliament holden this grant was adjudged void [...]. Also admit that such grant or dispensation were good, yet [Darcy] cannot maintain an action upon the case against those who bring in any foreign cards, but the remedy which the act of Edward the third, in such case gave ought to be pursued. And judgment was given and entered, "quod querens nihil caperet per billam" [that the plaintiff take nothing by his bill]. [...]*[6]"

The court concluded:

[5] *Darcy v. Allin*

[6] *Darcy v. Allin*

> "*[...] it is true "quod privilegia quae re vera sunt in praejudicium reipublicae, magis tamen speciosa habent frontispicia, et boni publici praetextum, quam bonae et legales concessiones, sed praetextu liciti non debet admitti illicitum" [that privileges which in truth are to the prejudice of the common wealth nevertheless have more specious frontispieces and pretext of public good than good and lawful grants; but an unlawful thing ought not to be admitted under the pretext of being lawful]. [...]*[7]"

The court concluded in favor of Allin that the queen's grant of a monopoly was invalid. Darcy, who was granted the monopoly, knew little about making playing cards. Judge Popham stated that monopolies were contrary to common law and customs, because they could prevent persons who may be skilled in a certain craft or trade from practising. At the same time Popham bolstered that under the exceptional conditions that "wit or invention" would bring good to the commonwealth the privilege of a monopoly could be granted. In other words a reification of know-how emerged during the court case *Darcy v. Allin.* After this court decision, the parliament made efforts to curtail the monarch's power to grant patents. In 1624, the findings of this court case resulted in the *Statute of Monopolies* law. This statute repealed all queen's patents, except those created in order to protect intellectual efforts, resonating attorney Fuller' arguments, "wit or invention" as a property.

[7] *Darcy v. Allin*

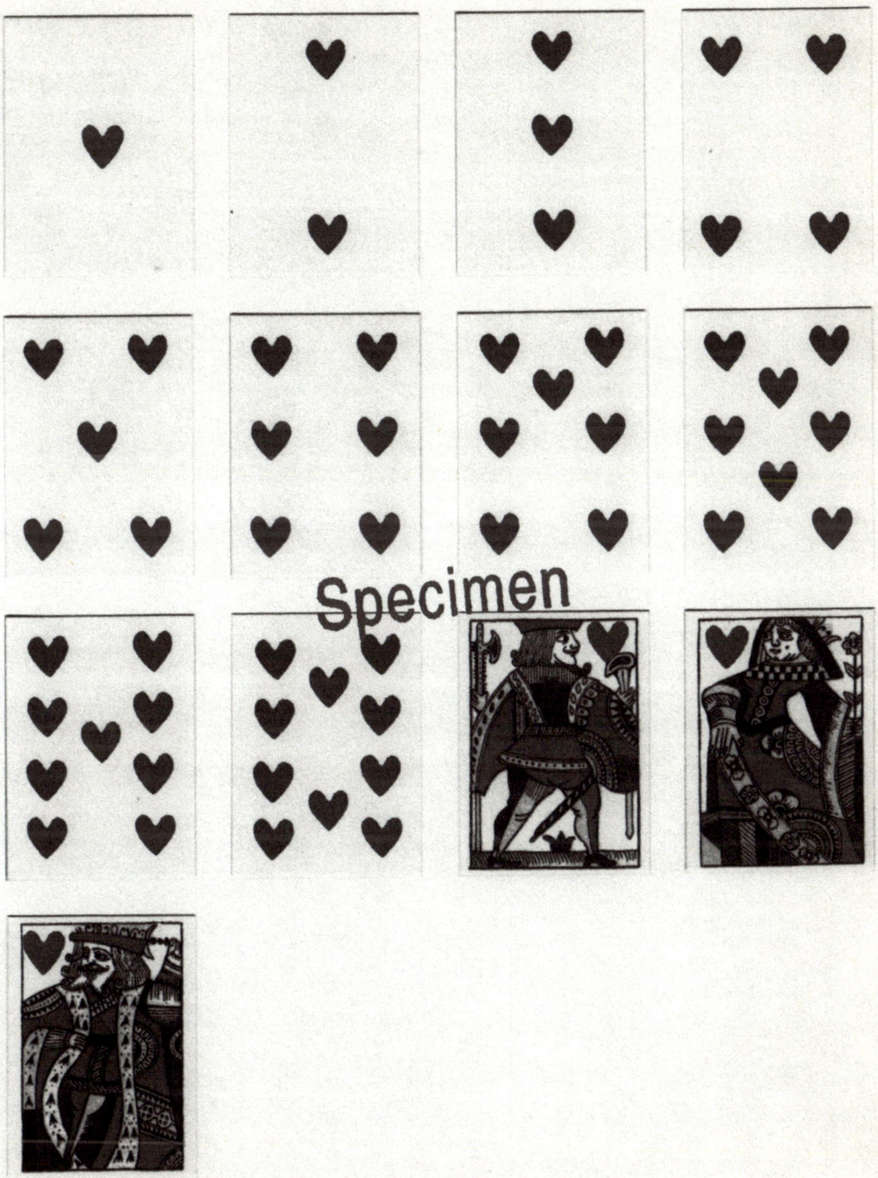

Thing 001895 (playing cards)

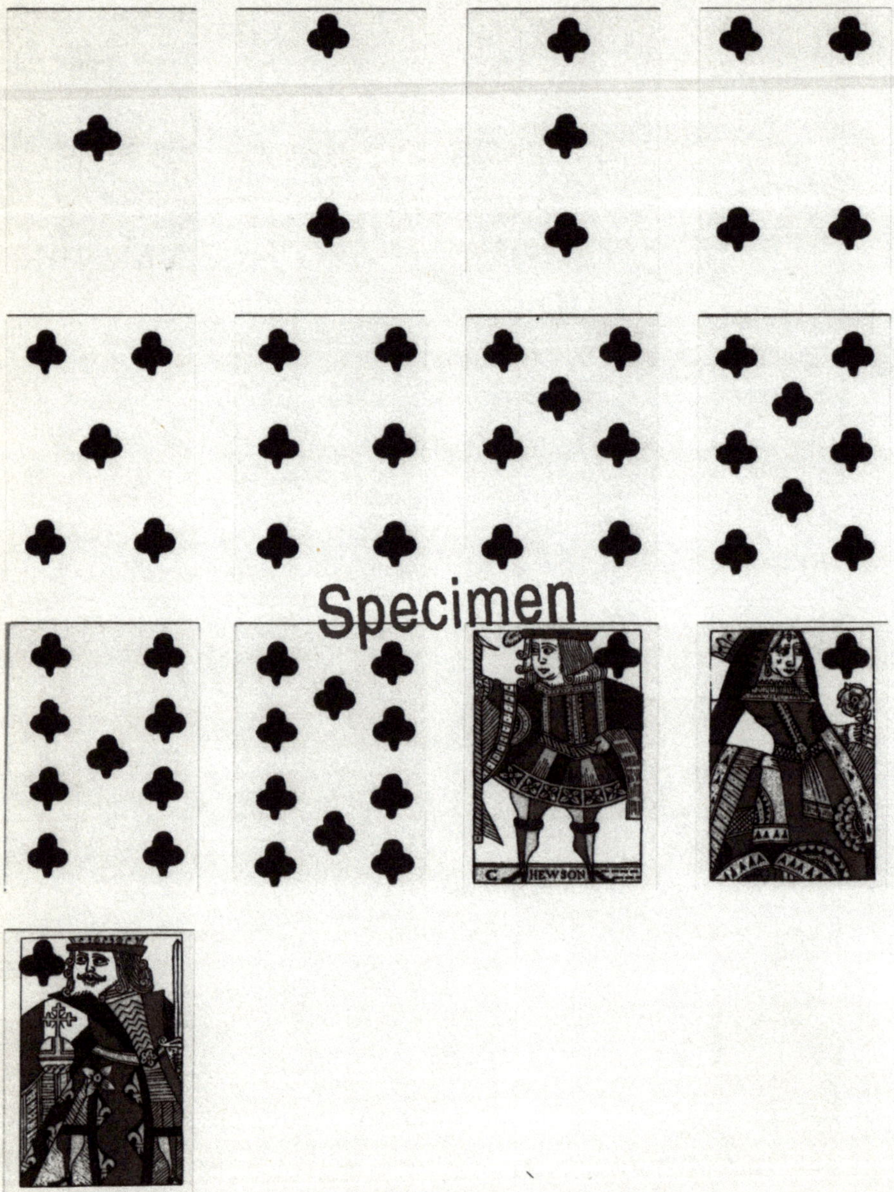

Thing 001895 (playing cards)

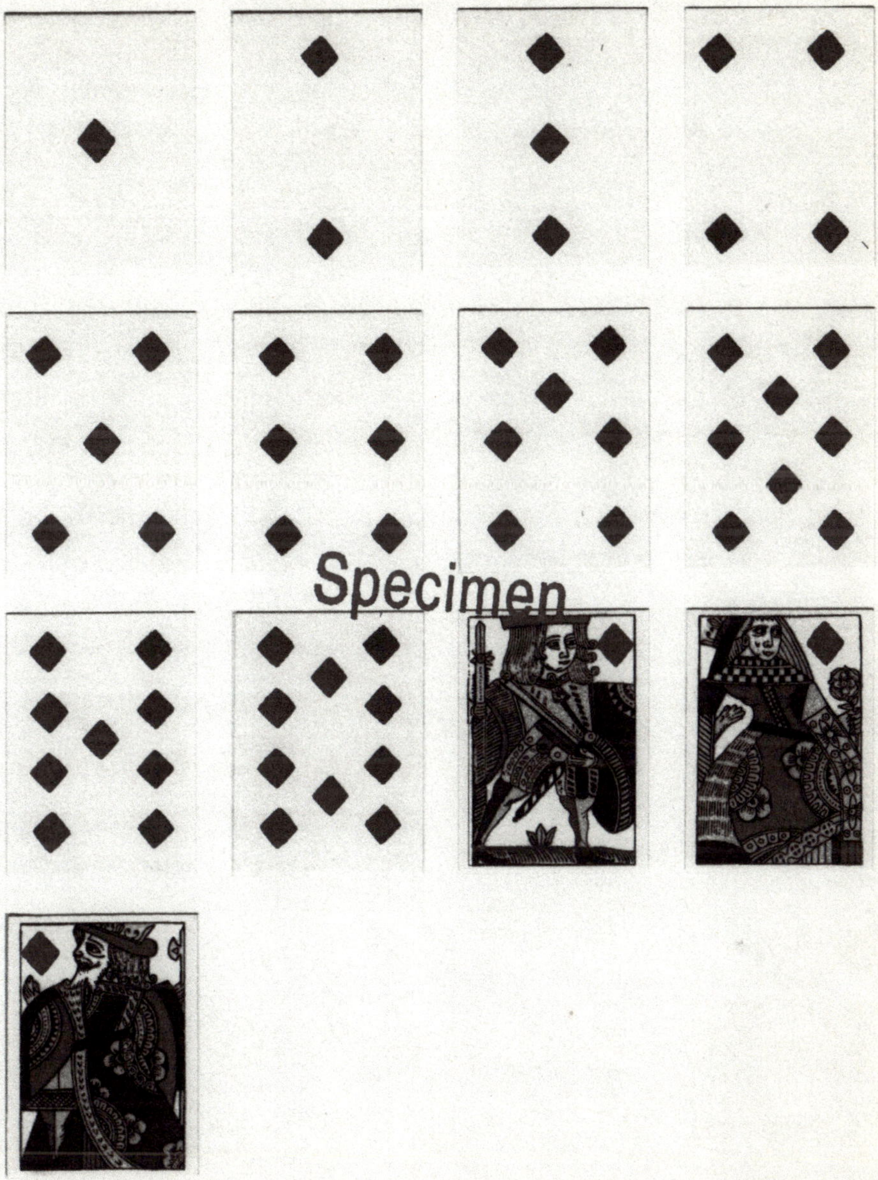

Thing 001895 (playing cards)

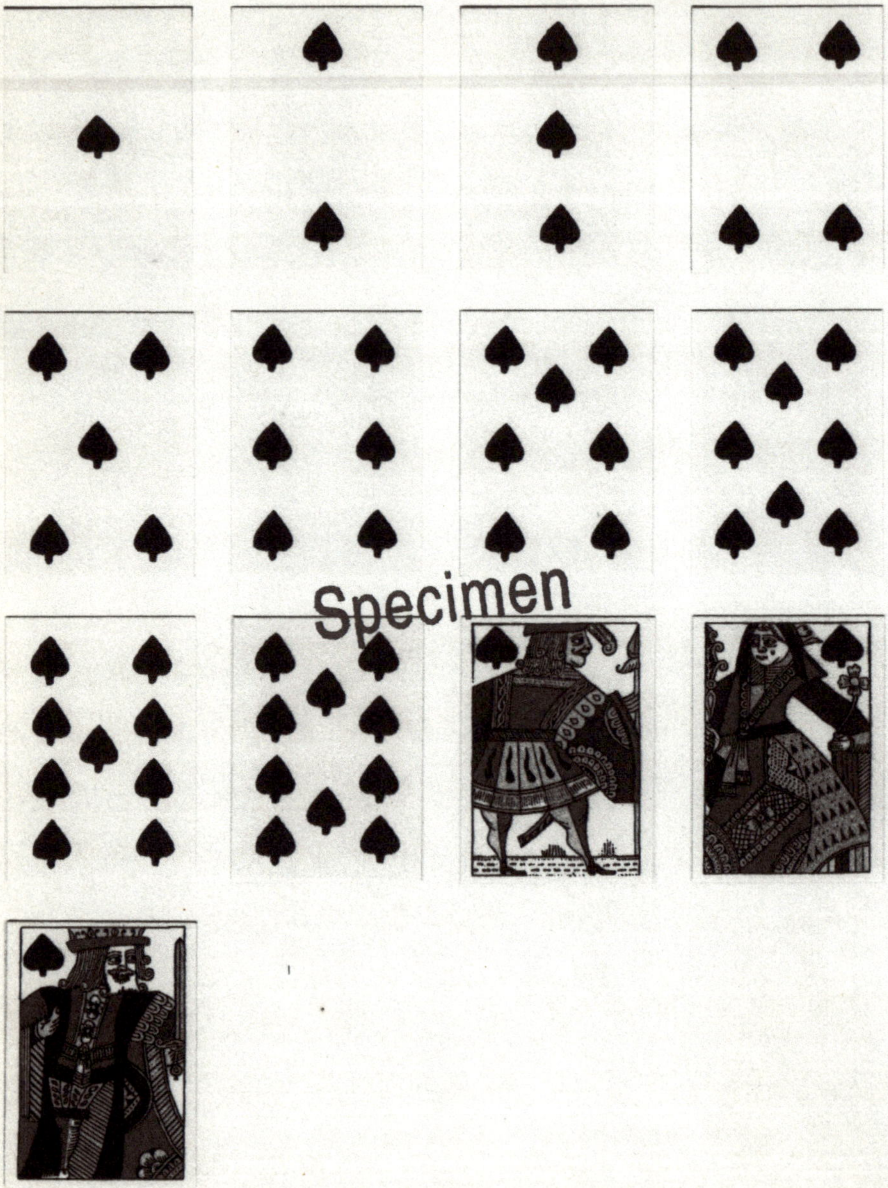

Thing 001895 (playing cards)

The Edges of the Public Domain

Open Music Archive, Eileen Simpson and Ben White

Cherish derelict spaces, forgotten works, dates of expiration.

Find loopholes, test boundaries, check motives.

Mired by unsustainable models of economic growth, we look to the archive and its potential futures.

To effect change we participate in alternatives. Seek out public spaces; rediscover generosity; value sharing.

We love pirates! Their lawlessness is inspirational. But beyond rebellion, we seek to hack antiquated systems of control, to build active resistance and test new models.

The public domain is not a safe zone. It is a mistake to ignore its potential as a site of political invention.

We oppose the dominant system of the artificial limitation of the flow of ideas and concepts, reinforced by a market that seeks to profit from restricting access to cultural materials.

Open Music Archive offers a collection of eighteen new recordings for publication and distribution in *Undoing Property?* The project identifies a gap in the present legal reality in order to obtain public access to sonic materials before they are closed down by impending changes to legislation. It extracts elements that are common, and forms part of an ongoing project to collect and freely distribute copyright-expired music recordings.

Source material for the project is gleaned from the edges of the public domain with a specific focus on audio material from early commercial releases presenting a divide in ownership between lyrics and musical composition—two discreet and essential elements of modern popular music and the subject of countless legal disputes throughout the history of the recording industry. This split exists in UK copyright law, and offers an opportunity for elements of material to be released once divorced.

New sonic sequences have been generated from archival recordings, which have been edited, redacted, cut-up, and processed to suppress copyright-secured elements, thus enabling the release of public domain layers from the proprietary control of commercial publishers.

Retrieved from the recesses of the British Library and beyond, recordings from the 1920s, '30s, and '40s have been dug out from record company back catalogues. Recordings have been altered and encoded using pervasive digital processing techniques ported from pop, R & B, and hip-hop. Melodic phrases are scrambled or reduced to a monotone and lyrics are flipped and reversed, rendered incomprehensible, to bypass legal frameworks and enable unrestricted playback.

Phonetic reversal and backmasking—techniques conventionally used to censor words or phrases in rap recordings for radio broadcast, or historically used to encode subliminal messages on vinyl releases—are here used to redact recordings with lyrics still under copyright control. Elsewhere, reedits strip the vocal content out of a recording—intros, outros, and instrumental sections are re-spliced to open out and free melodic layers. Vocal production technologies of vocoder and autotune are folded back into their original military functions of speech coding and encryption in order to suppress controlled melodic elements and release copyright-expired lyrics.

This processing allows recordings of songs—such as the 1924 song "Golden Days," not scheduled to return to the public domain until 2022 (perhaps to a future world suffering overpopulation and depleted resources as depicted in the 1973 film *Soylent Green*), or the 1937 song "Sentimental and Melancholy," whose copyright is due to expire in 2047 (the same year rescue vessel *Lewis and Clark* answers a distress signal from starship *Event Horizon*)—to be released in part, right now in 2013.

We must remember that the legal frameworks that define the limits of the public domain are not fixed. The future of the public domain is precarious—the field of culture is increasingly colonized for private interests as proprietors of intellectual property continually lobby for the extension of their control. We are well aware that intellectual property has been declared the oil of the twenty-first century.

On September 12, 2011, following aggressive lobbying by private interests, the Council of the European Union adopted an extension of the term of copyright in sound recordings. The British government is using this opportunity to bring other elements of copyright law under tighter control. These upcoming legal enclosures are due to take effect across Europe in late 2013: some public material will be returned to proprietary ownership, in other cases, material on the threshold of escape will be forced under control for a further twenty years.

In response to this moment we offer a "record catalogue": a collection of newly processed recordings that are freely published and distributed online. This timely and urgent action ensures that copyright-expired recorded lyrics and melodies are distributed publicly while still free.

Source manuscripts and recordings for this collection are currently scheduled for full release into the UK public domain between 2018 and 2069. Here, we present a series of prerelease leaks for free distribution. Audio has been hacked for the present legal reality.

Download and listen to the recordings at:
www.openmusicarchive.org/undoingproperty

GOLDEN DAYS
~~Music by Sigmund Romberg~~
(died 1951) © expires 2022,
lyrics by Dorothy Donnelly
(died 1928) © expired 1999.

MY ONE AND ONLY
Music by George Gershwin
(died 1937) © expired 2008,
~~lyrics by Ira Gershwin~~ (died
1983) © expires 2054.

DEEP IN MY HEART, DEAR
~~Music by Sigmund Romberg~~
(died 1951) © expires 2022,
lyrics by Dorothy Donnelly
(died 1928) © expired 1999.

THE CONTINENTAL
Music by Con Conrad
(died 1938) © expired 2009,
~~lyrics by Herbert Magidson~~
(died 1986) © expires 2057.

THE FREE AND EASY
~~Music by Fred E Ahlert~~
(died 1953) © expires 2024,
lyrics by Roy Turk (died 1934)
© expired 2005.

LOVE ME OR LEAVE ME
~~Music by Walter Donaldson~~
(died 1947) © expires 2018,
lyrics by Gus Kahn (died 1941)
© expired 2012.

GOLDEN DAYS

LYRICS BY
GERSHWIN
MUSIC BY
MY ONE AND ONLY
WHAT AM I GONNA DO

DEEP IN MY HEART

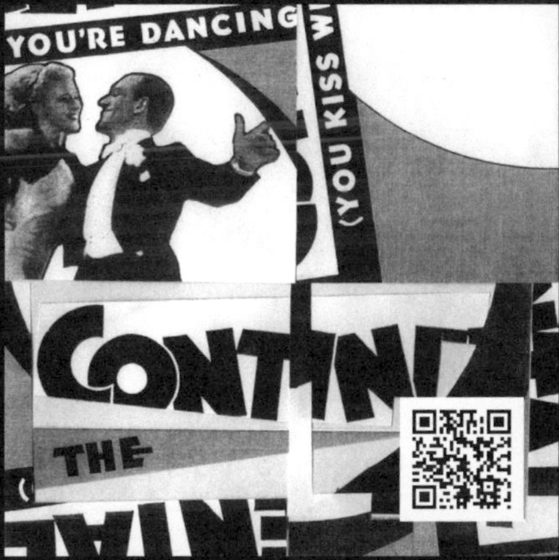
YOU'RE DANCING
(YOU KISS
THE

Free
And
Easy

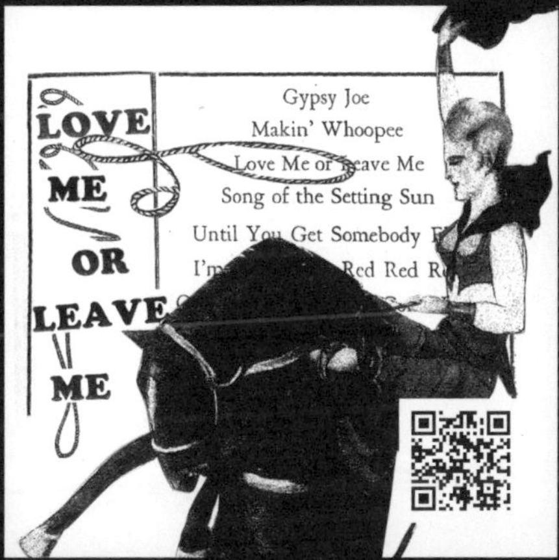
LOVE
ME
OR
LEAVE
ME
Gypsy Joe
Makin' Whoopee
Song of the Setting Sun

SENTIMENTAL AND MELANCHOLY
Music by Richard Whiting (died 1938) © expired 2009, ~~lyrics by Johnny Mercer~~ (died 1976) © expires 2047.

I'M GONNA SIT RIGHT DOWN AND WRITE MYSELF A LETTER
~~Music by Fred E Ahlert~~ (died 1953) © expires 2024, lyrics by Joe Young (died 1939) © expired 2010.

TILL THE SANDS OF THE DESERT GROW COLD
Music by Ernest R Ball (died 1927) © expired 1998, ~~lyrics by Geo. Graff Jr~~ (died 1973) © expires 2044.

TOO MARVELLOUS FOR WORDS
Music by Richard Whiting (died 1938) © expired 2009, ~~lyrics by Johnny Mercer~~ (died 1976) © expires 2047.

DROP A NICKEL IN THE SLOT
~~Music by Fred E Ahlert~~ (died 1953) © expires 2024, lyrics by Joe Young (died 1939) © expired 2010.

COLORADO SUNSET
Music by Con Conrad (died 1938) © expired 2009, ~~lyrics by L Wolfe Gilbert~~ (died 1970) © expires 2041.

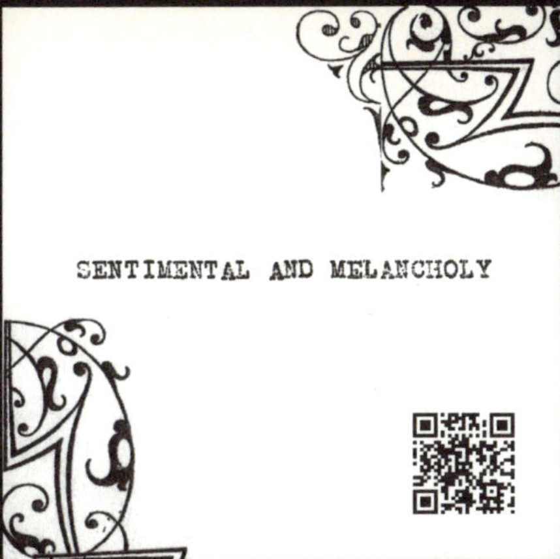
SENTIMENTAL AND MELANCHOLY

I'M GONNA SIT RIGHT DOWN
AND WRITE MYSELF A LETTER

Till The Sands
of The Desert
Grow Cold

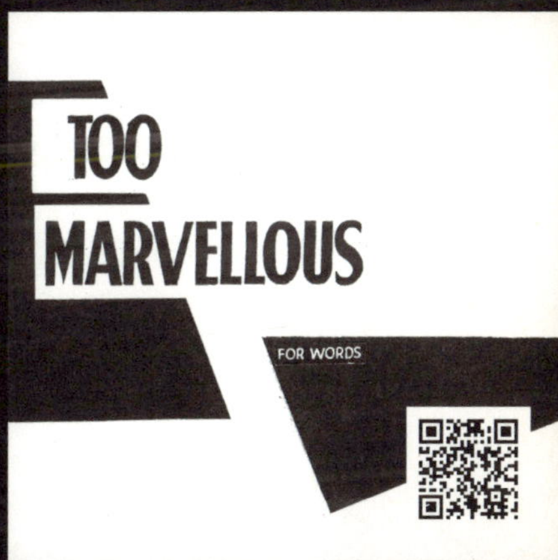
TOO
MARVELLOUS
FOR WORDS

DROP A NICKEL
IN THE SLOT
UNG
A. S. C. A. P.
HLER Inc.
New York City
1619 Broadway
MUSIC PUBLISH

COLORADO
CINEPHONIC
“DE
SUNSET

DREAM A LITTLE DREAM OF ME
~~Music by Fabian Andre~~ (died 1960) ~~and Wilbur Schwandt~~ (died 1998) © expires 2069, lyrics by Gus Kahn (died 1941) © expired 2012.

YOU'VE GOT WHAT GETS ME
Music by George Gershwin (died 1937) © expired 2008, ~~lyrics by Ira Gershwin~~ (died 1983) © expires 2054.

WHISTLING THE BLUES AWAY
~~Music by Harry Tierney~~ (died 1965) © expires 2036, lyrics by Anne Caldwell (died 1936) © expired 2007.

SOMETHING'S GOING TO HAPPEN TO YOU
Music by Theodore Morse (died 1924) © expired 1995, ~~lyrics by D.A. Esrom~~ (died 1953) © expires 2024.

GOOD TIMES ARE HERE (WHEN MY BABY IS NEAR)
~~Music by Fred E Ahlert~~ (died 1953) © expires 2024, lyrics by Roy Turk (died 1934) © expired 2005.

SPRINKLE ME WITH KISSES
Music by Ernest R. Ball (died 1927) © expired 1998, ~~lyrics by Earl Carroll~~ (died 1948) © expires 2019.

DREAM A
LITTLE DREAM
OF ME

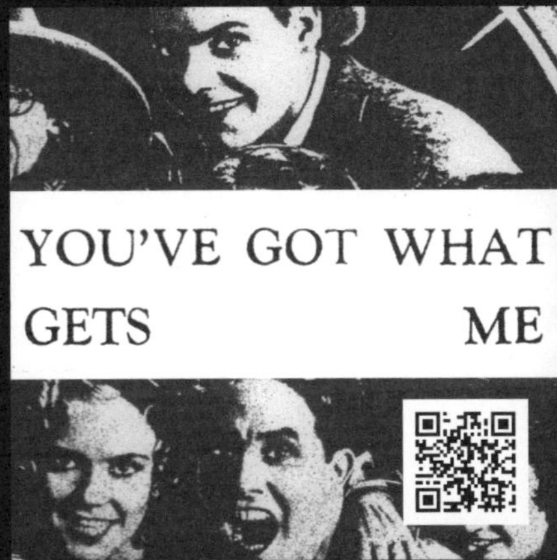

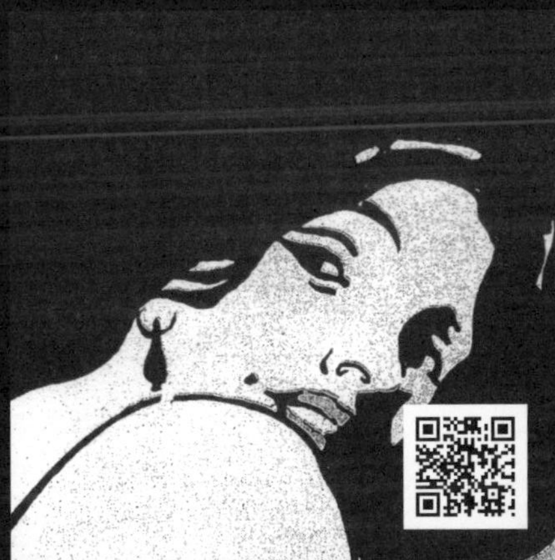

GOOD
=TIMES=
ARE
HERE

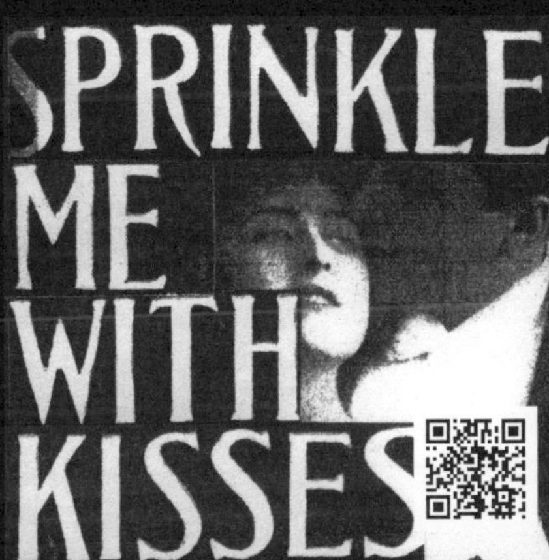

Seat Belt Patent 1962

Nils Bohlin

141

July 10, 1962 N. I. BOHLIN 3,043,625

SAFETY BELT

Filed Aug. 17, 1959

FIG 1

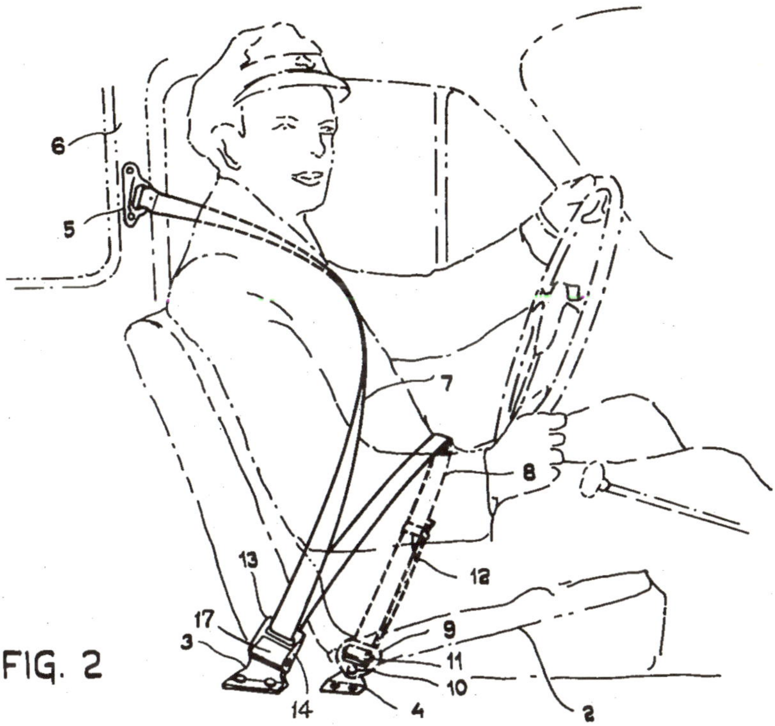

FIG. 2

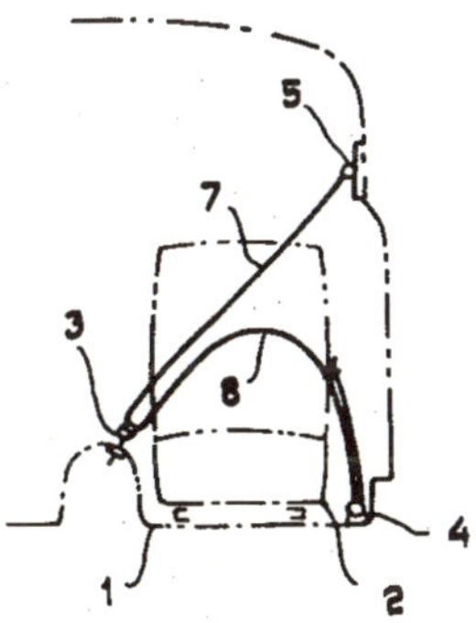

FIG. 3

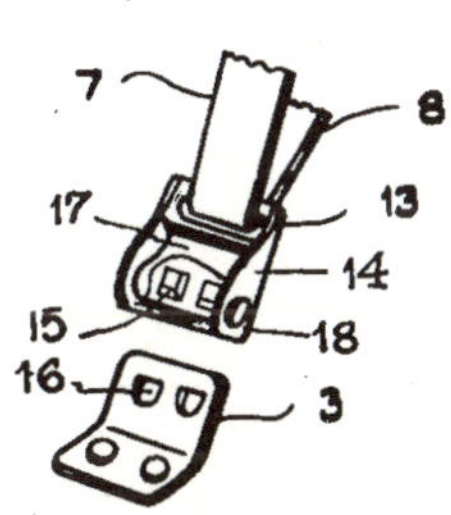

The Artist's Trust
Marysia Lewandowska

145

Michael Asher's work is an example of an artist's practice that consistently attends to its own formulations, while proposing an inquiry into the processes and procedures institutions use to frame, control, and reproduce their values. In June 2003, Asher and curator Charles Esche (who, pertinent to this context, would become director of the Van Abbemuseum) were in public conversation at the Serpentine Gallery. That evening, Asher and I sat together talking about working with museums and more specifically about William Morris. I had just completed *Free Trade*, a project for Manchester Art Gallery, and Michael was interested in its catalogue. Soon after sending him a copy I received a publication accompanying his exhibition at the Renaissance Society. This was accompanied by a single-page letter written on July 27, 2003, referring to the influences of Morris on the professors at the University of Chicago, which Asher researched in relation to his work on patents. Almost ten years later, his gesture inspired me to approach him with an invitation to develop a project for this book. By the time I wrote to him in the summer of 2012, he was already too ill to be able to respond to such a request.

After Asher's death in October 2012, I felt compelled to acknowledge his lifetime engagement and interest in questions of property. In 2010, reading *Situation Aesthetics: The Work of Michael Asher* by Kirsi Peltomäki, I was drawn to one of the projects she discusses and began researching the correspondence surrounding two proposals the artist made for the Van Abbemuseum. As a public institution, the museum is, under Dutch law, committed to making information regarding its holdings accessible to the public. Their current digitization project is exemplary in setting standards for access to exhibition histories contained in its archive, all of which is available online. This progressive approach assures that its documents remain in the public domain, and, more importantly, continue their relevance as part of a public discussion.

Having been given access to their archives, my intention was to reproduce the letters written between Asher and the Van Abbemuseum between 1975 and 1987. The set consists of fourteen letters relating to two proposals made by Asher for long-term projects investigating the status of property and permanence as embodied by the museum's permanent collection. They trace a unique relationship between artist and museum. Encouraged by the openness of the

Van Abbemuseum, I wrote to the trustees of Michael Asher's estate, requesting permission to reproduce his letters. Three months later, this permission was denied. As a result, reproducing his letters here is barred, as is referencing their content. This is just one indication of how a private interest and a public good can collide. It exposes the need for activating attention around the benefits of the public domain. My account below has been constructed in the spirit of reciprocity and respect of one artist for another.

Access to the Van Abbemuseum archive:
alexandria.tue.nl/vanabbe/public/correspondentie/
asher_michael/Scan-10071611360.pdf.

ON JULY 24, 1975, Rudi Fuchs, Director of Van Abbemuseum in Eindhoven (1975–1986) writes to Michael Asher, inviting him to take part in an exhibition scheduled for the spring of 1977. On SEPTEMBER 8, Asher responds favorably to his letter. Nine days later, on SEPTEMBER 17, Fuchs sends the museum plans and requests photographs of Asher's work, which he will later include in a documentation file. On MARCH 3, 1976, Fuchs informs Asher of the development of a new wing at the museum, which he expects to be completed within a year. A month later, on APRIL 2, Asher responds. Six months later, in a letter dated FEBRUARY 15, 1978, Asher is in contact again. Around this time he submits a draft entitled *Permanent Collection*. His proposal stipulates buying the deeds to two museum rooms and acting as the "landlord" while leasing them back to the museum for the period of two-and-a-half years. By establishing a landlord-tenant relationship, both in title and economic mechanism, the work is incorporated into the institutional system. On OCTOBER 19, 1979, Fuchs sends a postcard, which features the interior of the Sir John Soane's Museum in London, informing Asher that his proposal has been accepted by the commission. Here, he raises the matter of payment arrangements, and their duration contained in the proposal. Almost five months later, on MARCH 4, 1980, he sends another postcard confirming that the authorities have accepted the artist's idea for the permanent collection, and that the legal department is dealing with the possible ramifications. He asks Asher to design a poster for documenta 7. After this, their correspondence regarding the Van Abbemuseum project ceases for a long time, until, on MAY 25, 1985, five years later, Fuchs sends another postcard, featuring Ely Cathedral in Cambridgeshire, making reference to their soured relations and encouraging a restoration of contact. He mentions obtaining Asher's new address from Anne Rorimer, and reassures him of the plans to keep the *Permanent Collection* proposal alive. In the fall of 1985, Asher sends a new proposal bearing a working title *The Michael Asher Trust Fund.* This second project extends the ideas contained in the first and establishes the artist as a trustee in a fund operating inside the museum under his own name. The purpose of the trust fund is the acquisition of artworks at "regular intervals" for the permanent collection. Asher attends with precision to multiple conditions and anticipates possible complications by setting them in a list with the heading "Questions

Regarding the Bank Trust." By the end of that year, on DECEMBER 28, Asher is in contact with the museum again. Having not heard from the curators for five months he sends another letter on MAY 12, 1986. Faced with a continuing lack of response, a week later, on MAY 19, he writes to the curator again. On MAY 23, Piet de Jonge, a curator at the Van Abbemuseum (1981–88), apologizes for the silence, offering the preparations for the anniversary exhibition as his reason. He declares that Fuchs had, as yet, neither approved nor rejected the idea of *The Michael Asher Trust Fund*, but mentions that the costs involved—nearing $100,000—would be problematic. He notes that he needs more time before he could return to the matter. Four months later, Asher renews his correspondence with de Jonge, and on OCTOBER 1, inquires about the state of preparations for the project. Just before the end of that year, on DECEMBER 28, he makes what will be the last attempt at clarifying the situation. Two months later, on FEBRUARY 12, 1987, Piet de Jonge, a curator at the Van Abbemuseum (1981–88), replies, admitting how difficult the letter is for him to write. He refers to the efforts he has made in trying to reach an agreement on the municipal level, and expresses hope on behalf of Fuchs and himself for the project to be realized "one day." It was not "the right day," as he puts it. He informs Asher that the project will have to be abandoned for the foreseeable future. Neither of the proposals has been realized in the twenty-six years since the last letter was written.

Mr. Michael Asher
1135 Amoroso Pl.
VENICE, Ca. 90291
U.S.A.

September 17, 1975

RF/jv

507/8.98

Dear Michael Asher,

I am very pleased that you agree to make a presentation in Eindhoven - and that the time schedule suits you. - Enclosed please find a ground plan of the museum; I will see that photographs are made as soon as possible. - I am sorry you cannot come now. When we are in a later phase planning I possibly could pay your ticket - preferably together with somebody else who wants you in Europe. If such an occasion arises, please let me know. - Then I would be grateful if you could send me photographs of work to start forming a documentation file. If necessary, send a bill for them.

With best regards,

R.H. Fuchs.

Michael Asher
1135 Amarosa Place
VENICE, Ca. 90291
U.S.A.

Marc h 3, 1976

RF/jv

223/8.98

Dear Michael Asher,

Kasper König was just here. He told me of a plan to make an exhibition for a new museum in Bottrop, Germany, about Southern California. He sees this exhibition, which has to be in Bottrop as in some other museums not too far away (Krefeld, Essen, Mönchengladbach and Eindhoven), in conjunction with Documenta which next year will concentrate a lot of things in Kassel under the heading, it seems, of decentralisation. Now he suggested that our exhibition in Eindhoven be part of his 'chain'. It then is important that the exhibition will beç there during Documenta, which will set a date of May-June 1977. Would such a plan be agreeable to you - as long as each exhibition will be basically independent?

Kasper also told me (without telling me much mofe) that you already a are working on installations here. Is there anything you care to divulge? Or is there anything you need, like for instance photographs of the (empty) rooms. Since just a few days ago the city council voted for a plan to enlarge the museum with roughly 80% of exhibition space, I very soon will become a building supervisor; that makes it difficult, I guess, to come to L.A. before, say, the fall. So we must continue to work by correspondence, or are you planning any European trips?
As soon as we have good diagrams, I will send you the plans for the new wing to be built. It is expected to be ready by March 1977, and you maybe could prefer the spaced there instead of those in the old building.

With best regards,

R.H. Fuchs,
director.

MICHAEL ASHER
1135 Amoroso Place
Venice, Cal. 90291
USA

GF· A GORDON FRASER CARD GF·

Dear Michael – unforseen circumstances make that I have to limit this US trip to NYC. Bad enough. I'll try again in the spring or so. I'd really liked to see you – but I need my time here. – The Commission has accepted your proposal – but with one question: how can the process be stopped at some point, or do we pay you until your death? (I'll write more fully about details) – The printer promised the catalog as finished in a few more weeks. FINALLY. Warmest regards

Rudi F

SIR JOHN SOANE'S MUSEUM
The Dome and galleries behind No. 13 Lincoln's Inn Fields.
Built 1808-24.

LSJSM-C4

Eindhoven 19/10/79

A SALMON CAMERACOLOUR
POST CARD
PRINTED IN ENGLAND

Michael Asher
1135 Amoroso Place
Venice, Cal. 90291
U.S.A

© J. SALMON LTD., SEVENOAKS

EINDHOVEN 4/3/1980

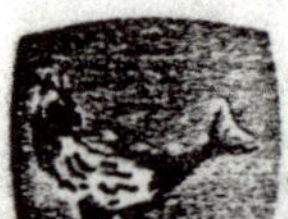

DEAR MICHAEL, NOW, FINALLY + REALLY, IN ONE MONTH FROM NOW THE CATALOGUE WILL BE READY. CHEERS TO ALL OF US. THE PRINTER, AND ALSO WALTER, ARE A BIT OVERWORKED. – THE COMITTEE HAS ACTUALLY ACCEPTED YOUR PROPOSAL FOR THE COLLECTION. BUT THEY WANTED TO HAVE IT CHECKED BY THE LEGAL DPT. – THEN: I WANT YOU TO DESIGN A POSTER FOR DOCUMENTA 7 (ONE OF THE POSTERS). IT SHOULD NOT BE A DIRECT REPRESENTATION OF YOUR OWN WORK: BUT A POSTER. 4-COLOURS. TEXT: <u>documenta 7 kassel 1982</u>

WALTER NICKELS WILL HELP. I WOULD APPRECIATE IF YOU CAN LET ME KNOW WHETHER YOU ACCEPT. THE FEE IS ± 2500 DM (+ EXPENSES). WARM REGARDS

Rudi F.

VAN ABBEMUSEUM
P.B. 235 EINDHOVEN

1-29-09-03

Ely. 25/5 85

to: MICHAEL ASHER

Walter Scott

POST OFFICE PREFERRED

Dear Michael –

Colour Series
Natural Colour
POST CARD

I wonder whether you are still angry with me. I am not. It would be silly and stupid to rupture relations because of the innuendo of others. You know what I mean. Luckily Ann Rorimer gave me your new address so I can write you – to tell you that the construction of a piece for the museum's permanent collection is still very much wanted by me. Secondly I would like you to see a new museum in which I am involved, in Turin Italy, in order to work there too if you want. It has been some time we've seen you in Europe. Please come. For tickets etc we will be responsible.

Warm regards,

Rudi Fuchs

(Copyright Published by Walter Scott, Bradford)

ELY CATHEDRAL.
Lantern interior, Ely's Special glory, built by Alan de Walsingham to replace the Norman tower which fell in 1322. The main timbers are oak trees 63 ft. x 2 ft. 7 ins. x 3 ft. 4 ins.

C.F.119

VAN ABBE MUSEUM

Stedelijk Van Abbemuseum
Postbus 235
5600 AE Eindhoven NL
Telefoon 040-389730

23rd May 1986

Michael Asher
2262 S. Carmelina Ave. apt. 6
Los Angeles Cal. 90064

Dear Michael,

I am sorry to keep you waiting so long in replying your phonecalls.
The reason is our anniversary, it consumes me totally and although I have mentioned our idea of a Michael Asher Trust Fund to Rudy, he has not yet refused or approved to the idea.
He likes it but as you will understand organising $ 100.000,- is quite some thing.
Not only the money itself but how to deal with this legally is difficult.
After our big show - eyelevel - I will have time to go into this matter so I hope you don't mind waiting that long.

Best regards,

for Wil Kloeppel
Piet de Jonge.

Bilderdijklaan 10
Telex: 51365 / Postgiro: 1094666
Bank: NMB Eindhoven 66.29.14.074

VAN ABBE MUSEUM

Stedelijk Van Abbemuseum
Postbus 235
5600 AE Eindhoven NL
Telefoon 040-389730

12th february 1987

Mr. Michael Asher
2262 S.Carmelina Ave. apt. 6
Los Angeles Cal. 90064

USA

Dear Michael,

Thank you for your kind letter. I am sorry you did not reach me during Christmastime but I took a small vacation (and fell ill). Anyway I am well again and very busy organising different exhibitions at the same time.

This letter is very difficult for me to write because I have tried very hard talking to different legal and tax people and with Rudi of course. We both feel it is a wonderful plan and would like to have it realised one day. This just does not seem to be the right day. The municipality is not willing to accept any of our proposals, on the contrary they are more and more difficult providing us money we should get anyway.
I feel we have to abandon the project for some time because there is no real chance in succeeding.
I have tried my utmost and do not think I can find other canals that will enable us to continue.

I am very sorry to disappoint you and I hope you will understand.

I hope all is well with you and hope to see you when you are in Europe again.

Warmest regards,

Piet

Piet de Jonge.

Bilderdijklaan 10
Telex: 51365 / Postgiro: 1094666
Bank: NMB Eindhoven 66.29.14.074

Abstraction and the Currency of the Social

Marina Vishmidt in conversation with Laurel Ptak

159

In a May 2013 exchange with Marina Vishmidt, I had the opportunity to engage her around her incisive thinking on labor and value-form. We spoke about concepts of property and the creation of value in relationship to the digital—addressing everything from social media platforms to alternative forms of currency. With respect to art, Vishmidt observes that while all kinds of work today comes with the imperative to be creative, art is making a turn toward its social usefulness, becoming directly implicated in economic and urban forms of development. Addressed throughout is the role of abstraction and how the obscuring of both labor and a belief in our ability to act is fundamental to capitalism's mechanisms. Given these circumstances, Vishmidt pushes us to ask what a real negation of property might look like today?

Laurel Ptak: Your writing has focused recently on what you term the "speculative mode of production" allowing us to see ways that value is produced across fields like art, finance, and digital media. Can you unpack this concept for us?

Marina Vishmidt: Sure. Speculation as a mode of production is a rubric I have settled on to talk about subjectivity and finance as they are expressed in and reshaped socially through contemporary forces of capital like art, finance, and the changing nature of work. I am trying to outline a speculative subject, which is how humans and capital come together—especially in fields like digital media. But this subject also engenders a kind of negativity or disidentification, which could be politically interesting. The idea of the attention economy, for example, is something I would like to approach through the Marxist concept of real abstraction, and align that with the different kinds of discussions that have been happening around artistic labor and the various historical proximities artists have charted for themselves in relation to labor, management, and expression. But that's definitely charting the outlines of an analysis rather than proposing one.

Can we think of artistic work as producing attention or managing it? And, conversely, can we think of art as the moment of suspension or unworking within regimes of production for value? Emerging from this would be the hypothesis of speculation as a mode of production, in which the speculative praxis of art and the speculative arenas of finance and human capital can be aligned, then brought into disjunction with the speculative politics of the common, and actualized as a possible outcome.

LP Inside this framework, how can we think about the digital in relationship to questions of property? What are its models of production and consumption? How are traditional ideas about work and value challenged through its economies?

MV The hypothesis of the attention economy gets applied to situations wherein value is generated out of modes of production and consumption that cannot be clearly distinguished and/or quantified—such as free software, peer-to-peer, and social media. Critical theories or political economic accounts of these activities sometimes refer to them as playbour, where recreation, research, wage work, and enterprise seem to mingle indiscriminately. It can be difficult to apply a Marxist labor theory of value to this realm. The moment of labor or the labor-content is hard to locate, particularly since the other mainstays of capitalist work, such as surplus-value production, alienation, and wage are not clearly evident. Commentators, including Tiziana Terranova and Simon Yuill, point to the notion that the digital economy, like the economy in general, relies on large quantities of unremunerated labor—which is often not recognized as labor in the interests of preserving the specious freedom of the (non-)contracting agents.

Monopolistic social media platforms like Facebook, with their ad-based profit models, are highly speculative. Facebook's profits are mercurial, albeit extensive. Their profit model is converting relationships and shared information into capital goods, but this conversion—like the realization process for capital in general—is always uncertain. What it does result in, as problematic but intriguing perspectives such as Jaron Lanier's have recently suggested, is a driving down of the value of labor across the board, with consequences for social and political infrastructures, especially in the West. Something like the Amazon Mechanical Turk model would be an illustration of that, and it also reflects the fractalization of work—the forms of time, place, and sociality of work—that erodes traditional methods of resistance to exploitation.

LP Our desire to share ideas and experiences beyond the alienation of wage labor or capitalist relations gets exploited here as forms of collective knowledge are expropriated. It begs the question, how we can care for or protect these collective forms from traditional or monopolistic models of ownership?

MV Established schemes of alternative licensing, such as Creative Commons, attempt to open up the strict intellectual property regime that form the bedrock of valorization in the digital economy. These also tend to reinforce the profit-making imperatives of that regime by acknowledging property and control of authorship as legitimate, without getting involved in the material conditions that reproduce property laws and authorship as exploitation and exclusion for most. They in fact confirm those structures by giving them an appearance of flexibility and agency, and are thus conservative rather than transformative.

However, that's only one model. I guess the question is about how embedded social relationships and social networks can settle on forms of production and distribution that have both their prefigurative moment (acting as if the world you want already exists) and their antagonistic moment (recognizing that durable and resistant socialities need to be built, which do not seek to find ameliorative interstices within or away from the totality but are forced to question its very logic). With regard to the social relations and social commodities of wholly-owned social media, for me, the question is increasingly posed in terms of time and affect as well as ownership. It has very specific pragmatic aspects to it, which are obviously considerable (due to the sheer presence of people and institutions in those networks). But any ways to reconsider how we communicate and produce across those networks, as the case of Creative Commons or indeed even piracy-based activism, have made clear that no challenge to digital property can succeed in isolation—on any scale—without a more far-reaching challenge to property in general, which may be informed and pervaded by commons-based practices or by something different. That's not to say that scale is homogeneous or that social networks are teleological, as a lot of analysis that falls on either side of the advocacy-condemnation vector would tend to suggest. For example, in a recent text on activism and entrepreneurship, I was exploring alternative currencies and how the historical contexts for these have been quite disparate. Bitcoin is a good contemporary example of this: it maintains the anonymizing function of money but without the sovereignty principles of fiat currency. I guess the point then would be to try to articulate, though not merge, these levels of critique that need to be happening at once: formal-logical ones (immanent critique), historical analysis, and something more strategic, for lack of a better term.

LP How do we start to think about producing conditions for a truly equitable commons? One that would not simply reproduce but instead transform the concept of property in a radical way?

MV A constitutive praxis of the commons would be one that questions the validity of these structures and does not negotiate with them, but renders them inoperable. This does not mean that direct and small-scale community control is the answer to exclusionary capitalist laws of production and property; the question must be posed on the same scale and level of abstraction on which we encounter it today. That is, if going beyond capital is to mean anything other than going beneath it.

In those instances where the economy of attention is linked to the social and political discourses of the commons, with its corollary scenario of peer production eventually out-competing commodity-based production, capital still largely provides the platform for this commons-based production. This will remain the case, as Dmytri Kleiner writes, so long as workers' disposable incomes continue to be diverted into alternative social or economic models and this tendency remains cut off from developing a shift in the relations of production themselves.

LP How do you think about the relationship between the political and the technological?

MV The political and the technological are neither conceptually nor pragmatically separable. Capital is contradictory, and if its contradictions can be used to destroy it, rather than it destroying us, all the better. But we cannot out-innovate or out-cooperate, much less form a "we" on technological or pragmatic bases that negate capital without thinking about how to produce and organize political subjectivity. The question remains, can capital be practically negated at the level of property and the value-form, which means acting in the material, the affective, and thus the political realm? Although technology influences social relations and their affects, it is a politicizing force only insofar as it provides new practical possibilities for envisioning and organizing other forms of collectivity.

LP How should we think about the commodity form inside a digital economy? Do existing economic models fail us here, and, if so, why?

MV We see that traditional or neoclassical economic paradigms strain to explain valorization models of digital or attention economies by using orthodox metrics like supply and demand. These categories don't function analogically to older kinds of marketing where the audience was a commodity in thrall to one-way advertising. Nor do they function at all as they do in industrial production. With social media conceived as a distributed attention economy, the commodity is temporal and affective in its circulation, although someone is still capturing value somewhere along the chain. With social media or the world of financial derivatives as guiding archetypes, it is clear that capital and cybernetic feedback loops are perfectly compatible as long as (intellectual) property laws apply.

LP Can you also address forms of exchange? And even alternative forms of finance? Are these similar to the relationship you described earlier between Creative Commons licenses and normative ideas about property?

MV Real abstraction refers to the concrete social experience of the dominance of abstract value and abstract exchange as the parameters of our lives. Abstraction is real because it is socially effective—objects really do enter into social relations. The general equivalent of money is fetishized as an independent actor, mediating but also erasing social relations of labor, power, and class. Money is an example of real abstraction—an abstract concept with real effects.

Currency reform and direct exchange propositions like time banks, LETS [local exchange trading system], and Bitcoin are increasingly being aired today, as they are in every epoch of capitalist crisis. The dominance of money and abstract value does not lose its force with the introduction of local currencies, since their adoption and circulation remains parasitic on that dominance. They rely on the spare time left over from employment, education, debt, and, increasingly, workfare, for those interested in supporting local economies by participating in these schemes. To the extent that their social relations can include a political dimension, their ability to foster local autonomy lends them to be as conducive to insularity and community policing as they are to systemic challenge.

LP Given all we've discussed so far, I'd like to return now to how your work connects this thinking more specifically to the realm of art.

MV I have been writing on the relationship between the art object, artistic subjects, and the logic of management. Management theory has embraced creativity, flux, singularity, and improvisation as its passe-partouts for decades. Management and art have a lot in common, perhaps most obviously that both of them make labor disappear, only later, if at all, to reintroduce it in the guise of a resource or a reference. Both distinguish themselves from labor (akin to the division between mental and manual labor). This is a labor subsumed in a final project of some kind that generates value for the manager of this labor.

LP Your observation that this managerial role is mimicked and performed by culture itself is striking because it is so contrary to how art tends to be represented.

MV Reflexivity is a highly-valorized term in critical art production and mediation. However, against a wider backdrop of mass consumption of critical cultural practice, it is also a highly normative term and technology. One need only look at the prominence of criticality in art school curricula to recognize it as a bureaucratic form of critique. Such a training in criticality nearly always marks the spot from whence critique has been expunged. Its descriptive or referential aspect is critical, while its performative or prescriptive side is stabilizing. It functions in analogy with instruments of feedback and measurement that signal management in other spheres, like consultation, evaluation, or assessment—it is the standard operating procedure.

LP Art presents a parallel with what you observed earlier about social media. As you put it, the moment of labor can be very difficult to locate and this leads to contested ideas that it is or involves work per se.

MV Art is defined and traversed by its antagonism with productive relations, with abstract labor. Artists have continually identified and misidentified their labor and their social relations with work, management, and entrepreneurship. Theodor W. Adorno located art as both the emblematic and oppositional figure of modernity—it has played out and mutated in the emergence of the artistic subject. According to Adorno, it thus internalizes the abstraction of capitalist relations as the innermost truth of its existence. The relationship between art and labor is always problematic, as is announced by the paradoxical term "art worker" no less than by the checkered history of the labor politics of art itself.

LP Have these dynamics changed over time? How specific is this to contemporary conditions of capitalism?

MV Michel Foucault saw the origins of neoliberalism in the shift from the subject of exchange to the subject of competition. Capital is internalized and the antagonistic relation between the different interests of worker and capital is eliminated. It seems no coincidence today that all kinds of waged work is supposed to become creative at exactly the same time that art is supposed to become socially *useful*—an aid to economic growth, social integration, and urban redevelopment.

The figure of capital, with its laws of expansion and growth, guarantees the division in social labor that produces the artist and the worker as ontologically distinct. It could even be said that it is precisely through the dissolution of the artwork into the field of wider social relations (social, participatory, and relational forms of art) that the recuperation of this dissolution as individual artistic capital is upheld most forcefully. The artist emerges as both a de-skilled service worker and manager and curator of social creativity.

The artist as both not-worker and as the figure of the utopian model of labor survives as an analogue of capital's boundless creativity and transformative agency. This is true especially in times of crisis and decline, when this figure takes on anticapitalist or oppositional content within social forms, which then remain very much the same.

The challenges to art's autonomy that have solidified into an orthodoxy in the past decades have by and large accommodated themselves to the results of these challenges with a conception of artistic practices and artistic institutions more and more defined by the heteronomy of the market. Thus, it is refined consumption and the effacement of labor that give law to this sphere of social practice objectively, while the modernist subject of autonomy continues to underpin it—mediated through the character masks of manager, researcher, or ethnographer.

LP Any last thoughts you want to add?

MV It might be generative to touch again on the notion of abstraction as a constitutive backdrop for the formal trajectories and the economic relations of art in the twentieth century. Sven Lütticken, for example, has drawn some apt constellations here. I'm quite interested in how a certain recurrent fascination with the utopian valences of modernist abstraction ends up performing some very similar ideological moves in the present as it did in its original era—that is, glorifying power as progress, or decorating untenable global inequalities as part of an ineffable force of material ambiguity.

The real abstraction of capital is as mediated by art as it is by money. It is an ambiguous and ultimately unresolvable field of social desires. It embodies forms of production that are too vast and complex to change and give us only a few positions to take if we don't want to be left out of the game. Such contemplative attitudes are always with us in art but specific circumstances can reveal a more violent or reactionary side to them, as we saw recently with the exhibition "Abstract Possible" at Tensta konsthall—a move that critics like Mikkel Bolt have surveyed with great detail and historical awareness.

Ultimately, the power of abstraction is to make us believe that our own power to act has to be severed from the conditions of that power, that is, from the contradictory and oppressive structures that allow us to have any kind of voice at all. This then generates both a deathly pragmatism of action and the equally torpid reproduction of the same, which activism can leave untouched. The abstract conditions of our experience, whether reflected in art, forms of immaterial property, or production, cannot be separated from the analysis that allows us to interpret it. They are one and the same and they have to form the substance of our politics.

From Ownership to Belonging

Matthew Stadler

171

We are asked to consider property and ownership as they shape an economy of publishing. These are the words of economists, and we are not economists. But their meanings and our understanding of them directly affect the vitality and circulation of things we value—literature and art, for example.

So, we will study economics and ask if these words can be turned to our advantage. I focus on literature because that's what I care and know about. Visual art is also published, and sometimes under very different pressures than literature. In visual art, scarcity is often rewarded; in literature, never. Whatever good it might do, scarcity also undermines some vital potentials of visual art—among them, relevance, equity, and complexity. I don't mean that what we make should never be unique or singular or meant for just one person; I mean that its value should not be increased by restricting access to it. Literature and art should both be managed as common-pool resources, a concept I'll borrow from economist Elinor Ostrom.

I love books. More, I love literature. By literature I mean writing that opens up meanings that no single party—not the author, not the reader, not the critic, not the fact-checker, or the lawyer—can ever hold full authority over. Literature is writing that opens up a space of mutually-negotiated meanings that never close or conclude: a unique political space. Negotiation and dialogue are the permanent condition of literature. We read and reread and never arrive at any single answer.

In this, literature differs from other writing. In nonfiction, there are established legal standards of fact that grant authority over the meanings in the work, and these can be argued in court, or informally outside of court, until they conclude with a binding judgment. Literature also differs from private communications that mean only what the writer says they mean. Literature must enter the public. It must be given up by the writer. In the act of relinquishing authority over the text—giving it up to an unbounded sea of readers—the writer creates what I call literature. This is a political act. The creation of a political space, also called "public space."

Which doesn't mean it can't be profitable. Art and literature are forms of inquiry. They resemble what's called "basic science" in that, while they do not provide useful, marketable products, per se, marketable products grow from them. Non-applied "basic science" is routinely paid for by large, profit-making companies—either through philanthropy to research institutions or by hiring scientists directly. Maybe art and literature could be funded by R&D budgets for the culture industry? It happens on a small scale at Wieden + Kennedy, the advertising giant headquartered in Portland, Oregon; artists are paid or kept "in residence," simply to work and be interesting. They produce nothing, except art, with all its unresolved insights. More famously, Walt Disney founded the California Institute of the Arts, CalArts, to train artists, the basic R&D from which Disney's "imagineers" learn and invent.

If we think of art and literature this way, as forms of cultural R&D, we quickly see the ways that they are unique. Where most inquiry—hard science, social science, journalism—drives toward resolution and agreed-upon truths, art and literature thrive on multiple plausibilities, many right answers rich with contradiction and paradox. Art and literature suspend us in a perpetually negotiated relationship with others, a deeply social arrangement that is never closed by answers, authority, or ownership. Basic science is more like this than we might think. But, without a doubt, art and literature cultivate inquiry, rather than seeking finality or closure.

In economic terms, we're talking about "intellectual property," but of a very unusual sort. This "property" is alive, exceeds us, is beyond our grasp. It is quite literally public space—that is, common ground open to all, where strangers recognize each other in common, and where meanings and value are shaped in perpetual dialogue. How do we own or sell that? Literature and art—these inquiries that are sometimes reconfigured as intellectual property—can suffer when practitioners fight over ownership, or draw boundaries to make owning and selling easier.

Relinquishing work to a public—what we call "publication"—has another more pragmatic meaning for writers. It is the moment when money can be made. The writer claims ownership so she has something to sell in a market, something she owns that others can pay money to buy. This exchange of ownership is the flashpoint of value—a price is named and the exchange is enabled. For convenience's sake, the exchange is organized around a material object, a book, that can be held and possessed, that can belong to someone, so that ownership is clear and uncontested.

In Ostrom's terms, the exchange rests in a confluence of two very different kinds of goods: literature, which she has called a "public good," and the book, inarguably a "private good." But money must move. So, we sell literature in books, or now in e-books. It's proven to be a workable "fix-it" for deeper contradictions. Literature can thereby be supported through the sale of easily exchanged private goods: books.

While physical books have suddenly become very hard to sell, publishers have rallied and found ways to "monetize e-books"—that is, organize a digital file so that it can be restricted or granted the same way as a physical book, enough so, anyway, that e-books can be bought or sold. This was really only a design problem. And already, a brief decade into the "crisis of publishing," which, for most publishers, shakes down to "how to rescue shopping as the engine of profit around literature"—the problem is well toward being solved.

The sale of an object, the book or e-book (the two should be considered as interchangeable), rather than the literature inside it, is necessary because literature itself is impossible to own. Even the writer never really owned it, which accounts for the common feeling, among literary writers, that at some level we are all charlatans, pretending to make something that never really was ours. We have to attach our names to it and make a claim of ownership—often despite our deep feeling that we are only ever participants in a process that far exceeds us—in order to sell it to others. And these others, who come to own the book, feel so little "ownership" of the literature within that they routinely share it, read it out loud, spill it out to any and everyone who will listen, loan the book, prattle on and on, giving away this thing they are said to "own," because in fact literature is not owned. It is, by definition, a space of mutually negotiated meanings that never closes or concludes, a space that thrives on—indeed requires—open access and sharing.

So, at their core, these accommodations run counter to the essential logic of literature, of what it is and what relationships it enables. Here is where the parallel to visual arts is strongest. The structures of ownership and exchange are hostile to literary culture, even as they move money into the hands of writers. We risk depleting the resource if that is all we think about. But there are other economic models that better suit goods like art and literature, including something Ostrom calls "the common-pool resource."[1]

Among Ostrom's contributions to economic theory has been her elaboration on the division of public versus private goods—in particular, her analysis that there are at least four distinct categories of goods. Remember, "property" is just a legal regime that is either appropriate or inappropriate to the management of different kinds of goods. Private goods are managed well through private property and all the relationships and exchanges that that tool enables. But other kinds of goods beg other considerations.

Ostrom divides goods into four types: public goods, which she defines as "a good that is available to all and where one person's use does not subtract from another's use"—for example, a television broadcast or a publicly available web page; private goods, which are those things we can prevent others from using and for which one person's use precludes another's (a hammer or a loaf of bread); and between these two, public and private, are distinct classes of goods that Ostrom calls "common-pool resources" and "toll good" or "club goods."[2]

Toll or club goods are resources that we buy membership into. Ostrom gives the example of a subscription to a journal. We might add Netflix, gaming site subscriptions such as Xbox, or membership in online services such as AppleCare. Those without membership are easily excluded from the club, and the use of the goods by one member does not deplete the resource for others. Common-pool resources are goods that we cannot exclude others from using, and that can be depleted by use. Unconstrained use threatens the resource's sustainability. Good examples are fisheries and forests. This distinguishes them from "public goods," which are used without risk of depletion, or what economists call "subtractability."

Ostrom's pioneering work has given us a deeply-researched understanding of club goods and common-pool resources. She proposes patterns of management for both that differ radically from the appropriate management of either public or private goods. Because her inquiry began by looking at material and biological goods, such as irrigation, fisheries, and forests, Ostrom only recently applied these distinctions to intellectual property. Her 2009 collection of essays, coedited with Charlotte Hess, *The Knowledge Commons*, sketches the outline of this new application. In it,

Ostrom says that art and theater are "public goods."[3] There is broad agreement on this.

Unconstrained use does not deplete art or literature, the common reasoning goes, and therefore they are public goods, rather than common-pool resources. At the simplest level, this is true. The use of literature or art does not subtract numbers from the pool, the way that overfishing will bring fish populations rapidly down to zero. The opposite occurs with literature and art—increased use breeds increased resources. But this surface abundance obscures a deeper depletion that follows from unconstrained use. For literature, and arguably for art, this depletion—what economists call "subtractability"—happens in a uniquely backwards way. The literature that disappears is that which users neglect. This paradox is crucial, and little understood. The contrast to something like fisheries or forests is complete. Fish not wanted by a market thrive with neglect—not so in art and literature. I'll repeat: the literature that disappears is that which users neglect.

However anomalous, this fact makes it impossible to treat literature or art as simply public goods. To do so risks depleting the resource. The economy of literature in the twentieth century is a case in point. Today, more books and e-books are bought and sold than at anytime in human history: a surface abundance. Yet there is a radical narrowing and homogenization in the range of books that are read and remain available.

Clustering, monolithic patterns of use—the sort that are shaped by mass production and marketing—leave vast parts of the field fallow by centering attention on fewer and fewer books. The rest of the field—the whole delicate ecology of literature—wanes and disappears. The end result, as with fisheries or timber, is the need for management quite different than that appropriate to "non-subtractible" public goods. Common-pool resources need locally based, mutually negotiated management to avert depletion.

Ostrom has identified five features of the most successful common-pool resource regimes, organizational tools that have been employed for thousands of years, around the world, to manage, for instance, shared irrigation in Valencia, Spain, canal building and maintenance in the Philippines, forest management in the mountains of Japan, and meadow management in the Swiss Alps. They include: (1) clearly defined boundaries, (2) proportional value between benefits and costs, (3) collective choice arrangements, (4) nested enterprises, and (5) a graduated array of monitoring and enforcement tools.

Now we have arrived deep within the specialist discourse of economics. Most of the concepts, and nearly all of the vocabulary, will bear only an accidental and passing relationship to the things we care or think about most in the hours and days of our lives. My mind naturally fixes on the surpassing genius of the late American writer, Guy Davenport, and his brilliant story, "O Gadjo Niglo," following a Swedish boy, Jens, as he discovers the joys of masturbation in the long empty hours of summertime with his friend Tarpy, the miller's idiot son. Obliged by this commission to consider property and ownership and the ways they shape an economy of publication, my mind is dragged away from Davenport's beautiful sentences— for example:

> We did it again later in the afternoon on the sand bank where the bears fish in winter. He let me feel his peter. He asked me if I could get him a piece of pie. I told him to meet me before sunset between the knoll and the river. I brought him the drumstick of a hen and a fair slab of gooseberry pie. I had never seen anyone eat so. He cleaned the bone with his teeth and broke it and sucked out the marrow. [...]
>
> We met every day. I saw Tarpy in the sunflowers from my window and put down my Fenimore Cooper or Baron von Humboldt and go out with my beetle bottle and kit. Matilda would cry that I needed a straw hat against sunstroke. I would head for the woods on the bluff over the sea. Tarpy would bob up to my left when we were out of sight of the house. In a glacial scoop ringed with a haw of bushes under a boulder we shed our breeches and fell to.[4]

Away from the beautiful language. And toward the puzzling market anomaly of Davenport's Balkanized, limited readership, and how his multiple professions as teacher, essayist, illustrator, translator, and prose writer divided his work among divergent markets that irreparably split his audience into non-communicating segments, no one of which was large enough to guarantee profits to the publishers that took a chance on him. While my heart and mind bend magnetically toward the captivating image of Jens naked among dappled ferns beside the woodland spring where he and Tarpy lay side-by-side, jerking off, my obligation reminds me that Davenport, the author, was paid $30.03, "a perfect palindrome," he once told me, for his first book. Scribner, the American publisher that paid him this miserly sum, published my first book, too. And among the accidents of history that have shaped my career was their provision of a copy of my novel to this man whose work has meant the world to me, an allowance that would have been at best unlikely with any publisher of smaller scope or less illustrious history. How do notions of property or ownership shape the vitality and future of these unlikely goods, literature or art? The question is absurd, a phantasm, a fiction. So be it. We love literature and are obliged to understand economics.

Notions of property and ownership are flexible and can be taught or codified in law. They are not facts, in any sense, but tools for the management of goods. Our common sense notions of both pertain to private goods—the objects we "own," that are our property because we have made or paid for them.

But with the addition of Ostrom's two other categories of goods —club goods and common-pool resources—ownership opens up along a broader continuum better delineated by the word "belonging." Private goods (say, the books you buy) belong to you; but literature—that unresolved, shared space of meanings within the books—does not belong to you, so much as you belong to it. You join that collective space by reading and caring. So, belonging occurs both in your ownership of the private good, the book, and in your obligation to the common-pool resource, literature, and it runs in opposite directions. The book belongs to you. And you belong to the literature. Similarly, club goods do not belong to an individual. The individual belongs to a group that shares the goods. Ostrom gives the example of a subscription journal.

Belonging, more so than ownership, describes the property relations of art and literature. Belonging aligns us with the logic of common pool resources. Where we used to speak of ownership, we should now speak of belonging. The two meanings of belong both relate to what we call possession, but these are curious, elastic ideas of possession. The first is our private possession of things, which are taken by law or force out of a kind of natural commons that would exist without property. We keep them, possess them, so that they lose their own future, becoming solely an extension of our own, the owner's, the one they belong to. The second, when we belong to a group, obliges us to cede our autonomous, unconstrained liberty and take on rights and obligations toward others. We agree to share what we hold in common. We are possessed by the group, linked by a shared resource and its future and well-being.

This paradoxical term, belonging, enables our humility in the face of resources that we both possess and are possessed by, goods that we share and are responsible for. It summons collective notions of value, encouraging us to move money and other kinds of capital to enable work that is not precisely owned, but which we treasure. So, it is not surprising to see recent initiatives in publishing turning toward collective work, collective management, and subscription and membership models, as artists and writers look for sustainable economies appropriate to art and literature.

If we are moved treat literature and art as common-pool resources, even without referencing that concept or learning directly from Ostrom, what specific shifts and changes should we encourage and cultivate? To return to Ostrom's list (obscured in the shadows back there behind the compelling image of Jens and Tarpy shaping their collectivity in the Swedish summer twilight that lingers and lingers) we ought to attend to four essential tools for effective common pool resource management: (1) clearly defined boundaries; (2) proportional value between benefits and costs; (3) collective choice arrangements; and (4) nested enterprises. Ostrom's fifth essential tool—a graduated array of monitoring and enforcement tools—might be unnecessary. That question, and the specific forms that (1) clear boundaries, (2) proportional value, (3) collective choice, and (4) nested enterprises, will take in a right and sustainable economy of art and literature, are the challenges that I believe we should now take on.

Notes

1 Elinor Ostrom, Roy Gardner, and James Walker, *Rules, Games, and Common-Pool Resources* (Ann Arbor: University of Michigan Press, 1994).

2 Ibid., 7.

3 See Charlotte Hess and Elinor Ostrom, eds., *Understanding Knowledge as a Commons: From Theory to Practice* (Cambridge, MA: MIT Press, 2006).

4 Guy Davenport, "O Gadjo Niglo," in *A Table of Green Fields: Ten Stories* (New York: New Directions, 1993), 108–9.

Interface, Access, Loss

Sean Dockray

183

Digital file sharing signaled the conclusion of that brief period in human history during which certain forms of culture were mass-produced and sold as commodity objects (records, books, etc.) to consumers.

Property has, in one sense, been undone.

On a massive scale, people have used *their* computers and *their* Internet connections to share digitized versions of *their* objects with each other, quickly producing a different, common form of ownership. The crisis that this provoked is well known. What is less recognized—because it is still very much in process—is the subsequent undoing of property, of both the individual and common kind. What follows is a story of "the cloud," the post-dot-com bubble techno super-entity, which sucks up property, labor, and free time.

OBJECT, INTERFACE

Amidst the development of "gas-works, telegraphy, photography, steam navigation, and railways," Karl Marx described how the progressive mechanization and automation of industry resulted in the irreversible expansion of an ultimately redundant "industrial reserve army."[1] It is difficult not to read his theory—and these technologies of connection and communication—against the background of our present moment, in which the rise of the Internet has been accompanied by the deindustrialization of cities, increased migrant and mobile labor, and jobs made obsolete by computation.

There are obvious examples of the impact of computation on the workplace: at factories and distribution centers, robots engineered with computer-vision can replace handfuls of workers with a saving of millions of dollars per robot over the life of the system. And there are less apparent examples as well, in which algorithms determine when and where to hire people and for how long, according to fluctuating conditions.

Both of these examples have parallels within computer programming, namely "reuse" and "garbage collection." Code reuse refers to the practice of writing software in such a way that the code can be used again later in another program to perform the same task. It is considered wasteful to give the same time, attention, and energy to the function, as the development environment is not an assembly line. Such repetition gives way therefore to copy-and-pasting (or merely "calling"). When a program is in the midst of being executed, the computer's memory fills with data, some of which is obsolete (and no longer needed for the computer to run efficiently). If left alone, the memory would become clogged and the program would crash. It is the role of the garbage collector to "free up" memory, deleting what is no longer in use.

In Object-Oriented Programming (OOP), a programmer designs the software that he or she is writing around "objects," where each object is conceptually divided into "public" and "private" parts. The public parts are accessible to other objects, but the private ones are hidden to the world outside the boundaries of that object. This is one instance of a "black box"—a thing that can be known through its inputs and outputs, even in total ignorance of its internal mechanisms. What difference does it make if the code is written in one way or another if it behaves the same? As the philosopher William James argues, "If no practical difference whatever can be traced, then the alternatives mean practically the same thing, and all dispute is idle."[2]

By merely having a public interface an object is already a kind of social entity. It makes no sense for an object to provide access to its outside if there are no other potential objects with which to interact. So, to understand the object-oriented program, we must scale up—not by increasing the size or complexity of the object, but instead by increasing the number and types of objects such that their relations become denser. The result is an intricate machine with an on and an off state, rather than a beginning and an end. Its parts are interchangeable, provided that they reliably produce the same behavior—the same inputs and outputs. Furthermore, this machine can be modified: objects can be added and removed, changing but not destroying the machine; and it might be, using Gerald Raunig's appropriate term, "concatenated" with other machines.[3]

Inevitably, this paradigm for describing the relationship between software objects spreads outward, subsuming more of the universe outside of the immediate code. External programs, powerful computers, banking institutions, people, and satellites have all been "encapsulated" and "abstracted" into objects with inputs and outputs. Is this a conceptual reduction of the richness and complexity of reality? Yes, but only partially. It is also a real description of how people, institutions, software, and things are being brought into relationship with one another according to the demands of networked computation (not to mention the often contradictory demands of business, government, or collective desire); and the expanding field of objects encompasses exactly those entities integrated into such a network.

Consider a simple example of decentralized file sharing: its diagram might represent an object-oriented piece of software, but here each object is a person-computer, shown in potential relation to every other person-computer. Files might be sent or received at any point in this machine, which seems particularly oriented toward circulation and movement. Much remains private, but a collection of files from every person is made public and opened up to the network. Taken as a whole, the entire collection of all files, which on the one hand exceeds the storage capacity of any one person's technical hardware, is on the other hand entirely available to every person-computer. If the files were books, then this collective collection would be a public library.

In order for a system like this to work, for the inputs and the outputs to actually engage with one another to produce action or transmit data, there needs to be something in place to enable meaningful couplings. Before there is any interaction or any relationship, there must be some common ground in place that allows heterogeneous objects to "talk to each other" (to use a phrase from the business-casual language of the Californian ideology). The term used for such a common ground—especially on the Internet—is "platform," or that which enables and anticipates future action without directly producing it. A platform provides tools and resources to the objects that run "on top" of the platform so that those objects do not need to have their own tools and resources. In this sense, the platform offers itself as a way for to externalize (and reuse) labor. Communication between objects is one of the most significant actions that a platform can provide, but it requires that the objects conform some amount of their inputs and outputs to the specifications dictated by the platform.

But haven't we only introduced another coupling, this time between the object and the platform, rather than describing how that coupling works in the first place? To work toward a description, we need to look at that meeting point between things, otherwise known as the "interface." In the terms of OOP, the interface is an abstraction that defines what kinds of interactions are possible with an object. It maps out the public face of the object in a way that is legible and accessible to other objects. Similarly, computer interfaces like screens and keyboards are designed to meet with human interfaces like fingers and eyes, allowing for a specific form of interaction between person and machine. Any coupling between objects passes through some interface and every interface obscures as much as it reveals: it establishes the boundary between what is public and what is private, what is visible and what is not. The dominant aesthetic values of user interface design actually privilege such concealment as "good design," appealing to principles of simplicity, cleanliness, and clarity.

CLOUD, ACCESS

One practical outcome of this has been that there can be tectonic shifts behind the interface—where entire systems are restructured or revolutionized—without any interruption (so long as the interface itself remains essentially unchanged). In pragmatism's terms, a successful interface keeps any difference (in the back end) from making a difference (in the front end). To use books again as an example: after consumers became accustomed to the initial discomfort of purchasing a product online instead of from a shop, they saw an act such as "buying a book" to be something that could be interchangeably accomplished either by a traditional bookstore or the online "marketplace" equivalent. In each case, one gives money and receives a book. But behind that interface—most likely Amazon—the online bookseller has positioned itself through low prices and a wide selection as the most visible platform for buying books, and uses that position to push retailers and publishers to, at best, the bare minimum of profitability.

In addition to collecting data about its users (what they look at, what they buy) to personalize product recommendations, Amazon has also made an effort to be a platform for the technical and logistical parts of *other retailers*. Ultimately collecting data from them as well, Amazon realizes a competitive advantage from having a comprehensive, up-to-the-minute perspective on market trends and inventories. This volume of data is so vast and valuable that warehouses packed with computers are constructed to store it, protect it, and make it readily available to algorithms. Data centers such as these organize how commodities circulate (they run business applications, store data about retail, manage fulfillment) but also increasingly hold the commodity itself—for example, the book. Sales of digital books started the millennium very slowly but by 2010 had overtaken hardcover sales.

Amazon's store of digital books (or Apple's or Google's, for that matter) is a distorted reflection of the collection circulating within the file-sharing network, displaced from personal computers to corporate data centers. Here are two regimes of digital property: the swarm and the cloud. For *swarms* (a reference to swarm downloading where a single file can be downloaded in parallel from multiple sources), property is held in common between peers—property is positioned out of reach; but on *the cloud*, the same file might be accessible through an interface that has absorbed legal and business requirements. It is only half of the story, however, to associate the cloud with mammoth data centers; the other half is to be found in our hands and laps. Thin computing, including tablets and e-readers, iPads, Kindles, and mobile phones, has coevolved with data centers, offering powerful, lightweight computing precisely because so much processing and storage has been externalized.

In this technical configuration of the cloud, the thin computer and the fat data center meet through an interface, inevitably clean and simple, that manages access to the remote resources. Typically a person needs to agree to certain "terms of service," have a unique, measurable account, and provide payment information; in return, access is granted. This access is not ownership in the conventional sense of a book, or even the digital sense of a file, but rather a license that gives the person a "non-exclusive right to keep a permanent copy... solely for your personal and non-commercial use," contradicting the First Sale Doctrine, which gives the "owner" the right to sell, lease, or rent their copy to anyone they choose at any price they choose. The doctrine, established within America's legal system in 1908, separated the rights of reproduction from distribution as a way to "exhaust" the copyright holder's control over the commodities that people purchased, legitimizing institutions like used bookstores and public libraries. Computer software famously attempted to bypass the First Sale Doctrine with its "shrink-wrap" licenses that restricted the rights of the buyer once he or she broke through the plastic packaging to open the product. This practice has only evolved and become ubiquitous over the last three decades as software began being distributed digitally through networks rather than as physical objects in stores. Such contradictions are symptoms of the shift in property regimes, or what Jeremy Rifkin called "the age of access." He writes: "Property continues to exist but is far less likely to be exchanged in markets. Instead, suppliers hold on to property in the new economy and lease, rent, or charge an admission fee, subscription, or membership dues for its short-term use."[4]

Thinking again of books, Rifkin provides the image of a paid library emerging as the synthesis of the public library and the marketplace for commodity exchange. Considering how, on the one side, traditional public libraries are having their collections de-accessioned, hours of operation cut, and are in some cases being closed down entirely, and on the other side, the traditional publishing industry finds its stores, books, and profits dematerialized, the image is perhaps appropriate. In photographs inside data centers, server racks strike an eerie resemblance to library stacks, while e-readers are consciously designed to look and feel something like a book. Whether it is in recognition of the centuries of design knowledge accrued in the form of the book, or simply to make the interface as consistent as possible while everything else changes behind the scenes, the e-reader's evocation of the book is undeniable. Yet, when one peers down into the screen of the device, one sees both the book *and* the library.

Like a Facebook account, which must uniquely correspond to a real person, the e-reader is an individualizing device. It is the object that establishes trusted access with books stored in the cloud and ensures that each and every person purchases their own rights to read each book. The only sharing that is allowed is sharing *the device itself,* which is the thing that a person actually does own. But even then, such an act must be reported back to the cloud: the hardware needs to be de-registered and then reregistered with credit card and authentication details about the new owner.

This is no library—or, it is only a library in the most impoverished sense of the word. It is a new enclosure, and it is a familiar story: things in the world (from letters to photographs to albums to books) are digitized (as e-mails, JPEGs, MP3s, and PDFs) and subsequently migrate to a remote location or service (Gmail, Facebook, iTunes, the Kindle store). The middle phase is the biggest disruption: that is, when the interface does the poorest job concealing the material transformations taking place, when the work involved in creating those transformations is most apparent, often because the person themselves is deeply involved in the process (of ripping vinyl, for instance). In the third phase, the user interface becomes easier, "frictionless," and what appears to be just another application or folder on one's computer is an engorged, property-and-energy-hungry warehouse a thousand miles away.

CAPTURE, LOSS

The enclosure of intellectual property is easy enough to imagine in warehouses of remote, secure hard drives. But the cloud internalizes processing as well as storage, capturing the new forms of co-operation and collaboration characterizing the new economy and its immaterial labor. Social relations are transmuted into database relations on the "social web," which absorbs self-organization as well. In this sense, the cloud's impact on the production of publications is just as strong as on their consumption, in the traditional sense.

Storage, applications, and services offered in the cloud are marketed for consumption by authors and publishers alike. Document editing, project management, and accounting are peeled slowly away from the office staff and personal computers into the data centers; interfaces are established into various publication channels from print-on-demand to digital book platforms. In the fully realized vision of cloud publishing, the entire technical and logistical apparatus is externalized, leaving only human laborers and their thin devices remaining. Little separates the author-object from the editor-object from the reader-object. All of them maintain their position in the network by paying for lightweight computers and their updates, cloud services, and broadband Internet connections.

On the production side of the book, the promise of the cloud is a recovery of the profits "lost" to file sharing, as all the exchange is disciplined, standardized, and measured. Consumers are finally promised the access to the history of human knowledge (that they had already improvised by themselves), but now, without the omnipresent threat of legal prosecution. One has the sneaking suspicion that such a compromise is as hollow as the promises to a desperate city of jobs that will be created in a new constructed data center, and that pitting "food on the table" against "access to knowledge" is both a distraction from and a legitimatization of the forms of power emerging in the cloud. It is a distraction because it is by policing access to knowledge that the middleman platform can extract value from publication, both on the writing and reading sides of the book; and it is a legitimation because the platform poses itself as the only entity that can resolve the contradiction between the two sides.

When the platform recedes behind the interface, these two sides comprise the most visible antagonism: they are in a tug-of-war with each other, yet neither the "producers" nor the "consumers" of publications are becoming wealthier or working less to survive. If we turn the picture sideways, however, a new contradiction emerges between the indebted, living labor of authors, editors, translators, and readers on one side, and on the other, data centers, semiconductors, mobile technology, expropriated software, power companies, and intellectual property.

The talk in the data-center industry of the "industrialization" of the cloud refers to the scientific approach to improving design, efficiency, and performance. But the term also recalls the basic narrative of the Industrial Revolution: the movement from home-based manufacturing by hand to large-scale production in factories. As desktop computers pass into obsolescence, we shift from a networked but small-scale relationship to computation (think of "home publishing") to a reorganized form of production that puts the accumulated energy of millions to work through these cloud companies and their modernized data centers.

What kind of buildings *are* these blank superstructures? Factories for the twenty-first century? An engineer named Ken Patchett described the Facebook data center in a television interview: "This is a factory. It's just a different kind of factory than you might be used to."[5] Those factories that we're "used to" continue to exist (at Foxconn, for instance), producing the infrastructure under recognizably exploitative conditions, for this is "different kind of factory," a factory extending far beyond the walls of the data center. But the idea of the factory is only part of the picture—this building is also a mine and the dispersed workforce devotes most of its waking hours to mining-in-reverse, packing it full of data under the expectation that someone soon will figure out how to pull out something valuable. Both metaphors rely on the image of a mass of workers (dispersed as it may be), and leave a darker and more difficult possibility: the data center is like the hydroelectric plant, damming up property, sociality, creativity, and knowledge, while engineers and financiers look for the algorithms to release the accumulated cultural and social resources on demand, as profit.

This returns us to the interface, the site of the struggles over management and control of access to property and infrastructure. Previously, these struggles were situated within the computer-object and the implied freedom provided by its computation, storage, and possibilities for connection with others. Now, however, the eviscerated device is more interface than object, and it is exactly here at the interface that the new technological enclosures have taken form (for example, see Apple's iOS products, Google's search box, and Amazon's "marketplace"). Control over the interface is guaranteed by control over the entire techno-business stack: the distributed hardware devices, centralized data centers, and the software that mediates the space between. Every major technology corporation must now operate on all levels to protect against any loss.

There is a centripetal force to the cloud and this essay has been written in its irresistible pull. In spite of the sheer mass of capital that is organized to produce this gravity and the seeming insurmountability of it all, there is no chance that the system will absolutely manage and control the noise within it. Riots break out on the factory floor; algorithmic trading wreaks havoc on the stock market in an instant; data centers go offline; 100 million Facebook accounts are discovered to be fake; the list will continue to grow. These cracks in the interface don't point to any possible future, or any desirable one, but they do draw attention to openings that might circumvent the logic of access. What happens from there is another question.

Notes

1 Karl Marx, *Capital: A Critique of Political Economy*, vol. 1, trans. Ben Fowkes (New York: Penguin Books, 1990), 573.

2 William James, *Pragmatism* (Cambridge, MA: Harvard University Press, 1975), 28.

3 See Gerald Raunig, *A Thousand Machines* (Los Angeles: Semiotext(e), 2010).

4 Jeremy Rifkin, *The Age of Access: The New Culture of Hypercapitalism, Where all of Life is a Paid-For Experience* (New York: Jeremy P. Tarcher/Putnam, 2000), 4.

5 Quoted in Frank Mungeam, "Facebook Building Facility in Prineville," KGW.com, February 11, 2011, www.kgw.com/news/business/Facebook-building-facility-in-Prineville-115964989.html.

Imaginary Property
Florian Schneider

195

The difficulty in fully grasping today's property relations—conceived as increasingly immaterial—through traditional conceptions of selfhood and objecthood is generally acknowledged. It has almost become a truism that the proliferation of "new technologies" has come along with substantial reinterpretations of the meaning and the effects of ownership and control.

In discourse critical of capitalism, the term "privatization" is used to characterize the "complex array of interconnected processes and relationships through which political rights, social membership, knowledge production, and the related spheres that constitute personhood are increasingly brought within the ambit of the capitalist marketplace."[1] The neoliberal agenda of "rampant privatization" is countered with widespread attempts to propose "commons" or "the common" as a central narrative that would fight the excesses of postindustrial capitalism, and abolish, delimit, or soften its effects.

The concept of "imaginary property" takes a different route. Rather than denouncing the private and therefore "privative" character of property while leaving the general abstract concept of property more or less intact—as is the case in the concept of Creative Commons—the focus has to be shifted to the very idea of property and its problems as such. And rather than discussing the dialectics of the private as substantially inalienable and alienable at the same time, this project draws attention to relations of production whose forces are considered as primarily speculative.

Property as the mirror image of a (self-owning) self may no longer be reserved for the reciprocal production of a responsible subject in the legal realm of bourgeois society; instead the illusionary character of property is set free as a specter, a ghostly force that seems to constantly mirror everything. Due to their endless mirror effects, postmodern economies have often been perceived as a funhouse where you can bet on anything, for, like in a hall of mirrors, reality is just the image of an image.

Meanwhile, it has become obvious that the incalculable effects of networked realities in globalized capitalism are not confined to a kind of virtual amusement park but have irrevocably changed the world and how we perceive it; they have pounded to pieces the relationship between property and personhood—a relationship formerly known as eternally valid and still promoted as universally applicable.

In its simplest form, the problem that is at stake in imaginary property is articulated as the absence of the object that is owned. The immaterial, intangible expressions of a creative mind is an issue the moment when it starts to circulate and proliferate in an uncontrolled fashion, when it escapes traditional forms of arrest and becomes fugitive.

The critical analysis of imaginary property has to depart from a specific understanding of the passage from a mechanical production of reality to a networked production of realities, which should not be mistaken as a similar binary to that of the analog and digital. In fact the concept of imaginary property presupposes no essential distinction between analog and digital, material and immaterial. Instead it marks the intersection or collision of two vectorial lines, two modes whose crossover characterizes contemporary means of production.

Mechanicity or the mechanical reproduction of the real turns everything into things, reifying living beings by abstracting from their concrete qualities, capturing their forces, arresting movement, and then remobilizing the stagnating entities as disciplined items in controlled environments.

The networked mode of production turns everything into images, while animating them as flows of information, concretizing the vast variety of data in the fluidity of constant exchange. At first sight, networked reality seems to be ungraspable, opaque, fugitive (expressed in the vulgar notion of "virtuality"). The real reoccurs only partially and only temporarily in the image as a storage unit for framed portions of psychic reality. In the digital, networked economy, a copy (no matter whether it is text, sound, image) appears as a mirror image that is not isolated, but refers to another.

Traditional forms of ownership are applied to new types of digital imagery, while the seemingly immaterial character of production and networked distribution has long undermined the vulgar concept of property as a somewhat stable relationship between persons and objects. We might sense intuitively that things themselves cannot be owned, only their social relationality. What one owns, when one owns, is always the imagined efficacy of an acclaimed ownership within a given social environment as long as the effects of that ownership remain subject to manipulations.

In order to make things ownable, to enforce a claim, things need to be turned into images. This is at least the concrete truth of the saying: "A picture says more than a thousands of words." This transformation of a thing into an image characterizes the very act of seeing. This is the very capacity of our eyes to appropriate reality as a visual property, or what Konrad Fiedler called *Sichtbarkeitsbesitz*.[2] But the process of appropriation is everything but seamless. On the contrary, ownership comes into being as a mistake, an oversight—or, in German, *Versehen*: watching, but always omitting something crucial.

The mistake is the actual success of representation. One has to forget that one can own things only by assigning or providing them with a self. The self of a thing is the surplus that is expropriated; it is conceived as "data," the abstract representation of the object that is given to sensual experience and prehension through "perspective."[3]

The self of the thing—its "soul" or "aura"—is the invisible that becomes visible in property. It stands for a creativity that is not subjective but objective; for it refers to creation and permanent recreation of the thing, the fact that it itself has been created in a former or ongoing activity.[4] Property therefore is the appropriation of that activity as the self of the thing and not as the thing itself.

Property establishes an imaginary social relationship between the owner and the self of a thing, its immaterial and yet invisible data relating to its creation or creativity. Against this backdrop we have to understand the widespread myth of photography as a "stealing of souls."

In everyday life, we are pretty much familiar with the animation of that self, insofar as it constitutes the commodity fetish under the regime of industrial capitalism: the abstraction of an exchange value that relates to quantified and expropriated human labor from a use value that remains inherent to the quality of the thing itself and may not affect property relations.

Things become complicated when they encounter the reproduction of that self, not only in legal terms. The division of a thing into two, its double character—as visible and invisible, use value and exchange value, original and copy—needs to be brought back into congruence, in particular when it is supposed to be reproduced and multiplied (as a picture, an investment, etc.).

The production of such coherence and consistency in time and space is ensured by the means of and for the sake of continuity. Continuity is the expression of property on "the screens of the symbolic"[5]: it is its appropriateness as far as it demonstrates the successful inheritance of data from one occasion to the other.

The main characteristic of contemporary image production is the fact that it also operates in the reverse direction: it appears as a force that alienates the image from itself in order to make it ownable as if it were a thing. This is indeed only possible by turning the image back into a thing—understanding it as data.

Again, it does not appropriate the image as such, but its potential social relations insofar as they are subject to an endless array of readings, manipulations, and recreations. The extraction of metadata, the production of algorithmic identities through indexing technologies, the reduction of the visible to the legible, the recognition of reiterating patterns—these are serving the very purpose of the reorganization of the image as the data of past events or former experiences.

But it is not possible to eliminate entirely all the ambiguities of an image, even if it is digital. The ghost that is haunting imaginary property is the self of the image: it is constituted by a failure rather than a success, by its contingency rather than its continuity. The estranged "anti-aura" of the digital image resides in its noise; that is, what cannot be compressed and therefore needs to be discarded in the moment when the image becomes ownable as a digital object or data. The provisional character of imaginary property is realized as a contingent remainder in the self of the image.

In imaginary property we reencounter the problem of "over-appropriation" as the appropriation of what already has been appropriated. Bernard Edelman coined this term in 1973 when he set out to analyze the emergence of French copyright law in the advent of photographic and cinematic technologies in the course of the nineteenth century. "Over-appropriation of the real" characterizes acquisition through superimposing on an already established property.[6]

How can one own an image of a thing that is already someone else's property? The creation of the image needs to become a property in its own right, assuming that it does not harm the property that is depicted (like in a quotation)—or that the property is everyone's property (like a landscape). But it is not enough to reproduce the real in the image, since then it would remain someone's or everyone's property (the public domain is the general abstract expression of property). Law assumes a certain threshold of creativity for "intellectual" appropriation: the real needs to be produced rather than reproduced and only in doing so does the law generate a subject that is creative.

In order to compensate for the technology's inability to reproduce reality exactly, the impossibility of a perfect analog copy has opened a wide space for a certain variety of privileged notions of professional creativity. The access to this space has been regulated through a relative scarcity of the means of image production.

Digital technologies have changed the situation dramatically: the general acceptance and accessibility of the tools to produce a hypothetically loss-free and cost-free copy and to distribute it in so-called real time shakes the juridical construction of property that is both immaterial but real, produced by the creative subject and producing a creative subjectivity.

The bourgeoisie "creative class" is panicking. It fears losing its traditional privileges. At the same time, a new mass-creativity has emerged in which anyone can be a filmmaker, photographer, writer, or artist. Anyone can therefore claim the right to produce reality and consider it their own property based solely on the appropriation of the means of image production—as opposed to their former role as wage-laborers essentially deprived from accessing the means of production for their own purposes.

While theory, politics, and jurisprudence insist on continuing to apply nineteenth-century protectionist models of "intellectual property," capital responds to the new situation, characterized by the inflation of imaginary property, by a devaluation of the real. The real has ceased to produce a creative subject, which produces reality as its property—as was the case when it was about turning things into images. Instead, creativity is produced by the imaginary. When images turn into things, creativity results from the extraction of rather precarious data from images. Currently, creativity is reified as a productive force; it has become a machine that does not reproduce but produces images.

Consequentially, there is no longer a need for a creative subject in order to solve the riddle of the over-appropriation of the real. The problem today is the over-appropriation of the image: how to own images that are already owned. It can be solved only by the production of data that produce new data.

If creativity refers to a model of data that is generated from images and simultaneously generates new images, imagination as the power to make images appears as algorithmic control imitating or simulating movement rather than confining it. This is the very nature of surveillance, which calculates desire based on data extracted from images.

In a similar way to how private property relates to the division of labor in industrial capitalism, the concept of imaginary property leads to an analysis of imagination as a "rule of production," which then triggers the question of the division of labor in digital, networked image production.

The traditional form of division of labor in industrial capitalism appears in the separation of manual and intellectual labor. It reflects the division of the thing and its self, its material and immaterial character, its value in use and exchange. It operates through the expropriation of surplus labor and generates a notion of exclusive ownership of the means of production that constitutes a specific form of private property.

In the algorithmic mode of computing, workload seems to be divided into a radically idealized version of the assembly line: code that is written by a creative human mind assigns a finite number of tasks to a machine; these tasks have to be executed logically, in a determined and deterministic fashion.

The algorithm, the chain of commands that foresees its outcome, can be characterized as an incarnation of *Vorstellung*, a notion of imagination usually translated as "representation." It is a "prepositing of a being-posited," as Jean-Luc Nancy comments on Martin Heidegger's considerations of Immanuel Kant's image theory in his "Kantbuch." Algorithmic control is creative as an imaginative force, as it refers to time as a pure image or "a schema-image" in the Kantian sense. "There is no given present that is not preceded by the pre-givenness of its givability, identical to its receivability."[7]

"The imagination is therefore time, since time is the nonpresent, the non-instantaneous, of a look that does not see its own unity (its concept) directly, but only in and as the Bildung (formation) of the unity of the manifold, many-folded (if you will) into itself and from out of itself in order to image itself."[8] Algorithmic control divides a task into a finite number of subtasks that are executed consecutively. Its power is twofold: it is the power of a look which is preempting positions that are essentially deprived of seeing the process in its unity; but it is also the power of foreseeing the allocation of time slots in which each task or subtask has to be fulfilled. Both culminate in a notion of real time, where chronological time seems to have collapsed into an instantaneity that is only imagined as the identity of giving and receiving.

In that sense, globalized economies of late capitalism are self-imagined economies. The social divisions of labor of industrial capitalism are not overcome but radically applied on a global scale: contract manufacturing, just-in-time production, clustering. At the same time, new technical divisions of labor have emerged through the advance of digital registration procedures ranging from the cadaster to the stock exchange ("algo-trading"). These processes claim to operate in so-called real time—run by algorithms, which exploit the asynchronicity of milliseconds and therefore cannot be critically evaluated.

These phenomena cannot hide the fact that even the most complex systems of algorithmic control are based on the quantitative increase in the number of operations in a given time frame and their constant reprioritization in an hierarchically structured operating system, which, in the end, simulates a Fordist division of labor.

Today, systems that are inspired by formal logic and are algorithmically controlled and equipped with digital electronics have reached their limits of complexity. Furthermore, the paradigms inherent to networked computing seem to be in contradiction to all principles that characterize the current challenges of "biopolitical" control: from self-organizing and self-learning systems to neural networks and creative infrastructure.[9]

The conceptual need for new models of organizing workflows creatively is obvious when it comes to artificial vision as the ultimate instance of imaginary property. It fails precisely in the moment when it is confronted with the self of the image. Ambiguities, paradoxes, productive misunderstandings, and contradictions form the poetic character of an image as an image that was made creatively.

What is at stake are hybrid divisions of labor, which actively involve the self of the user in the actual creation of code; that combine algorithmic and poetic work, disciplined and undisciplined activities, deterministic and precarious states, paid and unpaid labor. The result will be automatization of a kind that we can already experience in rudimentary forms within corporate notions of social networking where the degree of freedom of movement correlates to the function of algorithmic control.

A hybrid division of labor requires a different conception of the self. It is not the mirror image of a subject that owns itself and through that acquires the capacity of ownership as such. It is not the creative self that mirrors its imaginative power in the product of its labor.

The charismatic notion of the self is characterized by a permanent sense of crisis and the resulting need to perform itself in real time. The charismatic self marks the arbitrary datum identified in the midst of exponentially growing relational value. It is the point zero that makes the measurement of imaginary property possible again (as clicks, followers, or friends).

It acts as a clearinghouse for heterogeneous streams of data that are extracted from the myriad of circulating images and need to be differentiated by ad-hoc judgments. The charismatic self is constituted by the very capacity to have a distinct opinion even in a networked environment where the hierarchical production of meaning is messed up and relational value is generated without a plan or purpose. Its ambition is to overcome the perplexity that results from the chaos of an inflation of data inherited from past events.

By interacting with it, the charismatic self makes itself immune against the threat of automatization as extinction of the individual or as the end of the specialist. The mythology of networked automatization has estranged creativity from the process of creation. In order to generate relational value, the image becomes valuable in an alienated context—one other than its own. Through relational value, the charismatic self reconnects the image and a self, which must not necessarily be either the original creator or authorized owner.

Notes

1 Bill Maurer and Gabriele Schwab, eds., *Accelerating Possession: Global Futures of Property and Personhood* (New York: Columbia University Press, 2006), 8.
2 Konrad Fiedler, *Schriften zur Kunst*, vol. 1, ed. Gottfrield Bohm (Munich: Wilhelm Fink, 1991), 169.
3 "Perspective" would be the literal translation of *Versehen*, according to the Latin root of the word.
4 "Even when they are nonliving, or rather inorganic, things have a lived experience because they are perceptions and affections." Gilles Deleuze and Félix Guattari, *What Is Philosophy?*, trans. Hugh Tomlinson and Graham Burchell (New York: Columbia University Press, 1994), 154.
5 Jacques Attali, *Noise: The Political Economy of Music*, trans. Brian Massumi (Minneapolis: University of Minnesota Press, 1985), 143.
6 Bernard Edelman, *Ownership of the Image: Elements for a Marxist Theory of Law* (London: Routledge, 1979), 38.
7 Jean-Luc Nancy, *The Ground of the Image*, trans. Jeff Fort (New York: Fordham University Press, 2005), 90.
8 Ibid.
9 See Ulrich Ramacher and Christoph von der Malsburg, eds., *Zur Konstruktion künstlicher Gehirne* (Berlin: Springer Verlag, 2009).

Reproducing the Future

Marilyn Strathern in conversation with Marysia Lewandowska

In late summer of 2012, I approached Marilyn Strathern with an invitation to consider contributing to this book. We have had little contact since Capital *(2001),*[1] *a project at Tate Modern for which she wrote an essay and led a seminar. More recently, I became aware of her current research—specifically her work in bringing questions of the gift into the contested terrain of the body and gender. Thinking about property in social and cultural terms led me straight back to her earlier writing. Her practice, born out of a lifetime of fieldwork, establishes a language away from legally motivated references to intellectual property or limited debates around networks and social media. I was inspired by the more fundamental questions that her research poses—about the spirit of generosity and a need to give up preconceptions of how culture is made and remade, produced and reproduced. The questions reverberate with my research and art practice, which is concerned with inquiries into ownership and how we conceptualize the boundaries between public and private interest. This return to Strathern's work was followed by a visit to her home in Cambridge in November 2012, a lunch together, and an audio recording of our conversation.*

Marysia Lewandowska: Prior to coming here, I read your text *Reproducing the Future.* The book was published in 1992, and it was a response to a public debate generated by the 1990 Act of Parliament regarding human fertilization and embryology. As I understand, you were part of a number of academics who were asked to contribute to that discussion and to form some kind of response.

Marilyn Strathern: Yes, there was certainly a lot of public debate at the time. As a response I organized a short research project with some colleagues that was funded by the ESRC [Economic Social Research Council]. One of the things that struck me upon returning from Papua New Guinea and becoming part of the English public again was the way in which new reproductive technologies really opened up questions around what I would call "kinship." Not necessarily around family, parents, and children, but kinship as being about ideas of what relatedness was and what it meant, and it seemed interesting that the act generated such a vigorous public discussion.

ML What attracted me to *Reproducing the Future* was the way in which it brings together some of the key notions addressing the new frontier of human intervention into the fundamental processes of life. The first notion is that of artifice, which in the context I work in—in art—bears a relation to artifact, but also artifice understood as a result of human labor and creativity.

MS It's interesting that you pick that up, because that was en vogue at the time in the way that these technologies were dubbed "artificial insemination," for example. AI was a long established procedure of course, but the concept of artificiality in these technologies was very much in the air. Certainly I, and I'm sure others, dropped the notion of the artificial very quickly from what we were writing about, and it was replaced by a much more informed interest in the issue of technology. Technology implied not just tools, but tools that have been knowingly constructed; they contain information within them, so to speak, and that was the beginning of what has become a huge topic in anthropology, which is the study of technology. So, that sense of artificiality was very current but didn't endure, at least in the anthropologists' writings. Did you want to talk about another kind of artifice, around artifacts?

ML It is my understanding that a very important part of anthropology is the study of artifacts. How was it present in that particular discussion you mentioned? Where was the contention?

MS It was undeniable that the offspring born from what became known as "assisted conception" were, in a sense, artifacts of human design. That wasn't a connection that was made—nor did people think of the technologies as artifacts—but it's very interesting *why* they didn't. I think partly because the whole status of the artifact in anthropology was a rather marginal one, and at that point in time really rather confined to the anthropology of art. Or, the artifact was associated with archaeology;

you dig up artifacts. So it didn't get into circulation as part of that argument, although clearly it could have done.

ML Lets explore another term, which seems to connect with how we might think of the processes of life and the processes of culture, and that is "reproduction"—reproduction as the origin of life, and reproduction as a "thing" or relation standing in for the original. Before the onset of the digital technologies, that version—the copy—was always treated as inferior, as less significant, and, certainly in art historical terms, not to mention market terms, less valuable. Art history as a discipline still insists on privileging the original. It's the logic of exclusivity; be it between artist and dealer, artist and curator, artist and critic, artist and collector. The original as a thing stands for access to the unique expression, and looking closely at the patterns of collecting in both private and public spheres supports such a conclusion. But the digital revolution has radically changed this, introducing doubt into the value system associated with the original. We are replicating and modifying everything from human, animal, and plant DNA, as well as producing unprecedented amount of data—texts, images, films, sounds. How do we create value inside this avalanche? And why does the thing or relation that is at the source of both terms remain so disparate?

MS There were in fact some commentators who were quite interested in the notion of the copy, and what was being copied, so to speak. Human reproduction is itself a very particular take on the whole notion of conception and birth, because the one thing that parents don't do is reproduce *themselves*—that is, they don't reproduce the combination of genetic materials that went into their makeup, because they are joined with another, and the outcome is always different and unique. [Social] identity is what parents reproduce; parents, within the context of being joint members of a household—their names, lifestyle, passing down property, reproducing values. But in all those ways, one is using "reproduction" simply to mean a kind of replication by which your identity endures.

ML Why is so much invested in the relationship between ownership, property, and the rights that one has to property in terms of inheritance? That seems, at least in our culture, overwhelmingly strong.

MS Absolutely. It's strong in quite an unusual way; one has to instantly create a divide between the law and legal definitions of property rights, and common understandings and common parlance. Most people would say that they own themselves, or they own their labor, and this gives them the right to do X or Y. In the law, of course, a person cannot have a property relationship with their own body, and the circumstances under which you can dispose of your labor are restricted by laws as well as market possibilities and so forth. But nonetheless, the colloquial notion that you "own what you are" is incredibly strong, and it keeps popping up. The lawyers can talk until they are blue in the face about how an individual does not own their person, but the very language of property and its close association with proprietorship, says the opposite. So there's an interesting disjunction. And also, out of the notion that people own themselves comes a sense that they can also talk about owning their name, or owning their house, or whatever. From all sides this forms a very general sense that your identity in the world and the activities associated with you are part *of* you, they are your *own* self, and the self can in that sense *own* the self: the self and all its expressions. That's a very strong folk construct.

ML I wanted to return to the idea that in terms of art, reproduction is always presented as inferior to the original, like a shadow. Yet, we also think of reproduction, which is culturally motivated as relating to value, and the role of institutions in the reproduction of values. This is very crucial in how I experience art and how I think of my own practice as an artist. It always functions within the institution; it is already coded while it participates in legitimating an existing system of value.

MS So art reproduces part of the institution?

ML Well, the institution is really the place of the reproduction of value.

MS So you mean that all the practices to do with producing works of art—commissioning them, displaying them—are the context that reproduces something as "art"?

ML Yes, and also confirms something as art.

MS But are you suggesting that this is somehow an echo or a shadow?

ML No, it feels like that is the primary function of the institution. Whether it is the public museum or a private foundation supporting that museum, it is through the exhibitionary practices that its core values are reproduced and disseminated.

MS Indeed.

ML So in that sense, the more reproduction there is, the stronger the institution is.

MS The fact that there are multiple connotations of "reproduction" to be reported upon is just a fact of the way language works. Coming to the point that you make about institutions and their need to reproduce values, that's close to the way a thinker such as Marx would use the term: reproduction in terms of the reproduction of labor, which involves looking at everything that goes into allowing someone to dispose of their labor—so you are looking into the domestic processes by which a worker reproduces him or herself—in order to be available to put his or her labor on the market. That sense of reproduction, which is to sustain the conditions under which something exists, can be applied to any activity. For example, a university wishes to reproduce the values of scholarship that it upholds, and it does so by sustaining the conditions under which people can be scholars.

ML A paragraph in the introduction to *Reproducing the Future* made me wonder: how are such direct interventions into processes of life (by allowing human cells to be reproduced artificially) threatening or altering property relations? Is it because it changes the role of the parents who are no longer the people having something to say about what is at stake here?

MS That is an exceedingly interesting question because there are still people making claims, but they're not making claims in relation to what they take as biological processes that they can't do anything about; instead, they are making claims in relation to the way other people have acted. Let us imagine a fantasy scenario: you have three mothers, a genetic mother, a bearing mother and a commissioning mother who might have had an embryo implanted in her uterus. The question, then, becomes not that property *itself* is threatened, not at all—property proliferates, and becomes more applicable—but raises the question, are we talking about property or about ownership here? Because, I would prefer to talk about "ownership" as the colloquial term: ownership is not threatened, ownership becomes distributed, and different kinds of justifications are made for it, so that the genetic mother will use the genetic argument, the birth mother will use the birth argument, and the commissioning mother will use the commissioning argument, which then becomes an argument about contracts. Any of them could make claims saying "the child is mine," and they use the possessive, but in English idiom they would be less likely to say "I own the child," which introduces us to a way of differentiating between subjects and objects, and, since slavery, everybody knows that persons should not be owned. So people tend not to talk of owning their children: they talk of "my own children," but they don't say, "I own my children."

ML So, what of the question of belonging? In another part of this book, Matthew Stadler—a writer based in Portland, Oregon—writes about literature, and introduces the difference between ownership and belonging. In the context you are referring to, the mother—when she feels she is the "natural" mother by saying, "my own child" or "my own children"—suggests that they *belong* to her.

MS It's perfectly appropriate in English to talk of my children belonging to me—it's a fairly benign word, it can be applied to all kinds of circumstances where you're trying to establish an authenticity or a relation of identity, and often to places and buildings, to anything, not just to people.

But going back to the fantasy scenario with three different mothers, the way in which it's often talked about, each one implying that the child is their own, is in terms of who the "real" mother is. And this is very interesting because despite the fact you quite clearly have this social relationship between the various possibilities, there is nonetheless an attempt to justify the "naturalness" of what is going on. So, for the genetic mother, her basis of being the "real" or "natural" mother is her genes, but to the birth mother, of course, birth is the basis; the commissioning mother may point to contract on the one hand, but on the other she may point to her desire, a maternal desire—even though it couldn't be realized through her own body, that desire is a "natural" instinct to motherhood—and that makes her a "real" mother.

ML So, it's the *desire* that is, for her, the origin of motherhood.

MS Indeed, and you've just touched on the jump that led me from the new reproductive technologies to intellectual property. There is a case of a contested parentage in which the commissioning parent claimed that although the embryo had been conceived by others, they were the *conceivers* of the relationship, conceivers of the *idea* of having a child, the prime cause. One of the judges in a case of this particular kind, picked up on that as an inappropriate introduction of intellectual property, and that woke me up to the idea. In this case, the judge pointed out that the analogy didn't work, because of course you can't have copyright on an idea, you can only have copyright over its expression.

ML Since the premise of this book is "undoing property," I wanted to see how this idea would reverberate with you: property as an image and property as a concept. Do both need "undoing" before a paradigm shift is possible? Where do we locate the image of property? And, also, how do we do this from the perspective of our separate practices? Art as a critical practice is where my work belongs, and yours in anthropology as a social science. How much attention do we give to the fact that in terms of knowledge production there might be an affinity between our positions? Might this be due to a shared desire for an embedded practice encouraging openness, dissemination, and public debate?

MS That's a very interesting question, which I suppose an anthropologist would translate into a question about context: what are the contexts in which this concept is used or not used? But that doesn't quite capture what you were getting at in terms of image. I don't know if I can speak for the discipline, so I will speak for myself: if I use the term property, I am implying some kind of subject–object relationship, in the sense that while property rights are a relation between persons—that is, I hold a right against you, to sell my teapot or whatever—so property is conventionally talked of in anthropology as a relation between people over things. However, a relation between people over things is very often collapsed into the notion of a subject who has rights over something, and objects (in English) tend to be equated with things. Now, one of the issues that fascinated me in Papua New Guinea is that you can't hold those stable subject–object person–thing terms—it doesn't cohere in the way it does in English parlance—and everyone has to be very clear about the terms one is using. So, in the comparative work I did on gender relations across New Guinea as in *The Gender of the Gift*, I did not use the term "property" at all for what was going on in the that context. The image that I would have is that property turns things into objects, and requires the exercise of subjective control over these objects. This is why in English you can't talk of owning persons without putting it all in quotation marks, or why having "property" rights over persons is not permissible.

ML I was reading Lewis Hyde's most recent book *Common as Air*. In it, he's exploring property relations through the idea of the knowledge commons, and what particularly interested me was that he talked about property in terms of activity, which connects with what you just said. It is the act of claiming the rights that unleash contention between generations, between parents and children, between nations. For example, the Elgin Marbles, as long as they are on display at the British Museum, will always be perceived as contentious property.

MS Yes, that makes a great deal of sense.

ML Can you say more about this idea? Until it is claimed—and therefore becomes activated—it remains invisible? You need the act. It is a moment of transformation.

MS Yes, because until that moment you could have all kinds of compromises and could be thinking that you really have a share in something—things can be undefined and implicit, but the moment of introducing a claim is a moment of creating boundaries, boundaries that some might not recognize. In general terms, it can be very provocative to declare property; having said that, it's only half the picture, because there are all forms and kinds of property that do their work without anyone really doing much about them. I'm thinking of capital, of course, and what capital can earn: all that happens is that property, having been exercised in relation to an investment, will go on doing things for the owner without him or her having to do anything other than remain the property owner.

ML Your work has been so focused on kinship, as in different kin arrangements, and I was very drawn to the fact that you call them biological and genetic *facts*.

MS That's the facts for the native, facts in the vernacular, yes.

ML But with kinship, your interest is how it is performed through social bonds. So again, this is something that has all to do with relationships.

MS Absolutely. Those facts are themselves, in being an object of interest, socially created. So to think of conception as a natural act already implies that you've given it social value, you've marked it out for attention. It is in this sense that facts are socially produced.

ML Something else that contributes to my interest in the knowledge commons has to do with awareness. I quote from your introduction: "Awareness takes shape against previous experiences [...] thus (new) ideas are thought through other (old) ideas."[2] It's really fluid—there has to be a movement in order for awareness to even take shape. In *Understanding Knowledge as a Commons,* James Boyle's essay suggests that "copyright has done its job and encouraged the creation, and the initial distribution, of the work. [...] But now it acts as a fence, keeping us out."[3]

MS Yes, he's very much an open source advocate, isn't he?

ML I think this is very interesting in relation to the genome project. In the UK, the sequences are accessible as open source. But in America, they are not. This example shows very clearly that the knowledge about our genetic material, which is so primary to our existence, is treated as private property and direct source of commercial gain. I wonder how that feels for you?

MS This is an area in which I've not been following recent arguments and I really don't feel qualified to comment on. At the time of the decoding, of course, there was this race between the people at Hinxton (home of the Wellcome Trust Genome Campus), which is just outside Cambridge, and the Craig

Venter's laboratory in the United States. There was a very strong sense, from what was happening here, that we were dealing with something that "belonged" to people in common. What has happened since then is an incredible amount of detailed work on how we might actually use this knowledge. Cambridge University, for example, has rules about patenting, and it encourages scientists to take up patents. So, to return to the notion of artifice and the artificially produced: in the case of the information produced from the genome, even though it might be a common resource, it gets entangled in artifice in producing useable versions of it. It's a bit like the idea and the expression: to make things useable implies a huge input of human labor and money and finance and so forth, so that gets entangled in proprietary relations, whether you like it or not.

ML So it's only through use that property really becomes a source of wealth, as well as the source of knowledge?

MS Yes, exactly, which is what patents are all about. But there are all kinds of experiments with different forms of copyright and copyleft, open source software, recognizing different kinds of commons. For example, there's a new online anthropological journal, called *Hau*, which comes from [Marcel] Mauss's "spirit of the gift," and the journal has a Creative Commons license, which allows people to publish there, but doesn't restrict them from publishing elsewhere. And it's been hugely successful.

ML That's what Laurel and I have negotiated with the publishers of this book. We opened up a dialogue with the publisher, which has led to an agreement of releasing the publication under the terms of nonexclusive rights. That way it is the generosity that gets reproduced and distributed widely. Everyone benefits.

Notes

1 Marilyn Strathern, "The Aesthetics of Substance," in *Capital*, Neil Cummings and Marysia Lewandowska (London: Tate Publishing, 2001).
2 Marilyn Strathern, *Reproducing the Future: Anthropology, Kinship, and the New Reproductive Technologies* (Manchester: Manchester University Press, 1992), 4.
3 James Boyle, "Mertonianism Unbound? Imagining Free, Decentralized Access to Most Cultural and Scientific Material," in *Understanding Knowledge as a Commons: From Theory to Practice*, eds. Charlotte Hess and Elinor Ostrom (Cambridge, MA: MIT Press, 2007), 127.

Exchange and Circulation

Antonia Hirsch

221

> Desire (v.) early 13c., from Old French desirrer (12c.) "wish, desire, long for," from Latin desiderare "to long for, to wish for; demand, expect," [...] from the phrase *de sidere* "from the stars."[1]

Earth's most important star, the sun, divides our existence into night and day, unconscious and conscious. It assumed what we today consider its rightful place less than 500 years ago. Nicolaus Copernicus gave his name to the eponymous revolution that produced the paradigm shift marking the departure from a concept of the universe as geocentric and toward a heliocentric model.[2] It is a lesser-known fact that the author of the Copernican Revolution also wrote on economics. *On the Minting of Coin* was published, in various iterations, between 1517 and 1526,[3] and so it is Copernicus who is also credited with inventing the quantity theory of money, which focuses on money supply in a given economy—in other words, on problems such as excessive proliferation, also known as inflation. At first sight, Copernicus's dual expertise may seem somewhat surprising. Yet the obvious connection between his two areas of interest is circulation: planetary and monetary.

Copernicus's famous astronomical discovery was closely preceded by another revolution, the invention of the printing press in the mid-fifteenth century, signaling a new era in the proliferation and distribution of information.[4] One might assume that the work of medieval astronomers contributed, metaphorically, to the broadening of worldviews in a way comparable to that of early mechanically assisted publishing. (For example, the circulation of the printed theses of Martin Luther, a contemporary of Copernicus.) However, although medieval astronomical inquiries were considered useful for the precise calculation of (religious) calendars and were utilized in astrological predictions regarding the fortunes of kings and empires, astronomical endeavors such as Copernicus's—literally broadening knowledge horizons—had to answer to a restrictive "information management" by the Church and other, secular, powers.

Both of these "circulatory systems," astronomical and monetary, evoke specific *arenas* pertaining to knowledge and economy in which an individual has the potential to attain some level of agency. And while the mere existence of discourse (information in circulation) does not eliminate, for example, illiteracy, and the existence of a viable monetary system does not in itself bestow financial power on an individual, it nevertheless sets out a stage that awaits its actors.[5]

The notion of circulation expands the idea of exchange from a simple give-and-take economy—a one-to-one exchange—to a more complex configuration in which "what goes around comes around," but perhaps not from the same direction and not necessarily from or to a single point, but multiple nodes.[6]

The expression "what goes around comes around" articulates equivalencies, viz., representation. Fundamentally, representation registers what can stand in for something else (what is of equal value), so that it is possible to state that a commodity costs a certain amount of money—a universal exchange equivalent and floating signifier—and so conversely, the commodity can also become representative of a certain amount of labor. It is through this floating signifier (money) that circulation is possible. This is different from a barter economy where in every single act of exchange anew, a parity in value has to be established and specific items are exchanged against each other. For example, two individuals may agree that a specific laptop and a particular bicycle possess equal value, which results in a trade, but should the bicycle subsequently be traded against another object, an entirely new negotiation—rather than the mere naming of a price—would have to ensue regarding the value parity of the respective items to be traded.

By extension of this logic of representation, an image of a thing can stand in for the idea of that thing. A color can stand in for a political party and thereby describe who can stand in, or who can stand up for what or for whom, and it becomes possible for these ideas or values—as representations—to circulate broadly.[7] Ideas, while specific to some degree, retain the quality of a floating signifier insofar as they can be represented materially, but, by definition, they remain in the immaterial realm of thought. Representation necessarily relies on abstraction, and the particular nature of that abstraction is determined by the context in which it is produced. Therefore representation of any kind is itself the result of an exchange: a negotiation, a bargaining.[8]

Considered in the context of the circulation of ideas, Copernicus's quantity theory, which addresses monetary circulation specifically, also brings to mind the complication and challenge that the proliferation of voices, inflationary amounts of information, and, by extension, any form of publication—from those generated before and by the first printing presses to those distributed electronically—has posed to epistemological systems. This kind of inflationary proliferation of information has created a situation in which it has become glaringly obvious that what permits us to navigate our lives in more or less sane ways is not principally the existence or accessibility of information, but how we are able to negotiate a convolution of "knowables" that are quasi-value-free until they are integrated into an ordered system (the Internet as a form of logorrhea). This active navigation of information, a kind of empirical process that tests a "knowable" as to its feasibility, making it, or dismissing it as, "viable," constructs an epistemological system, something that by determining viability assigns value.[9]

The formation of an epistemological system is driven by curiosity —a desire for information, ideas, and knowledge. Desire—whether intellectual, erotic, or of a less savory variant (desire for power, for example)—is both the force that moves things, that makes the world go round, and it is the force that *builds* worlds through the centrifugal force emanating from a point of perception, a point momentarily condensing to form a center of gravity: a self. This desire must not be virtuous at all. It is value-free as a force that merely commands movement and action.

REPRESENTATIVE MONEY—REPRESENTATION OF IDEAS

Copernicus's *On the Minting of Coin* concerns itself fundamentally with the problem of a currency's face value being incommensurate with its exchange value. By diagnosing this problem of differing values, Copernicus did not only anticipate Adam Smith's identification of money as a commodity, but, in the very problem he apprehended, the astronomer also confronted the conceptual foundation on which fiat money[10] would later come to be based.[11] Representative money deploys a similar divergence in value strategically, as in, for example, paper money beginning to circulate in Europe in the seventeenth century, where face value and material value obviously no longer stood in any relation to each other as would have still been the case with, for instance, silver coins.[12]

Copernicus pointed out the need for restraint with regard to the minting of money. He argued in support of a single controlling power to oversee the issuing of currency against the background of a church apparatus that claimed exactly such a monopoly on the dispersal of information and learning. Without the church losing, at least to some degree, its stranglehold on the circulation of knowledge, Copernicus's theory would never have come to light, and, importantly, would not have been improved upon in the wake of its publication.[13] However, it was also the Catholic Church that, contemporaneously with Copernicus's research on astronomy, partially financed itself through a prototype of representative money: the so-called letters of indulgence that granted absolution from sin in exchange for a fee. Ironically, printing presses were used during that period to undermine the Church's knowledge monopoly, but they simultaneously also permitted an accelerated trade in the letters of indulgence (as their production, too, could now be expedited), initially fortifying the Church's economic power.[14] Ultimately, however, the emergence of modern money, the explosive proliferation of thought—unsanctioned thought, that is, thought by authors rather than authorities—and the secularization of power went hand in hand.[15]

I propose parallels between a monetary economy and an economy of ideas by emphasizing money's character as a universal exchange equivalent that can actualize itself (its value) in varying forms in the material world (as, for example, commodities). Similarly, ideas are able to circulate independently from their materialization, and, in a material economy, it is exchange that gives ideas their currency and also what gives them value.[16] It is the sharing and transacting of either (money or ideas) that creates realities.

Conversely, we might consider money as information; this "information" is not only expressed through exchange value—and here it is possible to find a more obvious and striking convergence with the notion of information in circulation—but in the form of paper money itself. At the time of the hyperinflation in 1920s Weimar Germany, emergency money was issued by municipalities or companies, somewhat haphazardly, as promissory notes in order to facilitate continued economic activity that had threatened to come to a halt due to galloping inflation. As banknotes became worth less and less, official institutions normally charged with printing the national currency could not keep up with the numbers of bills required to pay for even small purchases such as bread, which suddenly cost thousands of marks, and thereby required incredible amounts of bills in circulation. However, since this emergency money was not issued by the regular authorities who would adorn their bills with insignia of the national state and emblems of national pride, the peculiar emergency money instead proffered poetry, contemporary artwork, and statistics as to the current economic situation, as well as unsanctioned political commentary. These semi-legitimate currencies resembled handbills or news bulletins normally considered an order of printed material wholly different from that of money—even though circulation is crucial for both.

To this day, representative money, the stuff that emerged in close simultaneity to the printed book, has essentially remained a promissory note that functions only by virtue of faith in its issuer. In the context of the proliferation of thought, with an increasing number of voices becoming available, the question of issuers—authors—and their reliability and substance, is similarly significant. Ultimately, all technological improvements and personal efficiency strategies notwithstanding, there is a limit to how much humans, as living entities with finite biological capacities, can process; how much information, services, and goods they can transact. Consequently, in a universe of exponentially growing multiplicities of voices and "knowables," there seems to be a more urgent need for a baseline, a path, or stable epistemological system.

By pointing to the problem of inflation, an inflationary explosion of voices, I have evoked the idea of a controlling body, an authority that would maintain a balance of values, maintain an epistemological system preventing it from collapse under its own weight. Yet the call to install "an authority" to regulate and filter this glut of information seems at the very best impracticable. Instead, the situation may require a completely different mode of relational thinking, a different way of accounting. ("To count" and "to tell" notably sharing the same etymological root.)

FORTUNES

Up until and beyond Copernicus's age, astrology, the telling of fortunes based on the position of the stars, and astronomy, the mathematical analysis of the position and movements of the heavenly bodies, were generally considered one and the same discipline. Scientific knowledge and belief had not yet parted ways (and some might question whether they ever truly did). Historically, astronomy and astrology share a close connection to myth, with its images of animals, gods, and quasi-ritual objects overlaying a chaos of stars illuminating the night sky. While astronomy today limits itself to an analysis and prediction of events pertaining to dead-and-dumb rock and ice hurtling through space, astrology—equally based on mathematics and geometry—claims knowledge as to the path and quality of relationships of living matter, in fact, beyond this: consciousness and spirit. Astronomy and astrology, each in their own way, do not only attempt to illuminate what already is, but promise a hold on the future, for example by way of calendars—yet astrology does so in patent speculation.

In this speculation, astrology shares a fundamental quality with the capitalist principle of "forward dynamism"—one of its defining characteristics. This similarity manifests not merely in the trading of the poetically named futures, but in the simple fact that *any* investment of capital will realize itself only in a future moment; each and every act in a capitalist economy is one of speculation—however minor, a speculation on a future outcome.[17] It is this notion of speculation that also registers a kinship between fiscal economies and economies of ideas—parallel universes for which circulation is axiomatic. And while speculation can be driven by a desirous impulse that projects an ideal (as a future outcome), brokers, like alchemists turning lead into gold, are also hedging bets on negative developments, turning losses into gains (for example, by "betting" on a stock's decline in order to realize a profit). Speculation in and of itself, once put into circulation, creates its own set of facts, resulting in an altered material reality. For a system to be operational, to gain a level of reality, it does not have to be true in any provable sense. Instead, as is well known, it has to function only as a communal fiction that is shared by a sufficient number of people.

REVOLUTION I have spoken of circulation in connection to Copernicus's ideas; however, with regard to heavenly bodies, he refers distinctly to "revolution"—a repeated return along a constant path. This is significant in so far as in contemporary usage, "revolution," oxymoronically, is more often intended to signify exactly the opposite: not a return to the known, but a break with the habitual.[18]

Yet during Copernicus's lifetime, this new conception of the term "revolution" as a drastic change—the speculation on, and by extension the instantiation of, another possible world—did not yet exist, and neither did the idea that the planets traveled along elliptical paths, as Johannes Kepler proved in 1609.[19] Copernicus still imagined perfect geometric symmetry, composed of conclusive circles focused on a single center, whereas the ellipse is a form that orders itself around a duality of points, thereby implying relationality. Imagining and reimagining a universe, it is therefore pertinent not only to think of Kepler's ellipses as related to the syntactical ellipsis—the three dots that commonly indicate either a deliberate omission or an unfinished thought—but also to Aby Warburg's Hamburg reading room: an elliptical space that held the Warburg universe in its orbit.[20] This reading room was at the heart of the Kulturwissenschaftliche Bibliothek Warburg, which was founded in Hamburg in the 1920s.[21] Warburg became interested in Kepler, and Kepler's ellipses, during a time when he was institutionalized due to his persistent struggle with what was later diagnosed as schizophrenia and manic depression. Facing his own demons, Warburg was fascinated by the power of symbols, so prominently present in astrology, that formed one prong of a dual mechanism—besides rationality and science—intended to conquer the profoundly human phobia of chaos and the unknown. Likely by deeply felt personal necessity, Warburg positioned "In place of the circle [...] the geometric ellipsis, and in doing so, on the path to a 'mathematical cosmophysics' accomplished a significant step toward de-demonization and de-anthropomorphization of the heavens. The ellipsis is, especially because of its di-polar shape, the symbolic form of 'forces that beget space for thought.'"[22]

Warburg's library proposed a new conception of an epistemological system that championed, through its unusual classification system, a circulation of ideas over the notion of physical books circulating among readers, as is the case in a common circulating library. In other words, his library favored an immaterial permeability among self-contained books—and thereby exceeded the notion of the book as property: a thing proper unto itself, in the sense of being particular to itself.

Astronomy and astrology, which I use throughout this essay to discuss aspects of circulation, also formed a fulcrum of Warburg's *Mnemosyne Atlas*. The Atlas is founded on two key concerns of Warburg's research: orientation and expression. Warburg recognized symbolic systems—for example those found in astrological, but also religious cosmologies—as a civilizational move to "manage" affect, which in turn expressed itself in what he termed "pathos formulas," embodiments of universal affective forces, effective across cultures and ages. Importantly, Warburg positions the spectrum of affect not only in the region of the desirous that I reference in the epigraph of this essay, but also in the domain of fear. While this focus on a phobic dynamic may well have been founded in Warburg's own personal history, it is obvious that the drive to "manage" information (in the broadest sense: sensory, image-based, textual) is not just to make it useful, but to sustain a self, something that the desirous force continually strives to exceed. This force field, this duality, between desire and fear finds its expression in the ellipsis, the "space for thought."

Accordingly, the isolated, specific items Warburg unearthed and made available in the irregular architectural space of his library seem less significant than precisely the way in which Warburg struggled to relate a vast number of items that crossed and recrossed classification systems which had traditionally allowed them to be made sense of. These classification systems sprang from authoritative systems, academic traditions that constituted distinct filters on knowledge and information. Yet it seems that Warburg did not intend to dismantle any of them, instead he moved through and among them with impunity. Hartmut Böhme writes of Warburg as having embodied "a kind of pantheism that turned its eye on epistemology."[23]

Copernicus authored a model not necessarily true in order for it to be real, but functional as a communal fiction, and he intended it, literally, to be *uni*versal. Four centuries later, Warburg embodied a very different mode of authorship that defined itself through the ongoing attempt to articulate a knowledge system constituted of a multiplicity of dynamic relationships, creating a space for thought to circulate. The particular quality of this space for thought is in itself polymorphic and dynamic. As Böhme writes, "it is important that the gap [the space] produced by mnemonic techniques [embodiments and symbolizations of affective drives] does not produce a duration that describes a linear arrow in time moving from ecstatic delirium to sensible prudence [...] but a 'rhythm,' a swing of the pendulum, a 'circulation.'"[24]

This space, or gap—a void that finds its simile in outer space—is produced in a proto-economic exchange that, in its active state, suspends any notion of property—and also of propriety. It is a transgressive state forced into being by devastating affective momentum. Inasmuch as it is a struggle of forces, it is an unstable, antagonistic space that nevertheless produces an arena—the aforementioned stage—the ring (the circle), and force field in which the encounter takes place, and the story unfolds. This is a space that makes culture possible, no less.

Notes

1 Online Etymology Dictionary, s.v. "Desire," www.etymonline.com/index.php?term=desire&allowed_in_frame=0.

2 Copernicus is thought to have begun working on his seminal book *De revolutionibus orbium coelestium* (*On the Revolutions of the Heavenly Spheres*) around 1510. The book was not published until 1543 in Nuremberg. See Dava Sobel, *A More Perfect Heaven: How Copernicus Revolutionized the Cosmos* (New York: Walker & Company, 2011).

3 Nicolaus Copernicus was educated in canon law and medicine. He commenced tenure as economic administrator of Warmia, in what today is Poland, in 1516, and in this capacity he wrote and later published *Monetae cudendae ratio* (*On the Minting of Coin*).

4 By the time Copernicus was born, there were approximately 110 printing presses operating across Europe.

5 See Patricia Reed's discussion of the "wrong in common" in her essay "Economies of Common Infinitude," in *Intangible Economies*, ed. Antonia Hirsch (Vancouver: Fillip, 2012), 197.

6 Jacques Derrida's *Dissemination* seems relevant in this context, but I admit that I have not engaged with it enough to properly fold it into my discussion here. However, it might be useful to consider the particular difference of terms: circulation indicates something that returns but in possibly circuitous, meandering, and maybe even devious ways; dissemination describes a kind of spreading of seed, sending something on its way, without expectation of return, or rather, where any return is a fortuitous gift, unaccounted for, so to speak. This outward movement of dissemination, a giving away without expectation of return, could therefore be deemed "uneconomic"—also in the sense that it escapes the Symbolic order. See Jacques Derrida, *Dissemination* (London: Continuum, 2008).

7 As I have set out elsewhere, I propose to consider "economy" more broadly as a form of exchange that is not limited, as is common in popular discourse, to transactions of capital, commodities, and labor that can be expressed in a fiscal dimension. See Antonia Hirsch, "Intangible Economies," in *Intangible Economies*.

8 Forms of exchange, therefore, as divergent positions confronting one another, compel questions of ethics. By this I am not only pointing to the categorical imperative implied by "what goes around comes around," but also to the ethical values that are negotiated alongside common economic transactions. For example, the purchase of goods to satisfy a basic need is never abstract or reduced just to the satisfaction of such a need, but in a capitalist economy, in the choices made around the mode of transaction and as to the particular commodity elected for the satisfaction of a particular need, an ethical value system is expressed that reaches far beyond the purchase of, say, a bottle of juice (organic or conventional? Regional or mass-produced? Brand-name or generic?).

9 The mere mention of a "knowable" must conjure the memorable 2002 press conference held by Donald Rumsfeld, then US Secretary of Defense, in which he stated with regard to the possible existence of weapons of mass destruction in Iraq: "There are things we know that we know. There are known unknowns. That is to say there are things that we now know we don't know. But there are also unknown unknowns." Rumsfeld was much lambasted for this philosophical excursus, yet not only was he correct in the point he made, but the context of the Iraq War also makes it painfully clear how the knowing of certain facts goes hand in hand with their ordering into a system that assigns value (e.g., the Axis of Evil), and that then compels actions that are justified under that value system. For the full text of the press conference see Donald Rumsfeld, "Secretary Rumsfeld Press Conference at NATO Headquarters, Brussels, Belgium," June 6, 2002, www.defense.gov/transcripts/transcript.aspx?transcriptid=3490.

10 Fiat money assumes its value not based on its material value, but by *fiat* of an issuing authority.

11 Copernicus recognized these two crucial aspects in the phenomenon of money; they are embedded in his assertion that all kinds of money have a value (*valor*) and an estimated value (*estimatio*). He asserts that "while the value of a given coin depends on the amount and quality of the metal bullion of which it is made, its *estimatio* is its nominal value set by the overall authority in the country." Leszek Zygner, "Treatise *On the Minting of Coin* and Copernicus Views on Economics," Nicolaus Copernicus Thorunensis, www.copernicus.torun.pl/en/science/economics/4/.

12 This value differential posed a difficult problem because, and this was Copernicus's core thesis, "bad money" drives out good, with "bad money" flooding the market. This thesis later became known as Gresham's law after Sir Thomas Gresham (1519–79), an English financier. Copernicus diagnosed that the value of a coin could, in circulation, end up being worth less than its face value either through an excessive dispersal of coins relative to the values being created in a given economy, or because the alloy (copper + silver or copper + gold) used to mint the coins was poorer than the pure precious metal it pretended to represent (as per its face value)—with the result that "good money" (undervalued by its face value) would be hoarded, thereby pulled out of circulation, whereas "bad money" (overvalued by its face value) would flood the market. In today's economies, value differentials play out in free currency exchange, that is, normally across the lines that divide national economies—and currencies. During Copernicus's time and in his home region of what is now Poland, there were Prussian and Polish coins in circulation simultaneously, so that the problem of competing currencies was only compounded by the issue of a degradation of the material values of coins through the minting process.

13 By the likes of Johannes Kepler, for example. Nevertheless, one of the

reasons why Copernicus hesitated to publish *On the Revolutions of the Heavenly Spheres* for almost four decades was, in part, due to his acknowledgment that his theory opposed church doctrine and contravened the then-current interpretation of scripture that announced that the earth stood still and the sun moved. See Sobel, *A More Perfect Heaven.*

14 Of course, the mere printing of texts did not immediately eliminate the illiteracy prevalent outside the clergy. As Jan Verwoert points out in his essay "Faith Money Love," it was the same printing presses that helped the proliferation of the letters of indulgence as well as Martin Luther's condemnation of exactly such practices in the Catholic Church of the time. I thank Jan Verwoert for drawing my attention to the fact that in the fifteenth century, the newly invented printing presses tied Luther and the Catholic Church into this strange technological union. See Jan Verwoert, "Faith Money Love," in *Intangible Economies.*

15 Here it might be useful to reflect briefly on the seemingly related terms of "author" and "authority." Etymologically, "author" stands for "originator, creator, instigator." "Authority," on the other hand, stands for that which "settles the argument." Both terms describe, in other words, almost diametrically opposed concepts relevant to the positioning of today's authors (artists) as the much-hailed public intellectuals, participating in a public discourse. As Hannah Arendt points out, authority is a form of power, yet it excludes the notion of violence, because where violence is required to enforce authority, the latter has already failed. Thus the concept of authority is incommensurable with conditions of equality, a condition required for argumentation and persuasion to take hold. See Hannah Arendt, "Was ist Autorität?," in *Zwischen Vergangenheit und Zukunft: Übungen im politischen Denken I*, ed. Ursula Ludz (Munich: Piper, 1994).

16 We obviously find ourselves today in an information economy where ideas have a value that can be expressed in dollar or euro figures and that can be traded in the marketplace. This has not always been the case. Although the British Statute of Anne (1710) could be considered the earliest decree instating something like a copyright, the Berne Convention, which is the modern copyright law on which today's international agreements are still based, was not established until 1886. See copyrighthistory.com/anne.html.

17 See Melanie Gilligan, "Affect & Exchange," in *Intangible Economies.*

18 Walter Benjamin advances that, "Marx says that revolutions are the locomotives of world history. But the situation may be quite different. Perhaps revolutions are not the train ride, but the human race grabbing for the emergency brake." Walter Benjamin, *Arcades Project* (Cambridge, MA: Harvard University Press, 2002). Thanks to Olaf Nicolai for mentioning this statement of Benjamin's.

19 After having published *Astronomia nova* in 1609, a work that postulated planetary orbits to be elliptical, Kepler went on to publish *Epitome astronomiae Copernicanae* in seven volumes. Despite its name, it did not

deal with Copernican ideas in great detail, but simply took Copernicus's heliocentrism as a point of departure to then elaborate Kepler's own theories on the ellipses. *Epitome* became Kepler's most significant book.

20 I thank Lisa Robertson for bringing Aby Warburg to my attention while writing this essay and also for her pointing out Warburg's intense interest in Kepler.

21 Under the threat of Nazism, it was relocated to London in 1933 and is now part of the University of London.

22 Hartmut Böhme, "Aby M. Warburg (1866–1929)," in *Klassiker der Religionswissenschaft: Von Friedrich Schleiermacher bis Mircea Eliade*, ed. Axel Michaels (Munich: C. H. Beck, 1997); my translation. Böhme goes on to state that: "Not without reason did Warburg allude with the elliptical room to a time to which he, in the midst of, and reflecting on, World War I, dedicated his longest study 'Pagan Antique Prophecy in Words and Images in the Age of Luther.'"

23 "Eine Art Pantheismus ins Epistemologische gewendet." Ibid., 9. Of course, this turn away from a "monotheist model" had been under way in the arts of the Western world for ages, and historically, art, in all its variants, as an offspring of religious practice has performed this multivalence in exchange and in signification parallel to fiscal/material economies—yet with an incredible acceleration since Warburg's lifetime. Where up to the Middle Ages artists worked anonymously (when still designated as crafts people), ostensibly giving voice to a divine vision of the universe managed and sanctioned by the Church, they increasingly became authors, authorized by none other than themselves. This change occurred concurrently with the transition from feudal structures to a civic society and the emergence of a middle class that owned private property through which, in part, it was able to give expression to a newly won sense of individuality.

24 Ibid.

Common Pool Resources

237

Arendt, Hannah. "The Public and the Private Realm." In *The Human Condition*. Chicago: University of Chicago Press, 1958.
Barbrook, Richard. "The Hi-Tech Gift Economy." *First Monday* 3, no. 12, December 7, 1998. Accessed May 14, 2008. www.firstmonday.org/issues/issue3_12/.
Bataille, Georges. *The Accursed Share: An Essay on General Economy* 1. Translated by Robert Hurley. New York: Zone Books, 1988.
Berry, David M. *Copy, Rip, Burn: The Politics of Copyleft and Open Source*. London: Pluto Press, 2008.
Berry, David M., and Giles Moss. "Libre Culture Manifesto." In *Libre Culture: Meditations on Free Culture*. Edited by David M. Berry and Giles Moss. Winnipeg: Pymalion Books, 2008. archive.org/details/LibreCultureMeditationsOnFreeCulture.
Berry Slater, Josephine, ed. "Underneath the Knowledge Commons." *Mute* 2, no. 1. www.metamute.org/editorial/magazine/mute-vol-2-no.-1-%E2%88%92-underneath-knowledge-commons.
Bettig, Ronald V. *Copyrighting Culture: the Political Economy of Intellectual Property*. Oxford: Westview Press, 1996.
Blackwell, Adrian, Adam Bobbette, Nasrin Himada, et al., eds. "Political Economy Issue 00 Property." *Scapegoat: Architecture, Landscape, Political Economy*, no. 1 (Fall 2010).
Boyle, James. *Shamans, Software, and Spleens: Law and the Construction of the Information Society*. Cambridge, MA: Harvard University Press, 1996.
Coleman, Gabriela E. *Coding Freedom: The Ethics and Aesthetics of Hacking*. Princeton, NJ: Princeton University Press, 2013.
Colin, Anna and Emily Pethick, eds. *The Otolith Group: A Long Time Between Suns*. Berlin: Sternberg Press, 2009.
Davies, Margaret. *Property: Meanings, Histories, Theories*. London: Routledge, 2007.
"Definition of Free Cultural Works." Last modified December 1, 2008. www.freedomdefined.org/Definition.
Diederichsen, Diedrich. *On (Surplus) Value in Art*. Berlin: Sternberg Press, 2008.
Doctorow, Cory. "The Coming Civil War over General Purpose Computing." Lecture presented at the Long Now Foundation, July 2012. www.boingboing.net/2012/08/23/civilwar.html.
——— *Content: Selected Essays on Technology, Creativity, Copyright, and the Future of the Future*. San Francisco: Tachyon Publications, 2008.
Drahos, Peter and John Braithwaite. *Information Feudalism: Who Owns the Knowledge Economy?*. London: Earthscan Publication Ltd., 2002.
Dyer-Witheford, Nick. *Cyber-Marx: Cycles and Circuits of Struggle in High-Technology Capitalism*. Urbana: University of Illinois Press, 1999.
Dylan, Bob. "The 50th Anniversary Collection / The Copyright Extension Collection Vol. I." Sony Music Entertainment, 2012. www.discogs.com/viewimages?release=4142612.

Ehlin, Fredrik, Andjeas Ejiksson, and Oscar Mangione, eds. "Opening the Open." *Geist*, no. 13 (2007).

Federici, Silvia. *Revolution at Point Zero: Housework, Reproduction and Feminist Struggle*. Oakland, CA: PM Press, 2012.

Fisher, Mark. *Capitalist Realism: Is There No Alternative?* Hants: Zero Books, 2009.

Friedman, Ken, ed. *The Fluxus Reader*. London: Academy Editions, 1998. www.hdl.handle.net/1959.3/42234.

Ghosh, Rishab Aiyer, ed. *CODE: Collaborative Ownership and the Digital Economy*. Cambridge, MA: MIT Press, 2005.

Gibson-Graham, J. K. *A Postcapitalist Politics*. Minneapolis: University of Minnesota Press, 2006.

——— *The End of Capitalism (As We Knew It): A Feminist Critique of Political Economy*. Minneapolis: University of Minnesota Press, 1996.

Graeber, David. *Debt: The First 5,000 Years*. Brooklyn, NY: Melville House Publishing, 2011.

Hann, Chris, ed. *Property Relations: Renewing the Anthropological Tradition*. Cambridge: Cambridge University Press, 1998.

Hardt, Michael and Antonio Negri. *Commonwealth*. Cambridge, MA: Harvard University Press, 2009.

Healy, Kieran. *Last Best Gifts: Altruism and the Market for Human Blood and Organs*. Chicago: University of Chicago Press, 2006.

Hemmungs Wirtén, Eva. *No Trespassing: Authorship, Intellectual Property Rights, and the Boundaries of Globalization*. Toronto: University of Toronto Press, 2004.

Hess, Charlotte and Elinor Ostrom, eds. *Understanding Knowledge as a Commons: From Theory to Practice*. Cambridge, MA: MIT Press, 2007.

Hirsch, Antonia, ed. *Intangible Economies*. Vancouver: Fillip, 2012.

Hirsch, Eric and Marilyn Strathern, eds. *Transactions and Creations: Property Debates and the Stimulus of Melanesia*. Oxford: Berghahn Books, 2005.

Hirsch, Nikolaus and Shveta Sarda, eds. *Cybermohalla Hub*. Berlin: Sternberg Press, 2012.

Hyde, Lewis. *Common as Air: Revolution, Art and Ownership*. New York: Farrar, Straus & Giroux, 2010.

——— *The Gift: How the Creative Spirit Transforms the World*. London: Canongate Books, 2007.

Illich, Ivan. *Deschooling Society*. London: Maryon Boyars Publishers Ltd., 2000.

Jacob, Luis, ed. *Commerce by Artists*. Toronto: Art Metropole, 2011.

Joint Academic Statement on Term Extension (CIPPM/CIPIL/IViR/MPI-IP). "The Proposed Directive for a Copyright Term Extension – A Backward-Looking Package." October 27, 2008. www.cippm.org.uk/copyright_term.html.

Joselit, David. *After Art*. Princeton, NJ: Princeton University Press, 2013.

Krikorian, Gaëlle and Amy Kapczynski, eds. *Access to Knowledge in the Age of Intellectual Property*. New York: Zone Books, 2010. www.zonebooks.org/pdf/ZoneBooks_A2K_.pdf.

Latour, Bruno and Vincent Antonin Lépinay. *The Science of Passionate Interests: An Introduction to Gabriel Tarde's Economic Anthropology*. Chicago: Prickly Paradigm Press, 2010.

Lazzarato, Maurizio. *The Making of the Indebted Man: An Essay on the Neoliberal Condition*. Los Angeles: Semiotext(e), 2012.

Leach, James. "Leaving the Magic Out: Knowledge and Effect in Different Places." *Anthropological Forum: A Journal of Social Anthropology and Comparative Sociology* 22, no. 3 (November 2012): 251–70.

——— and Richard Davis. "Recognising and Translating Knowledge: Navigating the Political, Epistemological, Legal and Ontological." *Anthropological Forum: A Journal of Social Anthropology and Comparative Sociology* 22, no. 3 (November 2012): 209–23.

Lewandowska, Marysia and Laurel Ptak. "On Intellectual Property." *Paletten* (Spring 2011). www.marysialewandowska.com/wp-content/uploads/2011/05/Paletten-text.pdf.

Lovink, Geert. "Do-It-Together*:* Digital Publishing Experiments at the Institute of Network Cultures." Lecture presented at the New School, Institute of Network Cultures, December 2011.

Lovink, Geert and Miriam Rasch, eds. *Unlike Us Reader: Social Media Monopolies and Their Alternatives*. Amsterdam: Institute of Network Cultures, 2013.

Maurer, Bill and Gabriele Schwab, eds. *Accelerating Possession: Global Futures of Property and Personhood*. New York: Columbia University Press, 2006.

Mauss, Marcel. *The Gift: The Form and Reason for Exchange in Archaic Societies*. Translated by W. D. Halls. London: Routledge, 1990.

McClean, Daniel and Karsten Schubert, eds. *Dear Images: Art, Copyright and Culture*. London: Ridinghouse, 2002.

McLuhan, Marshall. *The Gutenberg Galaxy*. Toronto: University of Toronto Press, 1962.

Metahaven. "Captives of the Cloud: Part I & II." *e-flux journal*, no. 38 (October 2012). www.e-flux.com/journal/captives-of-the-cloud-part-i/. www.e-flux.com/journal/captives-of-the-cloud-part-ii/.

Moglen, Eben. "Anarchism Triumphant: Free Software and the Death of Copyright." *First Monday* 4, no. 8 (August 2, 1999). Accessed May 21, 2008. www.firstmonday.org/ issues/issue4_8/moglen/index.html#author.

Osten, Marion von. "In Search of the Postcapitalist Self." *e-flux journal*, no. 17 (June 2010). www.e-flux.com/journal editorial—"in-search-of-the-postcapitalist-self"/.

Pasquinelli, Matteo. *Animal Spirits: A Bestiary of the Commons*. Rotterdam: NAi Publishers, 2008.

Proudhon, Pierre-Joseph. *Property is Theft! A Pierre-Joseph Proudhon Anthology*. Edited by Ian McKay. Oakland, CA: AK Press, 2011.

——— *What is Property?*. Cambridge: Cambridge University Press, 1994.

Purves, Ted, ed. *What We Want Is Free: Generosity and Exchange in Recent Art*. Albany: State University of New York Press, 2005.

Radin, Margaret. *Contested Commodities: The Trouble with Trade in Sex,*

Children, Body Parts, and Other Things. Cambridge, MA: Harvard University Press, 1996.

Seijdel, Jorinde et al., eds. *Open: Cahier on Art and the Public Domain* 4–19 (2004–10).

Sennett, Richard. *The Fall of Public Man*. London: Faber and Faber, 1986.

Sharp, Lesley A. *Strange Harvest: Organ Transplants, Denatured Bodies and the Transformed Self.* Berkeley: University of California Press, 2006.

Sheikh, Simon. "Public Spheres and the Functions of Progressive Art Institutions." *transversal* (2004). www.eipcp.net/transversal/0504/sheikh/en.

Shershow, Scott Cutler. *The Work & the Gift*. Chicago: University of Chicago Press, 2005.

Sholette, Gregory. *Dark Matter: Art and Politics in the Age of Enterprise Culture*. London: Pluto Press, 2011.

Smiers, Joost and Marieke van Schijndel. *Imagine There is No Copyright and No Cultural Conglomerates Too: An Essay*. Amsterdam: Institute of Network Cultures, 2009.

Steyerl, Hito. "In Defense of the Poor Image." *e-flux journal*, no. 10 (November 2009). www.e-flux.com/journal/in-defense-of-the-poor-image/.

Strang, Veronica and Mark Busse, eds. *Ownership and Appropriation (ASA monograph 47)*. Oxford: Berg, 2011.

Strathern, Marilyn. "Gifts Money Cannot Buy." *Social Anthropology* 20, no. 4 (2012): 397–410.

Terranova, Tiziana. *Network Culture: Politics for the Information Age*. London: Pluto Press, 2004.

Virno, Paolo. *A Grammar of the Multitude: For an Analysis of Contemporary Forms of Life*. Translated by Isabella Bertoletti, James Cascaito, and Andrea Casson. Los Angeles: Semiotext(e), 2004.

Vishmidt, Marina. *The Economy of Abolition/Abolition of the Economy. Variant*, no. 42. www.variant.org.uk/42texts/EconomyofAbolition.html.

——— "Human Capital or Toxic Asset: After the Wage." *Reartikulacija*, no. 10, 11, 12, 13 (2010). www.reartikulacija.org/?p=1487.

Willats, Stephen. *Artwork as Social Model: A Manual of Questions and Propositions*. Sheffield: RGAP, 2012.

ARTISTS' PROJECTS, EDUCATIONAL INITIATIVES, EXHIBITIONS, PUBLISHING PROJECTS, URBAN INITIATIVES, ETC.

AAAAARG
aaaaarg.org

Amy Balkin, This Is the Public Domain, 2003–present
thisisthepublicdomain.org

AND Publishing Piracy Project
andpublishing.org

Andrew Norman Wilson, ScanOps, 2012
andrewnormanwilson.com

Archive.org
archive.org

Artist Run Credit League
artistruncreditleague.wordpress.com

Arts & Labor Alternative Economies Resource Guide
artsandlabor.org

Bitcoin
bitcoin.org

Caroline Woolard, Work Dress for Barter Only, 2008–present
carolinewoolard.com

Cassie Thornton, Fedora Archive, 2012
cassiethornton.com

CDR / Burntprogress
cdr-projects.com

Claire Fontaine, Some Instructions for the Sharing of Private Property, 2011
clairefontaine.ws

Co-op Bar
visitsteve.com/co-op-bar

Copenhagen Free University
copenhagenfreeuniversity.dk

Disclosures
disclosuresproject.wordpress.com

Disobedience Archive
disobediencearchive.org

e-flux, Time/Bank, 2010–ongoing
e-flux.com/timebank

Evolution of Art
evolutiondelart.net

Exyzt
exyzt.org

Fallen Fruit
fallenfruit.org

Feral Trade
feraltrade.org

Free Kevin
freekevin.info

Goldin + Senneby, The Decapitation of Money, 2010
goldinsenneby.com

Hinrich Sachs, Kami, Khokha, Bert and Ernie (World Heritage), 2012
tenstakonsthall.se

Hollis Frampton, Public Domain, 1972
hollisframpton.org.uk

Indeposito
indeposito.net

Interference Archive
interferencearchive.org

Institute for Distributed Creativity
distributedcreativity.org

Kollektiv Kreativität
(Collective Creativity), 2005
whw.hr

LA Urban Rangers
laurbanrangers.org

Lets Re-Make
letsremake.info

Marysia Lewandowska, How Public Is the Public Museum?, 2010
marysialewandowska.com

Mess Hall
messhall.org

Model For Qualitative Society, 1968/2013
amodelforaqualitativesociety.info

Monoskop
monoskop.org

OccU
university.nycga.net

Offer & Exchange: Sites of Negotiation in Contemporary Art in London, 2008
electra-productions.com

Open Congress, 2005
tate.org.uk

Open Source Publishing
osp.constantvzw.org

Open Source Video
osvideo.constantvzw.org

OurGoods
ourgoods.org

P! Reading Groups on the Copy, 2013
p-exclamation.org

P2P Foundation
p2pfoundation.net

Pad.ma
pad.ma

PAGES
pagesproject.net

Philippe Parreno and Pierre Huyghe, et al., No Ghost Just a Shell, 1999–2003
noghostjustashell.com

Pil and Galia Kollectiv
kollectiv.co.uk

Pirate Cinema
piratecinema.org

Publication Studio
publicationstudio.biz

Publish and Be Damned
publishandbedamned.org

Public Collectors
publiccollectors.tumblr.com

Public Works
publicworksgroup.net

Publishing In Process: Ownership In Question, 2012
tenstakonsthall.se

REPOhistory
repohistory.org

Rolling Jubilee
rollingjubilee.org

Society Without Qualities, 2013
tenstakonsthall.se

Sixteen Beaver
16beavergroup.org

Stephan Dillemuth, The Hard Way to Enlightenment, 2010
societyoutofcontrol.com

subRosa Soft Power, 2012
cyberfeminism.net

Sukey
opensukey.org

Sunday Soup
sundaysoup.org

Superflex, Copyshop, 2005–present; Free Sol LeWitt, 2010
superflex.net

Tania Bruguera, Disseminate, 2010
taniabruguera.com

Telekommunisten, Octo, 2013
telekommunisten.net

Temporary Services
temporaryservices.org

The Baltimore Development Cooperative
baltimoredevelopmentco-op.org

The Commons Brooklyn
thecommonsbrooklyn.org

The Diggers
diggers.org

The Digital Tipping Point
digitaltippingpoint.com

The Directory of Open Access Repositories
opendoar.org

The Free University of Liverpool
thefreeuniversityofliverpool.wordpress.com

The Free University of NYC
freeuniversitynyc.org

The Institute for Wishful Thinking
theiwt.com

The League of Moveable Type
theleagueofmoveabletype.com

The Metropolitan Complex
themetropolitancomplex.com

The Pickpocket Almanack
pickpocketalmanack.org

The Pirate University
pirateuniversity.org

The Public School
thepublicschool.org

The Resource Exchange
theresourceexchange.org

The School of Missing Studies
schoolofmissingstudies.net

The Silent University
thesilentuniversity.org

The Social Life of the Book, 2011–ongoing
castillocorrales.fr

The Surplus Library
thesurpluslibrary.com

This Is Not a Gateway
thisisnotagateway.net

Trade School
tradeschool.coop

UbuWeb
ubu.com

Walid Raad, Scratching On Things I Could Disavow (Pension Arts in Dubai), 2009–present
scratchingonthings.com

Who Makes and Owns Your Work
whomakesandownsyourwork.org

Will Holder, Common Knowledge
commonknowledge.at

X Marks the Bökship
bokship.org

Contributors

Agency is a Brussels-based initiative that was founded in 1992 by Kobe Matthys. Agency constitutes a growing "list of things" that resist the split between the ontological classifications of nature and culture. Agency calls things forth from its list via varying "assemblies" inside exhibitions, performances, publications, etc. Each assembly speculates on a different question. All those questions explore in a topological way the operative consequences of the apparatus of intellectual property for an ecology of art practices.

David M. Berry is Associate Professor in Digital Media at the Department of Political and Cultural Studies at Swansea University and affiliated researcher at the Department of Media and Communication at University of Oslo. He is author of *Critical Theory and the Digital* (Continuum, 2013), *The Philosophy of Software: Code and Mediation in the Digital Age* (Palgrave Macmillan, 2011), *Copy, Rip Burn: The Politics of Copyleft and Open Source* (Pluto Press, 2008), co-author of *New Aesthetic, New Anxieties* (V2_, 2012), and editor of *Understanding Digital Humanities* (Palgrave Macmillan, 2012) and *Life in Code and Software: Mediated Life in a Complex Computational Ecology* (Open Humanities Press, 2012). He tweets at @berrydm.

Nils Bohlin (1920–2002) invented the three-point safety belt while working at Volvo in Sweden. His invention changed the world through preventing car crash injuries. Though Bohlin held the patent to its design, he decided to make the safety belt free for public use.

Sean Dockray is an artist and a founding director of the nonprofit organization, Telic Arts Exchange, an organization established for critically engaging with new media and culture. His practice radiates outward from writing—both software and texts—occasionally into complex platforms that involve many people over long durations, taking on a life of their own. Dockray initiated the Public School and AAAARG.ORG.

Rasmus Fleischer is a Swedish historian, writer, and musician. He completed his PhD at the Institute of Contemporary History at Södertörn University College. In 2003, he helped to found the Piratbyrån, an organization opposed to copyright laws for digital media. He is a frequent lecturer on what he calls the impending "collapse of copyright."

Antonia Hirsch is an artist whose work has been exhibited at, among others, the Contemporary Art Gallery, Vancouver; Power Plant, Toronto; the Taipei Fine Arts Museum; Tramway, Glasgow; and ZKM Museum of Contemporary Art, Karlsruhe. Her work can be found in public collections such as that of the Vancouver Art Gallery, the National Gallery of Canada, and the Sackner Archive of Concrete & Visual Poetry, Miami Beach. Her writing and projects have appeared in *artecontexto*, *C Magazine*, *Fillip*, and *The Happy Hypocrite*.

David Horvitz is an artist born in California. His work shifts seamlessly between the Internet and the printed page. His recurring interests include attention to strategies of information circulation and the impermanence of digital artifacts. Recent projects include *POST*, a mail-art exhibition at the Charlottenborg in Copenhagen; *Sad, Depressed, People*, an artist book released in 2012 by New Documents showing a collection of stock images of depression; and *Watercolors*, a two-year e-mail correspondence project with Natalie Häusler.

Konst & Teknik is a graphic design studio based in Stockholm, Sweden. The studio was founded in 2006 by Mattias Jakobsson and Peter Ström, and works on commissioned and self-initiated projects, most often for print or screen. This includes graphic identities, books, catalogues, websites, apps, type and web design, as well as teaching, lecturing, and curating. Most recently they launched "Publishing as (Part-Time) Practice," a seminar, exhibition, and online platform for small-scale publishers, in collaboration with Matilda Plöjel and Iaspis.

Marysia Lewandowska is a Polish-born, London-based artist who, through her collaborative projects, has explored the public function of media archives, collections, and exhibitions in an age characterized by relentless privatization. Her practice critically explores the property of others. Her recent projects that engage questions of ownership include the *Museum Futures: Distributed* (with Neil Cummings, 2008), *Tender Museum* (2009), *How Public Is the Public Museum?* (2010), *Re-Distributed Archive* (2011), "Publishing in Process: Ownership in Question" (with Laurel Ptak, 2012), *Open Cinema* (with Colin Fournier, 2012). She is Professor of Art in the Public Realm at Konstfack in Stockholm.

Mattin You've got a right to scream. When the dark one's here to stay. You've got a right to be. What you want and where you wanna be. You've got your own voice so sing. You've got two hands, let's go and make anything. We all got rules we all have to break. We all have to make those mistakes. When I say I know the way, I'm only trying. No, don't nobody know where the road to life really lies. See the people on television get shot in their very own street. People just like you, people just like me. Can't you see you cut your hand on the advantages. You could stand to manage your damages. You, my dear, are a force to feed, not to fear. You've got a right to anywhere, anything. You've got a right, you've got a right. You're a human being.

Open Music Archive was initiated by Eileen Simpson and Ben White in 2005, as an ongoing project to source, digitize, and distribute out-of-copyright sound recordings. The archive is a vehicle for collaborative activity including exhibitions, events and projects at: de_sitio, Mexico City; VBKÖ, Vienna; Camden Arts Centre, London; Gasworks, London; Women's

Library, London; 17th Biennale of Sydney; Institute for Contemporary Art, London; and Cornerhouse, Manchester.

Matteo Pasquinelli is a writer and academic researcher. He completed his doctorate at Queen Mary University of London with a thesis on new forms of conflict within the knowledge economy and cognitive capitalism. He wrote the book *Animal Spirits: A Bestiary of the Commons* (NAi, 2008) and edited *Media Activism: Strategie e pratiche della comunicazione indipendente* (Derive Approdi, 2002) and *C'Lick Me: A Netporn Studies Reader* (Institute of Networked Cultures, 2007). He writes and lectures frequently at the intersection of Italian operaismo and French philosophy, media theory and life sciences. Together with Wietske Maas he wrote the Manifesto of Urban Cannibalism and is currently developing the art project *Urbanibalism*. He is a member of the international collective Uninomade.

Claire Pentecost is an artist whose work engages collaboration, research, teaching, fieldwork, writing, lecturing, drawing, installation, and photography. For years she has focused on the political, social, and ecological dimensions of food. Her project on soil was part of dOCUMENTA(13). She lives in the Midwest Radical Cultural Corridor and teaches at the School of the Art Institute in Chicago.

Laurel Ptak is a curator of contemporary art based in New York City. She is Associate Curator at Tensta konsthall and teaches at the New School. Her recent collaborative projects include "To Have and to Owe" at the Elizabeth Foundation for the Arts, an exhibition that considered debt's aesthetic and affective dimensions as part of its economic register and "Publishing in Process: Ownership in Question" at Tensta konsthall, a series of public seminars looking at changing notions of production, property, ownership, and exchange at a moment when what is privately owned and publicly shared is being contested in numerous parts of the world.

Florian Schneider is a filmmaker, curator, and writer who currently lives in Brussels and Munich. He is an advising researcher at the Jan van Eyck Academie in Maastricht. He teaches at the Academy for Fine Arts in Trondheim, and is working on a doctoral project on the subject of "Imaginary Property" at Goldsmiths College in London. Schneider is one of the initiators of the "Kein Mensch ist illegal" campaign at documenta X, and subsequent projects such as the "noborder network." He is the founder of the online network kein.org and was the director of the new media festivals *Makeworld* (2001) and *Neuro* (2004). Between 2006 and 2010 he developed the multimedia performance project "Dictionary Of War" and organized "Summit: Non-Aligned Initiatives in Education

Culture" in close collaboration with Irit Rogoff. In 2012 he launched *Issue Zero*, in collaboration with Hila Peleg, a magazine for documentary practices in networked environments.

Matthew Stadler founded the Back Room, a peripatetic series of drunk dinners with publications; Clear Cut Press, an independent subscription press; suddenly.org, a periodic multi-scalar assemblage inquiring by foot and mouth into the new shapes of cities; and Publication Studio, a print-on-demand publishing house working under the motto "free is bullshit." He was previously literary editor of *Nest Magazine* and is the author of five novels for which he received a variety of prizes. Most recently he and Canadian poet, Lisa Robertson, have together compiled and annotated *Revolution: A Reader* (Publication Studio, 2012). He lives in Portland, Oregon.

Marilyn Strathern is an anthropologist initially trained through fieldwork in Papua New Guinea, and latterly involved with anthropological approaches to new reproductive technologies, intellectual property, and audit cultures. An emeritus professor at the Department of Social Anthropology, Cambridge University, she is currently working on issues in the conceptualization of relations.

Kuba Szreder is a curator of interdisciplinary projects, which actively engage in public spheres, combining artistic practices with other forms of cultural production and the critical examination of contemporary society. He is a curator within the collaborative initiative Free/Slow University of Warsaw. As part of his curatorial practice he organizes research projects, seminars, and conferences; writes articles; and edits publications which coalesce critical reflection with art theory and sociological analysis of the contemporary art field. In 2009 he started his PhD research at Loughborough University School of the Arts, where he scrutinizes the apparatus of project making and its relation to independent curatorial practice.

Marina Vishmidt writes on art, labor, and the value-form. She holds an MA from the Centre for Research in Modern European Philosophy, Kingston University, and a PhD from Queen Mary, University of London. Research posts have included the Montehermoso Research Grant, critic-in-residence at the FRAC Lorraine, and a fellowship at the Jan van Eyck Academie. Vishmidt is coeditor of the books *Uncorporate Identity* (Lars Müller, 2010) and *Media Mutandis: Art, Technologies and Politics* (Node, 2006). She is a frequent contributor to catalogues, edited collections, and journals such as *Mute*, *Afterall*, *Parkett*, and *Texte zur Kunst*. She takes part in the group projects Unemployed Cinema, Cinenova, and Signal:Noise.

ACKNOWLEDGMENTS

Many have contributed to this book and we would like to give recognition to their efforts within the complex process that publishing entails. *Undoing Property?* is a collective work and we have benefited greatly from engagement with its many contributors.

Discussion of the themes originally began at the Center for Curatorial Studies at Bard College in New York in 2009. Thanks are owed to the students and faculty there who were also part of this dialogue. Former director of graduate studies Maria Lind was crucial, and we wish to thank her for encouraging our project to continue inside the unique hub she has created at Tensta konsthall. Her ongoing support has meant a lot to us.

In the fall of 2010 we were hosted by Emily Pethick at the Showroom in London, where we sat around a table sharing ideas together with Binna Choi, Magnus Edensvard, Daniel McLean, Mike Sperlinger, who, in addition to some of the book's contributors—namely, David Berry, Kobe Matthys, Mattin, and Marina Vishmidt—introduced many important questions.

In the spring of 2011, Antonia Hirsch, Florian Schneider, Matthew Stadler, and Marina Vishmidt graciously accepted invitations to lead public seminars as part of "Publishing in Process: Ownership in Question" hosted by Tensta konsthall in Stockholm. The collective insights of the speakers and audience at these events was key to the development of this book.

Tensta konsthall's excellent team including Hans Carlsson, Jan Ekman, Emily Fahlén, Ulrika Flink, Safiya Guleed, Katrin Ingelstedt, Sanna Lampiainen, Maria Lind, and Hedvig Wiezell were all a true pleasure to work with. We owe special thanks to Eric Nylund for his precision and openness in designing the printed matter for these events. We are also grateful to Tomas Nygren and Pål Sommelius for their sensitive approach to the audio and video recordings made during the seminars, all archived online at www.tenstakonsthall.se. Sincere thanks go to Lisa Rosendahl and Sara Teleman at Iaspis and Olof Glemme at Konstfack for providing additional financial support for hosting the speakers.

Along the way we have appreciated the involvement of Basia Lewandowska Cummings who has committed much of her time offering editorial support and fresh insights to many of the texts. Antonia Blocker carried out in-depth research, Luke Gould shared some of his design experience early in the process, Helen Kaplinsky helped with funding applications, and Emily Ballard made transcripts from audio recordings.

Kirsi Peltomäki's excellent book on Michael Asher led us to his unrealized projects proposed to the Van Abbemuseum in the 1970s and 80s. Willem Smit at the Van Abbemuseum, Eindhoven, has guided us through the archival documents pertaining to Asher's exchanges with the museum.

Peter Ström and Mattias Jakobsson at Konst & Teknik are responsible for designing the book. Working closely with them has been rewarding and we cannot emphasize enough how impressed we are with the result.

At Sternberg Press we wish to thank Caroline Schneider for her openness to exploring new models of rights ownership and digital distribution with us in light of the book's subject matter. We have also been guided by Tatjana Günthner and are grateful to Leah Whitman-Salkin's close attention throughout the editorial process.

The project as a whole is part of COHAB, a collaboration between Tensta konsthall in Stockholm, the Showroom in London, and Casco – Office for Art, Design and Theory in Utrecht. We thank their respective directors, Maria Lind, Emily Pethick, and Binna Choi for a sustained curatorial dialogue and for making a distributive model of practice a reality. With the help of these institutions, direct financial support for the book has been provided by the Culture Programme of the European Union and the Henry Moore Foundation.
At various stages of the process we relied on conversations as well as friendship of Ute Meta Bauer, Ann Butler, Anna Colin, Maureen Connor, Saskia Holmkvist, Anthony Spira, and Måns Wrange. They all offered valuable critical comments, which, in one way or another, have enriched our endeavor. Thank you all.

Those closest to us continued to provide intellectual sustenance and unconditional emotional support; Marysia's thanks go to Basia Lewandowska Cummings, Joanna Grabiańska, and to Colin Fournier; Laurel's to Eric Nylund as well as Linda, Francis, Katie, and Elijah Ptak.

And finally enormous thanks go to Agency, David Berry, Nils Bohlin, Sean Dockray, Rasmus Fleischer, Antonia Hirsch, David Horvitz, Mattin, Open Music Archive, Matteo Pasquinelli, Claire Pentecost, Florian Schneider, Matthew Stadler, Marilyn Strathern, Kuba Szreder, and Marina Vishmidt whose ideas fill these pages. Their openness and diverse critical approaches have been incredibly inspiring to be in dialogue with and their contributions here will substantially enrich and extend existing debates around property and ownership well into the future.

Undoing Property?
Copublished by Sternberg Press and Tensta konsthall

Editors: Marysia Lewandowska and Laurel Ptak
Copyeditor: Leah Whitman-Salkin
Design: Konst & Teknik
Printing: Göteborgstryckeriet, Sweden

Templates and design for this book are released for free use with the open source layout software Scribus at www.scribus.net. The book is set in Universelle Free by Aron Kullander, Tallys Regular by Jos Buivenga, Junicode Italic by Peter S. Baker, and Free Sans Regular by Free Software Foundation—all in modified and updated versions by Konst & Teknik. Download and continue the development of these files at www.github.com/konst-teknik/undoing-property.

ISBN 978-3-943365-68-9

Sternberg Press
Caroline Schneider, Karl-Marx-Allee 78, D-10243 Berlin
www.sternberg-press.com

The project and book has been realized with financial support from
The Culture Programme of the European Union
The Henry Moore Foundation

Undoing Property? has been realized in the framework of COHAB, a two-year project initiated by the Showroom, Casco – Office for Art, Design and Theory, and Tensta konsthall, with the support of the Culture Programme of the European Union.

This project has been funded with support from the European Commission. This publication reflects the views only of the authors, and the Commission cannot be held responsible for any views which may be made of the information contained therein.

Marysia Lewandowska's research is part of *Public Speaking* (dnr 421-2007-2539), which is funded by the Swedish Research Council (Vetenskapsrådet).